Miscegenation Blues

Voices of Mixed Race Women

EDITED BY
Carol Camper

ISBN 0-920813-95-X
1994 © Copyright Carol Camper
Individual selections © copyright by their respective author(s)

Canadian Cataloguing in Publication Data
Main entry under title:
Miscegenation Blues: Voices of Mixed Race Women

ISBN 0-920813-95-X

1. Canadian literature (English) — Women authors.*
2. English literature — Women authors.
3. Canadianliterature (English) — Minority authors.*
4. English literature — Minority authors.
5. Miscegenation — Literary collections.
6. Racially mixed people — Literary collections.
7. Canadian literature (English) — 20th century.*
8. English literature — 20th century.
I. Camper, Carol

PS8235.W6M5 1994   C810.8'09287   C94-930679—7
PR9194.5.W6M5 1994

Sister Vision Press acknowledges the financial support of the Canada Council and the Ontario Arts Council toward its publishing program.

Managing Editor: Makeda Silvera
Production: Leela Acharya
Design: Stephanie Martin
Author Photograph: Michael Chambers
Printed and bound in Canada by union labour

Published by:
SISTER VISION: Black Women and Women of Colour Press
P.O. Box 217, Station E
Toronto, Ontario, Canada M6H 4E2

Miscegenation Blues

Voices of Mixed Race Women

EDITED BY

Carol Camper

Sister Vision
Black Women and Women of Colour Press

To my two children, Michael and Cicely,
who will always be a part of me.
To Camille, whose presence in my life is a true blessing.

Acknowledgements

I would like to thank the following individuals and groups: Sister Vision Press, Makeda Silvera, Stephanie Martin, Leela Acharya and volunteers for their support, encouragement and for all their hard work for this and many other projects. The Lesbian and Gay Community Appeal of Toronto. *Fireweed*, for the opportunity to learn as a member of the editorial collective, especially Sandra Haar, who was one of two people who suggested this anthology. Clarissa Chandler, for being the other person to suggest this topic and for her creativity and encouragement. To my family, both by blood and by choice and to the many friends who drive me crazy, inspire me, encourage me and make my life one where love is shared. Thank you.

Contents

The Unmasking... *betrayals, hard truths*

Are We Home Yet?... *return to self and cultures*

7/30   1-93   Doris R. Heggie

Etching by Doris R. Heggie

Into The Mix

MISCEGENATION BLUES: VOICES OF MIXED RACE WOMEN comes at a time when more than ever, mixed race people must speak. Identity, loyalty and belonging are issues which reside at the very heart of our existence and it is up to us to define who we are and identify our needs. This book emerges out of an increasing urgency in the lives of many women to end isolation and to understand racial multiplicity within our own bodies, families and cultures.

My decision to create this anthology sprang from my awareness that more and more young mixed race women were experiencing a difficult and sometimes lonely struggle to find identity. I felt that after forty years of living, I had something to share from my own experiences. Isolation was something I had known well, having survived adoption by White people and growing up in an all-White suburb of a small city (London, Ontario). I had considered running support groups but I decided that anthologizing a book would actually mean that more mixed race women would be involved and become connected either by writing for the anthology or reading it. Connections feel very important. Some of us don't even have a sibling that looks like us let alone anyone else. No one wants to feel this alone. To be perceived as a racial oddity is isolating and confusing.

Initially, I was not confused as a child about my race. I didn't know my race at all. I was not informed by my parents that I was Black. I knew that I didn't resemble anyone else in my world. The only Black people I knew were entertainers on television and I didn't quite look like them either. My confusion started when I moved to London and heard those first identifying cries of "Nigger" and the question, "What are you?" On some level I could see why I was called 'nigger' but there was still no discussion, no explaining, only urges to ignore the nasty words. These were the firsts of many times that I would be called upon to declare my loyalties, to identify myself.

When I was ten years old I was reading books about anthropology and discovered information about racial mixing. For the first time I had an idea of how to explain myself to myself. I went to the mirror and made my own assessment of what I was and then confronted my adoptive mother. "What am I, Mum? Am I part white and part Black?" "Yes" the reply came, along with sketchy information about a Black birth mother. I thought that my Black mother may have had non-Black ancestry as well, because of my light skin. I found out many years later that she has First Nations' ancestry and that this is very common. My mother's family are descendants of American slaves (escapees via the Underground Railroad) from the Carolinas who had mixed with Native people.

Prior to this discovery, the only people I knew that resembled me were Polynesian. I eagerly watched movies that featured actual Polynesians (rather than Dorothy Lamour) like the first two versions of *Mutiny on The Bounty*. I poured over an early sixties issue of *National Geographic* which featured articles about the people of Tahiti and the filming of the 1962 version. I was so uplifted that I resembled such a beautiful people and in my lonely efforts to be treated as a worthwhile and not-ugly person, I decided to claim that I was Polynesian. I needed tangible evidence to prove that my looks were good after all and so I stole the *National Geographic* issue. Once I learned of my Black identity, and of the existence of a relative who would resemble me (my half-sister is mixed — it actually turned out that I had several siblings who are), I no longer needed to believe I was Polynesian. But I still remember fondly the Tahitian people who were not my relatives, but made me feel beautiful when I needed to.

In my attempts to understand race and mixing I began to search for faces like mine in my immediate world. I had no idea how dangerous that could be. In grade eight my discussions with apparently-White Gayle about what her full lips and broad nose could mean, led to her grandmother's instruction to slap my face the next time I dared to say such a thing. I had ventured into forbidden territory. In grade ten, when beautiful Paula walked into class the first time, I knew she must be mixed. I knew this, but because her hair was light brown, because she never said anything to me about being like me and because I might get my face slapped, I said nothing about race to her. I had learned the earlier lesson well and had been effectively silenced. For the next three years of school with her, we friends never said a thing to one another. I saw on an inner level the lovely Blackness in her face, but I had learned that we could not meet at the place of our Blackness, but only at a place where her race would not be spoken. A shade of skin and two shades of hair colour and texture meant she was passing, whether she intended to or not. I forgot Paula's blackness for twenty years until new lessons about being unsilenced came to me. Now, I would like to reach out again and speak the truth.

In creating this anthology, I had to look at some truths about race itself. I actually had to examine how race physically or genetically exists. This is not just political. I had to do this because, the truth is, many people have passed completely into one race or the other and mixing from previous generations has had no impact on their lives. Many people have fairly recent mixed heritage deliberately hidden from them and have virtually become White, for example. They may be guessing about mixed race heritage and their guesses may be correct. Do these people's stories belong? Ultimately, I feel unable to address issues of possible mixing unsupported by any evidence. If this is the case, then the mixing has probably had no impact on the life experience that is the point of this anthology.

In my calls for submissions I asked that contributors identify their racial background either in their piece or their bio. One contributor was concerned about this request. It appeared to be a demand to authenticate herself, which for her (and many of us) recalls the troubling demands for "proof" of race that we sometimes experience. In truth, I *was* asking for some kind of authentication. I did not want to end up publishing White women whose racial mixing was no more than a fervent, baseless desire on their part. People often come to this belief because they wish to escape oppressor status and not deal with their own racism.

This book is about the lives and experiences of mixed race women who are affected by the socio-political aspects of racism. I will not give a platform to White women who believe they must be mixed because they "feel connected" to a non-White culture. Because of my upbringing, I am forever connected to White North American culture, but this does not mean I am White. I don't believe it is relevant to have been another race in a past life, therefore previously mixed race women 'need not apply.' This book is for racially mixed women of colour who want to say something about their lives and for anyone wishing to read about it.

Ethnicity and race are not the same thing. Racial differentiation in human evolution happened long ago, has never been static and there are racially mixed people all over the world. I chose to restrict this anthology to issues of racial and not ethnic mixing, therefore I had to decide what I thought race actually was. I am not an anthropologist who might be able to give a more scientific definition of race. But should it even be the anthropologists' role to define race? Science is not without race bias. In the end, I had to return to my experience. Race is an experienced thing. We are part of a race, or races, because experience, history, genetics, physicality, family and politics evidence it. The same can be said for ethnicity but to a lesser degree. Ethnicity focuses more around cultural and national boundaries. Persons of the same race can belong to different ethnic groups. For the purposes of a book that had to have some parameters, and as a lay person, these were my guidelines in determining the existence of race as different from ethnicity.

Because of my existence as a Black woman with a White parent, I experience my races in a certain way. I identify as a Black woman. If anyone chooses to inquire, I may also say that I have other racial ancestry. I have not taken on a mixed/Native identity because this is new information for me. I am still processing its meaning. I have very little information about it and I don't feel comfortable rushing into a new culture to which my claim is questionable. I do not wish to take from Native cultures as others who do not belong there have done. If I fill out a form that asks for my race I say Black. I do this because it is my Black self that has shaped most of my experiences in life. I don't experience myself as parts but as one whole and if that is a paradox, so be it. This paradox of existence in two or more races is crystallized in Faith Adiele's poem "Remembering Anticipating Africa" where she writes:

> *crowds of children churning up the dust*
> *they chase me shouting*
>
> ...
>
> *white lady! white lady!*
> *at me*
> *a nigger for 25 years*

I recognize that due to skin colour, I am certain to have received privilege from Whites (and later from Blacks) but having been the only Black person I knew for fourteen years, I never had a Blacker person in my life to compare experiences with. I only knew I was treated like dirt.

It was when I was a teenager, with a Black American boyfriend, that I discovered the hierarchy of skin tone. I seemed to be prized by him and his friends because of my "Red" colouring. My light skin, freckles, green eyes and looser hair meant that I was sought after, exoticized. After messages of ugliness and worthlessness, exoticization was okay by me. So this is who I became. I was the voluptuous, café au lait sister. The gypsy/Creole woman, big breasted, big afroed courtesan, welcome in any man's bed, as Camille Hernandez-Ramdwar experienced in "Ms. Edge Innate."

In grade one I was called "sex maniac" by gangs of six-year-old boys... and in later years, acquired the trappings of that myth — the over-sexed mama, the hot tamale, hot Latin blood, ball-busting black woman who could fuck you in half.

But then I was tired of being exoticized. This was not who I was either. It didn't get me anywhere but into bed, where I was a slightly more desirable piece of dirt. I realized that all I needed was a vagina to get into a straight man's bed. Sex was not an indicator of worth but only of gender and availability. I realized that to commodify myself as exotic meant incredible loss. Loss of self, family, community and spirit. I began working to reject the hierarchy of colourism.

Colourism is one legacy of colonization. The invasion of women's bodies is always a device of war. The creation of a mixed European and local "class" helped ensure division and conflict among the indigenous people. This has happened all over the world. The mixed race progeny often were given access to things their unmixed sisters and brothers would never have. The lighter-skinned people were also indoctrinated into the colourism hierarchy and believed themselves to be superior, creating their own history as oppressors and justifiable mistrust which is still having impact on our lives today. Even in countries no longer under white rule, the colour hierarchy is often still intact. Many people, including those of mixed race, need to look at this history and excise any lingering colonization of ourselves. As Joanne Arnott states in "Speak Out, For Example."

Participating in the diminishing of ourselves and of others is how we learned to survive, and it takes conscious effort, storming and weeping, and courageous collaboration to turn things around.

I chose to present mixed race women's stories in this anthology partly because my life and creativity revolve so much around women's energy and partly because women of mixed race experience a unique stereotyping that is compounded by gender bias.

Here in North America, popular culture's tiresome, racist images of racially mixed women show up in characters like Julie in Edna Ferber's *Showboat* (a recent production in Toronto, that has caused great pain in Black communities). If you look for us in these places, we are always either "good," self-sacrificing creatures, like Julie, who have just enough White in us to have nobility; to know when it is time to go back to our "places": or, we are "tragic Mulattos (or Halfbreeds or Eurasians...)" like Freddi Washington's character in the 1934 version of *Imitation of Life* (played in the remake by White woman Susan Kohler). Washington's character is the light-skinned child of two Black parents who is thwarted in her attempts to "pass" each time her darker mother comes on the scene. Usually, mixed women did not survive long in movies but in this case the character loses her mother who dies of a broken heart due to her daughter's rejection. As for Freddi, she left Hollywood, bitter at the racism of the movie and of Hollywood itself. She resumed her career at the Negro Federal Theatre in Washington D.C. where her radicalism was welcomed.

The other stereotype of mixed race women is that of moral and sexual degeneracy. It is as if our basic degeneracy as women of colour is magnified by White ancestry. Our so called "Whiteness" increases our "beauty" along with our awareness of it, driving us to a frenzy of bitter abandon so agreeable and piquant to our White male pursuers. It is this particular stereotype that affects our understanding of the word miscegenation itself. Literally this word means simply, "mixed marriage" and "mixed race," the prefix "*misc*," meaning mixed. Post-emancipation fear, outrage and racism in Whites resulted in anti-miscegenation laws in the United States. Other countries such as South Africa, have also had such laws. Not only were miscegenates abominations, but the word miscegenate became virtually synonymous with degenerate. This negative aspect still affects understanding of the word. I had assumed that the prefix of this word was "mis," which would indicate "error" or "wrong," relating its meaning to the idea that we should not exist.

Not only have White supremacists created race laws, they have also dictated our understanding of words such as miscegenation. I had to examine the reasons why I initially had a negative reaction to this word. For me, it came down to the fact that I had taken on the White mainstream view of this word and, therefore, had agreed with the racist interpretation of it. Since I now know the factual meaning (as well as knowing the historical misuse), I use the word without any reservations. Having this word in the title of this anthology has been a challenge to some, but this is the word I have chosen.

The way White North American culture sees the word "blues" and the art form of the "Blues" is also negative. This is because White culture's opinion of the creators of this art form is essentially negative. It has been comforting to White supremacists to see Blacks as lowly, powerless unfortunates coping with their lot in life by creating music to soothe themselves. I don't see the Blues this way at all. I see it as a powerful, defiant, creative expression claiming victory out of oppression. This is what I believe *Miscegenation Blues: Voices of Mixed Race Women* is. It does chronicle and analyze our lives and our experiences of difficult circumstances. It also proclaims that we lead positive, powerful lives and that we are not tragic. There have been objections to the use of the word "blues" in the title. Again, this is the word I have chosen. As a Black Canadian descended from Black Americans, the Blues are a part of my culture and so I use the term as a metaphor that I understand. I cannot speak for other cultures, which is why this is an anthology. Mine is not the only culture represented in this book and it is not entirely about a White versus colour struggle or North American situations.

Women of mixed race have many different experiences and points of view. We live and think about our lives in ways that may not seem at all feminist or political. I am a feminist but I feel that women do not need feminist analysis to speak about their lives. The women whose writing and artwork appear in this book are not all "political" women. They do not all describe their lives through a political framework. Even those of us who do, have not necessarily escaped our own racism or gender bias. We are simply in a process of living and learning our lives. Many of the contributors have never written or been published before. Some submissions were from such a colonized point of view they were painful. I did not include these because they represented a negative and misguided place where I did not want this anthology to go. One such place is the idea that racial mixing would be the so called "future" of race relations and the future of humanity. One or two contributors do mention it, briefly, without necessarily agreeing with it. I strongly disagree with this position. It is naive. It leaves the race work up to the mixed people and it means the annihilation of existing racial groups and our entire histories and cultures as if we are obsolete. It is essentially a racist solution.

For this reason I think it is important for mixed people who have White ancestry to not identify only as mixed but to stress identity with their coloured ancestry. This would be different for those who have no White ancestry, though there can still be oppressor/oppressed history in their lineage which may require examining.

Our existence is not meant to annihilate. We simply exist. We should not be forced into a "closet" about White or any other parentage, but we must recognize that our location is as women of colour. Recent U.S. census taking has helped to create a political hotbed in that country about how mixed Black and White people identify. Some mixed people loving and not wishing to erase White parentage opted to identify as "other." They may not have seen themselves as Black. They may have been challenged or disputed about their Blackness by White or Black people. Many Black people felt that it was internalized racism that led these folk to apparently opt out of Blackness. There was also the concern that this would lower the numbers of Blacks in America and possibly lead to a decreased power-base along with decreased attention to Black community goals in federal and state initiatives. I identify as Black for the purposes of census-taking or any other purpose, but I am not ashamed of my non-Black ancestry. I should be allowed to be who

I am and so should everyone else. Just let's do it with enough awareness to know where we are really located.

My goal for *Miscegenation Blues*, over the three years of working on it, was to create a book where mixed race women can document their lives, define themselves, connect with one another and examine some of the challenges they face. Because what we look like is such an issue, I have included many photographs of us along with artwork. I wanted to create a visually beautiful book that I would be proud to own and proud to have brought into being. And I am proud.

CAROL CAMPER
February 1994

Edge to the Middle

location, identity paradox

Camille Hernandez-Ramdwar

Ms. Edge Innate

DO YOU KNOW WHO I AM? I'M THE ONE YOU CAN'T LEAVE alone. The one who puzzles you, intrigues you. I am the original definition of "exotic." Acceptable in many ways, the cafe au lait of life, more palatable because I am diluted. Not as offensive, not as threatening — you think. Certainly not as obvious. But hard to ignore.

They call me white, they call me black — they've called me everything in between. Honestly, if one person could claim global citizenship, it would be me, because who could dispute? But then again, looks count for everything, and I *know* people see what they want to see. If they're looking for a new member, I'm it. If they're looking for a scapegoat, I'm it. If they're looking for a specimen, I'm it. If they're looking for an excuse, I'm it. I'm *It*. I'm *It*. I'm *It* — a glorious game of tag and everyone wants to participate.

I don't think my parents realized the complexity of what they were getting into. Like most interracial couples, they just closed their eyes and ears and hoped for the best. Of course the children would be beautiful, of course both sides would ooh and aah over the benefits — the dark (but not too dark) complexion, the wavy (not too curly) hair, everybody should have been happy, everyone should have been satisfied. Those large dark eyes, like the eyes of orphan poster children: "Is she adopted? Where did you get her?" Looks of bewilderment as my mother tries to explain her husband is "foreign," "dark." Dark like the night? Like tar? Like a rapist? Oh dear, you didn't marry one of *those*.

I went to my mother's family reunion when I was sixteen. I guess I went out of respect for my mother, because I didn't go for myself. There was no reason for me to be there, as far as I could see. I didn't resemble anyone in the crowd, and there were over three hundred people there. I remember leaving in the middle of the big barn dance, because I couldn't relate to anyone, and was tired of being asked whose (half-breed; bastard; darkie; nigger) offspring I was.

My mother raised me, she loved me, but upon reaching adulthood, I've never realized that there was something very important my mother could never give me — a culture which matched my colour. If women are the bestowers and the keepers of culture, the ones who pass on language, nuance, myth, food, spiritual teachings and values to children, then I have been culturally malnourished. It wasn't my mother's fault. In fact, through many years of struggle, I have learned that there is no one to blame. I could have blamed my parents — my mother for wanting an "exotic" experience, my father for coveting a white woman, but they made their choices, and now I am the one who must deal with the consequences of their actions.

Because I was raised in my mother's homeland, and not my father's, I grew up with my mother's culture. And my parents wanted it that way. If there were women who could have taught me things about my "other" culture — my paternal grandmother and aunts — I was removed from them by an entire continent and a sea.

My mother loved me, she raised me, but she could never quite understand me. She did not live in my skin. In fact she seemed oblivious to my colour, as my father had become oblivious to his. These issues to them were irrelevant, or, in retrospect too painful. They hoped my acculturation would make up for my colour. They hoped I would automatically assimilate — perhaps even marry white, continue the dilution of our blood, whiten the grandchildren. They never spoke of this, but it was inferred in their actions and statements. I, having had no choice, subjected to the isolation of an all-white community (save for the few foster children sprinkled amongst the middle-class white families), almost made their wishes a reality.

Because I grew up in this country, because I can speak the language, understand the nuances, the not-saids, the thought patterns, because I can decipher the white response, I am considered Canadian. But I hate this indefinable term.

"Oh Edge, you're so Canadian!"

You know what Canadian means to me? And remember, I know whereof I speak. A Canadian is someone who likes hockey, likes the winter, the whiteness. A Canadian is someone who spends every summer going to "the lake" ("a pool of stagnant water" my father used to call it.) A Canadian is someone who thinks this is the greatest country on earth. Someone who wants to perpetuate the status quo. Someone who travels to the Third World and hangs out with other (white) Canadians, Australians, Brits and occasionally Americans. Someone who thinks of Third World women and men as "an exotic experience." Someone who is ignorant of world history, geography, and is profoundly culturally ignorant. All black people are "Jamaicans" or "from Africa." All South Asian people are "Pakis." East Asians are invariably "Chinese." First Nations people are drunks, or militant troublemakers.

My friend's brother said that the Mohawks at Oka had no right to pick up guns. Oh? I've heard this many times — from all kinds of mouths. No, they have no right to be angry, no right to defend their land, no right to seek retribution. Canadians have become so accustomed in their psyches to the docility of people of colour that it is reprehensible to them that these "non-whites" are no longer behaving like children, accepting what is thrown at them.

But I digress. It is obvious that, to me, a Canadian is not a person of colour, nor an aboriginal person. A Canadian is white — one of the "two founding nations" or one of the following stream of later immigrants — Jewish, Ukrainian, German, Italian, Portugese, etc. Therefore, upon meeting black Canadians, I am heard to say "Well, you are black first, then a Canadian by fault of birth," to which they reply,

4

no, my people have been here for five generations and you'd better damn well believe I'm Canadian. To which I counter-attack — Oh yeah? When was the last time you *weren't* asked where you are from? How many of "your people" are represented in government — at *any* level? Why are there race riots in Halifax, where black people have been living as long as white people? Why are black people being shot by police?

Because I could not identify with my mother's culture, and because I could not acquire her colour, I strongly adopted my father's culture. I wonder how much of this was choice, how much necessity, and how much instinct. I know I gravitated towards thinking black and Caribbean long before I knew what those two intertwined, yet distinct, cultures represented. Everything else (literally) paled in comparison.

When I was small, I would go to parties with the other kids, and someone would put on a record, and I would get up and dance — perfect rhythm, hips, feet — and everyone would stare in amazement and ask — Where did you learn how to dance? Who taught you? How do you do it? No one taught me, I would respond — and then think, Edge, you're different. I would sit down to play "Peanut Man" on the piano with my Jewish friend, try to teach her the syncopated beat, but no matter how many times she rehearsed it, it just wouldn't come out right. And I'd think, doesn't she hear what I hear? It's so simple! Again — "I'm different."

And boys — white boys — fascinated by some myth of my sexual powers — dark, musky, hypnotic — would taunt, tease and abuse me. In grade one I was called "sex maniac" by gangs of six-year-old boys... and in later years, acquired the trappings of that myth — the oversexed mama, the hot tamale, hot Latin blood, ball-busting black woman who could fuck you in half. They bought it, I dished it out — desperate for love and acceptance and to be considered beautiful in the era of Farah Fawcett and Cheryl Tiegs. Because black women were to fuck, not to love, because I was a nymphomaniac *anyway*, it was alright to sexually abuse me.

And I've paid a price for all this acting, this "assimilation" if that's what it's called. A Trinidadian man told me years ago that people like me were schizophrenic, would always be schizophrenic because we are living in a world that does not allow us to integrate ourselves, our psyches. I don't know about this — there may have been a time in my life when I truly had a hard time feeling whole, but I now know who I am, what I am and where I fit in the scheme of things. Other people may have a problem defining me, but that is their problem. I know where I stand.

(Oh the words of the strong, of the self-knowing — Where have I gained such courage? How long have I envied people who simply look into the mirror and state "I Am?" People who can point to one nation on a map, or even continent, and say "This is where I/my people are from." The urge for wholeness, completeness in a world that consistently denies it.)

I watch couples on the street very carefully, mixed couples interracial couples, and I always think of the children. If you make children, who will be raising them? Who will be teaching them? Are these white women who mother children of colour really prepared for the struggles that child will endure? Are they willing to accept that they can not and have not walked in that child's shoes? Are they prepared to confront their own ignorance? Can they truly offer support and guidance to that child?

I watch with interest the conflicts over black children placed in white foster homes. The whole movement to end this, end the assimilation, the "loss of the race," and I can't help but think, yes, but what about those of us who grew up in a mixed race home and *still* did not get culturally nourished? Does it really matter if you are raised by your "blood" parents or not when the issue is culture? That is to assume that your parents' culture is always your own — which isn't necessarily the case. I know I had to fight for my culture; I had to wade and sift through endless genetic memories; I had to tune into ancestral voices and dreams; I had to see myself in eyes that easily reflected my own

6

because they were similar. Eyes that knew richness, pain, history, joy, rhythms of life. I had to seek that, and it was a long journey. I had to leave icicle stares and snow-capped schooling, literally and figuratively, in order to see myself in my natural habitat.

And they call me Ms. Edge Innate, precipice girl, riding on the wave of something wholly internal, a calling I can't explain save to say it is in my soul. Innate: ie., inborn, not acquired. I had to revert to myself. I had to struggle to claim what was already mine. Something that explains myself to me, something that makes sense.

But I can not expect you to understand — not yet. I watch as people become further divided, departmentalized, tribalized... and I wonder on the choices I will have to make — again — and that my children will have to make. There is no camp for us to fit easily into, there never has been, and we are always asked to choose, but by reason of our appearance the choice is often made for us.

I am tired of choosing; I long to be whole. The mirror lies, it confuses — appearances are so deceptive and so subjective. My inner voice tells the truth. Ms. Edge Innate — here I am, on the periphery of *your* world, but knowing that what is mine is wholly and soully my own.

A. Nicole Bandy

Sorry, Our Translator's Out Sick Today

You, a Black
> don't see why you should take Chicano studies, Asian-American
> studies, or even Native American studies — or why I do

You, an Indian
> ask me over and over why Blacks hang more with each other than
> they do with tan people

You, a white
> think I have a duty to answer any goddam personal question that
> comes into your head

You, a Black
> get offended when I tell you you're not capable of advising me
> on how to put together a powwow

You, an Indian
> look at me like I just told you I'm going to the moon and say, "Why
> do you want to go to *Nigeria?*"

You, a white
> don't believe me when I say it doesn't work to teach about Native
> Americans the same way you teach about African-Americans

YOU
> ask me questions
> and won't believe the answers.

Did you ever think that
maybe I get tired of translating?

8

Culture Is Not Static

Black girls
In a sista session
gossiping, laughing
Deep throaty Southern
Detroit composure
L.A. fast-as-a-machine-gun speaking
New York calm
Halter tops, low-slung jeans, hip-hop stylin'-

It is not my story.

Indian girls
strolling through the powwow grounds
looking for a snag, joking — *aiyeee!*
Pueblo, wishing for the deer dance
Creek, thinking of green corn ceremony
Seminole, noticing the Lakotas noticing her dark skin
Miwok, missing the sound of clapper sticks
Sunglasses, earrings, jeans over cowboy boots —

It is not my story.

White girls
In the locker room mirror
lacquered bangs, talking about boys
Blonde, clipped speech
Redhead wondering about a Friday-night date
Brunette angry with her wiry hair
Blonde number two adds another layer of mascara
Crop tops, tight jeans, fake smiles —

It is not my story.

Mine is complicated, complex.
I am many people at once, all living in me.
Sometimes one speaks through my mouth,
         using my lungs,
         curling my tongue,
         shaping my lips
Sometimes another
And those who don't believe in the
         many inside of me
Stare

Surprised
At the me they never wanted to know about.

         "You could tell you're Indian when you said that."
         "You sounded like a black girl right then!"
         You're letting the white come out in you."
(Surprised! What did you expect?)
I told you but I guess you weren't listening.

Crazy how folks refuse to believe.

Lisa Jensen

journal entry 25/10/92

...something so basic as *food:* basic in that it is at the *base* of life. and illustrates just how colonized our minds are.

I used to say, while pondering whether I identified myself as a woman of colour or not, that I wasn't sure, because I hadn't experienced really "blatant" racism, e.g. being called names, being denied employment. Though by then I had tired of being "exotic" looking, and wondering if perhaps there was some reason I was chased home from school, pushed down in the school yard — other little girls were too, but not all of them and I can't quite remember who else. So getting back to food: this might be an illustration of identity. For example, if I am talking about "comfort foods" with a white woman, I am fairly certain hers will be different from mine and that it is highly likely she won't know what some of mine are. And chances are, I will know what many of hers are, and some of these may be mine also...

Elehna de Sousa

I WAS BORN AND RAISED IN THE BRITISH CROWN COLONY OF HONG Kong. Although I did not identify with any cultural heritage in particular, I knew that I was not Chinese. They were the other 99.9 percent of the population.

My parents never spoke to us about our roots, and we did not have the benefit of an extended family in that part of the world. in retrospect, I think that my mother decided we were to be "cosmopolitan." At home, we learned to acquire a taste for food from all parts of the world and, at school, we mixed with children of all nationalities, Caucasian, Eurasian and Chinese.

The truth is, I didn't even have a personal identity when I was young. For one thing, I was a female child, fifth in a large family, and therefore, a "non-person." For another thing, children were to be seen and not heard.

Paradoxically however, in the early years of my childhood, I was also placed up on a pedestal for all to admire, a puppet-princess with no personality... a mere extension of my mother's vanity. I believe it was my fair complexion and pretty face that saved me from the unhappy fate of the darker ones in the family. From my elevated position, I watched helplessly as my mother directed the full force of her irrational anger toward those she did not favour.

It quickly became evident to me that in the cosmopolitan scheme of things, white was the most desirable colour to be. All other colours were tolerated with some disdain and derision.

"Mummy is milk, Daddy is coffee, and we are chocolate," rang the popular refrain in our household. I was glad that I was light chocolate and not dark. I quickly learned the value of being good, non-demanding, and numb. I also knew that I was the fairest of them all... next to my mother, that is. With her on my side, my safety and survival were thus assured.

My mother grew up in East Africa, a Goan, of Portuguese East Indian[1] descent. She lived within the shelter of a large extended family in an insular world that was neatly segregated into Whites, Asians and Blacks.

Here, in South East Asia, and so far from her roots, she could blend in as a white woman. In this new kingdom, she became the fantasy queen of her domain, wielding her power dangerously, instilling fear and dread in her subjects.

At the tender age of fifteen, I spread my wings and flew far from the unhappy place of my childhood.

For some years I travelled on Portuguese and British passports, interchanging them according to convenience. I spoke Chinese in the East and English in the West, and was equally comfortable with both.

Occasionally, I made the dutiful visit back across the seas to the place of my birth. I would obligingly attend social functions with my mother, standing by helplessly as she apologized to her friends for my darkened appearance and loudly scolded my foolish, foreign, sun-loving ways.

In time, I settled down with a husband, became a Canadian citizen, and gave birth to a winsome child, fair-skinned, blue-eyed and blonde.

I smile ruefully as I recall the time when her dad and I, starry-eyed and innocent, announced our forthcoming marriage to his parents. "My dear, what about the children?" his mother asked, with genuine anxiety and concern, echoing racist fears from long ago.

When our daughter was born, beautiful, white and perfect, I'm sure more than one grandparent breathed a sigh of relief and delight.

They looked at her with pride. "Must be a recessive gene somewhere," I was told. "Perhaps a trace of Dutch blood. They were great explorers and colonizers too."

So now my daughter grows up, Scandinavian looking, with a genetic heritage of Portuguese, East Indian, Scottish, Irish, French and perhaps a trace of Dutch. She is proud to be a Canadian. Her identity is intact. And for myself?

I am content to travel through life as I have done for many years, carrying the colour of skin and features that allow me to shapeshift through different cultures with ease.

I have been able to smile pleasantly in response to friendly locals who inquire about my place of origin, often insisting that I must be from their country, but perhaps from a different part. It has been my honour to have been graced with a variety of different nationalities as I have journeyed around the globe. Among others, South American, Spanish, Italian, Indonesian, Malaysian, Indian (East, West and Native), Jewish, Arab and... only in North America, WHITE WITH A GREAT TAN!

As my inner identity continues to grow and strengthen, my outer identity becomes even more flexible and tenuous. It is of no real importance to me. From where I write this, in Kauai, Hawaii, I have had the privilege of being called Kamaaina, or "child of the land."

Here, in this spiritual land of mixed race, I feel at home. I have been able to drop the last vestiges of my urban lifestyle, freeing myself for total immersion in the magic and Aloha of the Island. My soul is replenished daily with the kind of love and acceptance that is uniquely Hawaiian. I give thanks for the ancient wisdom I have learned here.

IKE: The world is what you think it is.

KALA: There are no limits.

And most importantly, *MANA:* All power comes from within.

That is what really matters to me. This is where my strength lies.

---

[1] Goa, formerly a colony of Portugal, was reclaimed by the Indian government in 1961.

Nadra Qadeer

Spider Woman

As a child I was fascinated by
tarantulas.
Their hairy bodies and predator approach
nobody could touch them on the other side
of the cage.

On the other side of the cage
I am the mystery that nobody touches.
Mimicking the colours of the spider;
Brown, White blends
One leg on land, the other dangling.

My hair is the fine silk thread
mixed with the raw fear of the venom.
I am the fascination in the cage.

Like the colonizer and the colonized,
I am the spider.
The Killer and the one
many times killed.

Deanne Achong

I THINK MY WHOLE LIFE I'VE NEVER HAD SKIN THAT FITS IN ANY-where. I have never been able to find a foundation make-up that matches — even the new ones made for darker skin. My skin colour is olive toned, I guess. It tans quickly. That is its colour.

Making the colour photograph was hard because the guy in the photo-lab asked me why I didn't like the orange tone of the skin on the contact sheet. I said my skin is not that colour. It's always been hard to identify, though, just what it is.

Fitting in seems like a vague anticipated memory. I can sometimes pass for white. People always ask me what my nationality is. Especially when they hear my name. And the thing I hate most is their response. *Oh, how interesting.* No, I want to scream, it's not interesting, it's who I am. And then, I remember, I don't even know what that is.

Now, I have a tatoo. A mark of colours that are my own. My skin carries a trace of uncertainty; I am unable to proudly wear the banner of race.

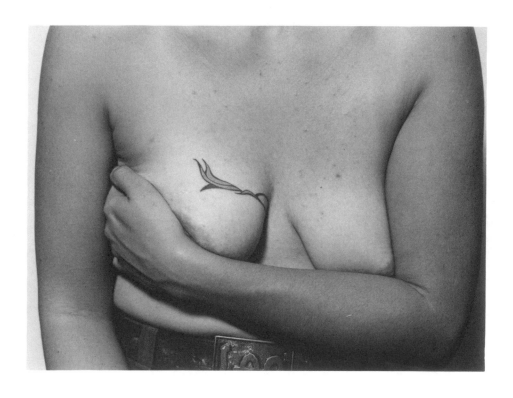

Michele Chai

Don't

ask me
to choose between you
Caribbean
 Blue (Red)
        Yellow (White)
                Black (Black)
over accented thighs
the freedom to love
who I feel

don't make me say
that I prefer
humming birds
        calypso
                salt-fish and coo-coo
over long harsh winters
        short humid summers
                and subtle racism
you know
I do.

and not just because we're here together
       fighting for a decent piece
           it's no easy business
remembering
      because it is far
          from perfect
and intolerance
      has caused this distance

so please
Don't
ask me
to choose between you
Caribbean
 Blue (Red)
      Yellow (White)
          Black (Black)
over accented thighs
the freedom to love
who I feel
 the freedom to express
      this openly
because although I am freer
      I can never
          enjoy freedom here
and I cannot choose —
I will not choose
between you.

Naomi Zack

My Racial Self over Time

DUE TO MY PHILOSOPHICAL WORK ON RACIAL THEORY AND some autobiographical information in the foreword to my book, *Race and Mixed Race*, (Temple University Press, 1993) I was recently asked to appear on a television talk show about "mixed-race kids," with a special focus on those who had first discovered that they were "black" in adolescence. I told the producer that it was true I was mixed race and that I had discovered that I was "black" for the first time in adolescence but that I preferred to direct my time and energy to scholarly work of some detachment, rather than situations in which I personally would be the subject. She said in that case, perhaps I would consent to appear as an "expert" on the show. I told her I did not think I was an expert on the psychological impact of adolescent discovery that one is partly, and therefore in American society wholly, black because social reality had changed somewhat since I was sixteen, I was not a psychologist, and again, I preferred not to deflect my efforts from academic concerns. She was disappointed, but not "unsympathetic."

I began to think again about autobiographical discussions of problems of identity as they relate to race and mixed-race, and it occurred to me that someone in my (demographic) position can experience sufficient changes in identity over time so that a main concern of autobiographical writing might be not the events in a life but successive stages of how one sees herself. Of course, probably everyone could write their autobiography in that way. At any rate, I am going to try to briefly describe how my own "racial self" has changed over time.

I was born in 1944, by caesarian section, in a hospital in Brooklyn, New York. My mother was one of seven children in a Russian Jewish immigrant family from Vilna. She grew up in tenements and every Saturday, her parents would spread newspapers on the kitchen floor and pour kerosene over their children's heads to kill lice. Her father was an herbalist and a Hebrew scholar and teacher. Her mother's father had been the mayor of a small village and he died when a canopy fell on his head during a public ceremony, leaving a suddenly-poor family of eight children. My grandmother was the oldest and she did not get along with her new stepfather, so she hastily agreed to an arranged marriage at the age of sixteen. She was said not to have loved her husband because he was strict and unforgiving.

My mother grew up as the baby in a house of discord. She caught polio at the age of two and wore iron braces on her leg until she was eighteen. She then began to walk with a cane, which she did for the rest of her life.

My mother was an artist and she raised me on her own in Manhattan's lower East side, working first as a janitor and then as a sketch artist. We were poor and we were Jews and my mother liked to refer to us as "little people." When I was seven, my grandmother came to live with us from Kings County Mental Hospital where she had spent some years — she probably had what was later called Alzheimer's disease. She was blind in one eye, sang boisterously in Yiddish and Russian and had a broken hip that had not mended properly. She was also incontinent when she laughed. She and I were good companions during the time I looked after her while my mother worked, although we often fought and threw things at one another.

My mother said she was a widow and that my father had been in the jewellery business and died as a soldier during World War II. On Canal Street, I saw refugees with concentration camp numbers on their arms and I understood that it was because they were Jewish. I usually felt content as a child although at times our neighbourhood seemed to have a dark gloom that made me dread going home.

In school, and around people who did not know me, I was sometimes asked what nationality I was. They thought I looked "Spanish" but I knew I was Jewish, even though I had never been inside a Synagogue. I was smart in school and not very active physically. I was always overweight but accepted my mother's pronouncement that I was "just right." My mother told me that I was beautiful but I didn't take her very seriously. I felt simply "alright." I liked to go to the movies and I could imagine myself to be anyone who was the main character, in any genre of Hollywood film.

D, a man with dark skin would come to see my mother on occasion, and stay overnight. He was usually drunk and angry. One morning he asked me for a glass of water which I gave him. Later, my mother praised me for having given him the water in our "good" glass. She said I might have thought he was dirty because his skin was so dark. I was glad my skin wasn't as dark as his or even as dark as some of the Puerto Rican kids in school. But that winter I saw that my bare wrists hung out of my grey hand-me-down coat and that they were a greyish-tan. They looked as though they should be covered up.

When I was twelve, my mother had enough money saved for a down payment on a house in a rural suburb in Westchester County. She, my grandmother and I went to live in that house. The school work was harder and there was no easy praise from my teachers. I was slow to develop physically and very clumsy at sports. My friends were the other girls who didn't fit in. My peers and teachers seemed to think that because I was from "The City," I was stupid and a bad influence on other girls. There were only a few Jewish kids in that school. Most of them formed a rich group that had nothing to do with me. Those who were not rich talked to me but they were both meek and disapproving. People didn't just ask me what nationality I was there, but told me they had thought I might be "coloured," although they were of course "not prejudiced," and "*for* integration." I didn't speak to my mother about this. A repulsive and scary feeling about myself began to grow. I lived in Westchester until I was fifteen, when I insisted on going to school in Manhattan again. But I think I lost my Jewish identity in any social sense that could be taken for granted, during those years.

I lost my virginity between fourteen and fifteen when I was seduced by H, a man twenty years older than I, who was my mother's business partner. This developed into a complex relationship that lasted until my junior year at college. H, whose parents had been Irish and German, made me ashamed of my non-white appearance. When I turned 16, he persuaded me to confront my mother about who — what — my father had been. She confirmed that D, her frightening friend before we had moved to Westchester, had been my father. She also told me that D was presently in prison for murdering his oldest son. D had been married for many years and had ten legitimate children. His father had been born a Negro slave and was six years old at the end of the Civil War. His mother was from the Sioux, and my mother described her as "an Indian princess and a granddaughter of Chief Sitting Bull." I found out later that my paternal grandmother had been at least partly Indian although I consider the Chief Sitting Bull descent unconfirmable. (It is on the same level as a claim that my maternal grandfather was a descendant of the prophet Zarathustra because the name "Zack," was a contraction of his Russian family name "Zarakadusha," which is phonetically a derivative of "Zarathustra.") I also found out years later that my father had not been in prison for murder but for assault: He had shot his oldest son, who was twenty-eight at the time, in the buttock with a .22 rifle, because he was lazy and rude to his mother.

I continued to mature with an unsure sense of myself, physically, and socially. Back in Manhattan, I was again accepted as Jewish by all who knew me well enough to ask, but on the street, it seemed to be assumed that I was Puerto Rican. I continued to do well in school and since my mother was making more money, it was assumed that I would go to college. I got a college degree and enrolled in graduate school. I married an Englishman, divorced him when I completed my Ph.D., turned down a college teaching position, left academia and went to live in London where I remained for three years.

In England, I was more open about having a black father than I had been in America. The English did not seem to find this particularly shocking, but their quiet anti-Semitism scared me. I was aware of being a Jew among them. I set up a small, independent film company in London that completed a feature film which never got distributed. I married again. My second husband was an American and we returned to the States. We lived in California and I wrote freelance. I had a son, divorced my second husband, married him again and divorced him. I got married a fourth time, had a second son and another divorce. There was a fifth marriage that was the limiting case of all my marriages — I married and divorced a writer who had spent most of his adult life in prison.

During those years of marriage and divorce I continued to write with minor success, made a videotape of my mother and her paintings while she was dying (which was shown on public television), buried my mother, set up and disbanded several small businesses and spent a lot of time wondering what my work was. I was very close to my sons when they were young children but both spent a lot of time with their fathers after the divorces. Both fathers were white. There were nasty battles over custody and I tended to give up on the rationalization that it was bad for the child to prolong such fights. I didn't think about race much over that time, perhaps because my marriages and eccentric projects isolated me socially — race was never uppermost in my mind during the ups and downs of personal life, and that may have been a mistake.

When I turned forty-five, I began to worry about money because (like Moll Flanders), I had spent most of my capital. I was still worrying about what my work was and I decided to try to return to academia. I began on an adjunct basis. Some of my preliminary writing about racial theory caught Affirmative-Action attention and I began a full-time tenure track job in 1991. I had begun to think about race as clearly as I could, with the use of the philosophical tools of my early training.

I wrote my book and made plans to follow it up with an anthology on mixed race (*Microdiversity!* forthcoming). I think that there isn't much to the concept of race as the ordinary American understands it.

The ordinary American understands race as something physical but there are no general racial markers on a chromosomal level and those physical traits that society has designated as racial traits have varied over time. No other nation at any time in history has developed anything as stringent as the American "one-drop rule" for black racial designation. "According to this rule, people of mixed black and white race do not exist because anyone with one black ancestor is all black, regardless of how many white ancestors he or she has.

Still, there are mixed-race people, because their parents belong to what are considered different races. Surely, I am one of those people, but I cannot decide at this time how close that *raciality* is to my present identity. Race, like class, is almost entirely part of one's social identity. There is no uniform biological foundation for it, even though people unthinkingly think and act as though there is. I first thought that the American problem with mixed race could be solved by showing up the absurdity of the one-drop rule. But I now realize that the problem cannot be fully addressed in that way for this reason: Black and White are invisible to each other in the United States. I have, in close relationships, been treated without prejudice by whites, all my life — or so it seems to me. Since I have been officially designated black for academic recording, I have been accepted without prejudice by blacks in my professional life — or so it seems to me. For a while I thought that I was in a unique position because both sides accepted me. But then I began to listen more carefully to what whites were saying about blacks — *among ourselves* — and what blacks were saying about whites — *among ourselves.* It became clear to me that generally speaking, among themselves, blacks do not consider whites to be human beings in the same deep sense that they are human beings; and whites, among themselves, do not consider blacks to be human beings in the same deep sense that they are human beings. So, among ourselves, within each race, the other race simply does not exist. We — they — are invisible to each other within the two races.

To have a foot planted on either side of this abyss is an emotional and conceptual impossibility. As far as I can tell about present social reality, at least in academic culture, the chasm keeps getting wider. It's too late for me to hop to either side because I can't lie about the presence of black ancestry and pretend to be white, and I can't remake my past and become black. Either I sink or rise. I have decided to rise. And I think that such *transcendence* is possible because I am defying the gravity of merely social reality. I have to function in social reality but I don't actually live there.

Many hours in a day go by when I do not think about myself in racial terms at all. I have lost any sense of that inferiority I had as an adolescent on account of my father's "race." I didn't deliberately set out to lose it. It went after I had done a certain amount of scholarly work on the topic. I am not so sure that my self-esteem has been repaired in that area so much as that my class status is strong enough to balance out my low racial status, (and possibly vulnerabilities due to female gender as well). And, I have not had the task of repairing the loss of self-esteem that the mixed-race person who is trying without recognition to be authentically black, suffers.

University scholars, who have books published, are part of those segments of society that used to be called the "upper classes," regardless of whether they are tenured or how poor they are, or what the ordinarily respectable middle-class person might think of them. So my identity has, in effect, come to rest on the identity of my profession. I am employed as a philosophy teacher which means that it is my charge to get students to think for themselves in the methodology of a distinctive discipline with a long history. That is a continually refreshing and exciting obligation.

However, I consider my most enduring individual work to be writing. Writing is a creative activity under my control in ways that love and family life never can be. It is a private activity that cannot be manipulated by the strings of social reality. What I write and how I write create me as a writer. I don't write fiction but what almost the whole world, except for some contemporary academic philosophers, would consider hard, dry prose. Still, there is art in it. I consider this activity of writing to be my real legacy and I am gratified that both my parents contributed to it. My mother was a painter, sculptor and sketch artist. My father worked most of his life as a landscape gardener. She rendered people as she saw them, for others to look at. He rendered the earth for others to find beautiful. These were both useless activities that bake no bread but have the possibility of nourishing what used to be called "the soul." I like to see myself as being involved in something like that, too.

In sum, over time, I have moved from being Jewish; to being Jewish but not looking Jewish; to being Jewish and black, which is to say black; to being mixed race. The impossibility of being mixed race in American social reality, at this time, has dissolved my racial identity as I write about it. Race has dissolved into writing, for me. I belong to the 'race' of writers who write hard, dry prose, i.e. the race of philosophers who are a type of artist who create themselves in writing. I do this for its own sake so that I can have an existence that others can read.

Ngahuia Te Awekotuku
Painfully Pink

SHE KNEW SHE LOOKED GOOD. THE WHITE PANTS FIT JUST RIGHT, hugging her narrow hips, but she wanted to look even better, she wanted to look perfect. Tonight was — might be — the night. Tahuri had to catch more than a smile from that pretty woman. They'd watched each other's moves for a few nights now; something more had to happen, and soon. And she had to break away from Master Blue Eyes, because it wasn't working. It was all wrong. It was going nowhere, and deep down, she knew it. Even if he was still too thick to face facts — he was fun, he owned a red convertible and an electric Gibson and had snowy blond locks crowning his hairy six feet, but he was male, and a white male, and she'd had enough of that. Enough. She remembered...

His father shouting at *Kuikui* about the Bantus and what happened when his family lived in Africa and how mixed race marriages never worked and by god my son will do no such thing I swear I forbid it! while silent *Kuikui* sat there, head downcast, fingers twining and plaiting black and golden fibres on her lap, shaping a tiny coin purse. Bulbous with frustration, snorting about natives being the same all over the world, the scarlet skinned englishman stormed back to his Rover. All the little kids were playing knucklebones under the plum tree, and they laughed at him in his hurry, with his red *pakeha* face. He jerked his classic car into gear, slammed his fist on the mellow mahogany dashboard, and thundered off.

Despite the diamond decorating her ring finger, she knew it was a summertime farce from the moment that Googelly Blue Eyes — the

Father — blinked over his sundowner, and pursed his slack mouth to stress each word, "University?" Syllable by syllable, each part of the word. "U-ni-ver-sit-y? YOU?" And then he guffawed, spraying himself with gin. A coloured girl at university? Preposterous!

His own son had dropped out of school at fourteen, blaming it on all the moving around from country to country; not that it mattered much, really. For Master Blue Eyes, cars were his thing. Cars, and girls with colour. Like this Tahuri. Café au lait to his milky pallor. They liked to dance, they liked to laugh. They liked him giving them a good time. Oh yes, he liked his happy-go-lucky coloured girls. And what they thought of him, he didn't really care. When things got complicated, he just moved on.

She got into the car, drew the door closed, and flipped him a smile. Within minutes, they were at the club. They could've walked, but dragging up in his chrome spangled Mustang was his statement for the night. Her relations — the male ones — glowered behind dark glasses, leaned against the weatherboard wall, and pretended not to notice their arrival. Maori voices murmered their contempt in Tahuri's mother tongue. She ignored them, counted the bottle tops and butts around her sandalled feet. The *pakeha* grabbed her wrist, and pulled her into the hall.

That pretty woman was there, dancing alone near the band. She moved like syrup, long and slow and easy, tuning herself to the music. Her fingers were spidering through thick lustrous hair tangled around a neck that strained and stretched, shadowing her throat in the dim light. No one else — no male, no female, seemed to be partnering her graceful sway. Tahuri edged over to her, slipped in to the rhythm, following her. The *pakeha* had gone to check out the bar. He was sure she was safe — safely — his. After all, he was the only white guy there, apart from the droogs tossing themselves off with their guitars. They weren't competition, not for a class act like him. One of the barmaids was quite a pretty little thing. So he just took his time, especially when he saw that his girl seemed to be quite happy gyrating with one of her sootier cousins.

She turned, and looked at Tahuri. Their eyes met; locked. Glittered bright signals of recognition. They moved towards each other. For a while, they continued dancing, maintaining careful space between each other. Master Blue Eyes was nowhere to be seen. Tahuri closed in on the pretty woman, who was closing in on her. "Me haere taua," the large upper lip curled over straight white teeth. "Let's get out of here."

No one noticed the two women leaving; they slipped along the ranks of dancing bodies, threaded in and out and around and between, close to the floor's edge, heading for the side door.

They they were out, breathing in the night, savouring fresh air.

Tahuri talked first. She had to, she was so aroused; she couldn't believe what she'd done. Taken off from Master Blue Eyes. Left the *pakeha*. By himself, in the hall, with all her relations, and that visiting team from up country, and all their supporters. Ha! No going back now; this was it. She couldn't believe what she'd done.

"Where shall we go?" she asked, conscious of her face in the flickering blue mauve of the lined up street lights. Town was that way. The pretty woman, who looked a bit older than her, grinned back, "My place. But we'll have to walk — it's not that far. Unless you can find us a taxi?" Her hands were doing things to her hair again.

"A taxi? Nope, not tonight." Not ever, the girl thought, not in this town, too many uncles behind the wheel. "Let's hit it then."

She felt cocky, she felt brave. She felt right. Hooking her thumbs into her belt, she stretched out her hockey-muscled legs, wondering at the woman next to her. Whose red dress was nipped in at the waist, belted in the same patent leather as her louie heeled shoes; long square pockets over her thighs repeated the square cut at the neckline; a plain black cardigan was draped across her shoulders. Earlier, she'd had it wrapped around her hips. From her ears, sharks' teeth set in scarlet sealing wax swayed as she moved. They didn't talk much as they walked. Every now and then, one would snatch a sneaky, appraising look at the other.

High concrete walls surrounded the staff quarters, and the hotel laundry's light caught the sag of clotheslines, drooping above the patchy stubbled grass. Ranks of louvres gaped open, half or three quarters, and cheap curtaining screened in the feebleness of low wattage bulbs. From one window came the sputter of contented snoring; from another, the three four three four grunt of heaving bed springs. Tahuri paused, listening, half embarassed. They'd stopped at a pale green wooden door, marked 31 with silvery letter box numbers. The key went into the keyhole.

Tahuri stood there, didn't know whether to take off her sandals, or leave them on, or just take off herself, or what. A strong palm against her back gently told her what to do. Click, and a light went on, as the red dress slid past her.

She was in someone else's world. Yet it was so familiar, too. Pictures of the Supremes, the Crystals, the Shirelles on the wall. Elvis in Hawaii, framed in a red crepe paper *lei*. And a *piupiu*, supple, exquisitely patterned, above the single bed. One stuffed animal on the quilted bedspread — a black teddy bear. "I made that myself from a *Women's Weekly* pattern," her question, unasked, was answered. "But I chose the colour. Ha. And my *kuia* made the quilt. Hey girl, nau mai, haere mai. Welcome! Sit down — there's only one chair, sorry. So it's yours. And what about a drink…" She stooped, took off her shoes, then unbuckled her belt and hung it on a hook behind the door. The red dress still hugged her shapely body.

"Anything for me," the young girl still couldn't believe what she'd done to the *pakeha*. And where she was. And why she was there. "Um.

You got beer or something? Even lemonade will do. Anything that's not too much trouble," she fumbled with her hair.

Master Blue Eyes liked it loose, hanging. She plaited it. "Hey, you know, we don't even know each other's names, eh..." She crossed and uncrossed her legs, scraping her ankles against each other; roped the braid tightly down her back. "I'm Tahuri, and I've lived here in Rotorua all my life and — "

"Kia ora, Tahuri," black eyes softened. With small, neat gestures, she removed her mako earings, placed them on the bedside cabinet, between a shaded reading lamp, and black plastic radio. "My name's Maka, and I've lived here in Rotorua just eight months — and you're the first one I've met who might be like me," she finished the sentence under her breath, and opened the small cupboard, lifting the embroidered doillie. She came up with a dark handkerchief, which she dropped by the radio, and then two glasses and a lemonade bottle. She balanced them on the cream leatherette glory box at the foot of the bed. She popped the top off, poured their drinks, then swivelled, and switched on the reading lamp. Over the off-white shade, she cauled the cotton square of purple bordered crimson. Then she crossed the room in two paces, and turned off the overhead light. "Lemonade," she murmered, offering bright crystal bubbles in a hotel tumbler. "No booze allowed in the staff quarters." Maka leaned forward; their fingers touched. Tahuri sought out the roundness of lush dark framed by the frock's square neckline, the warmth waiting there. Something inside her smiled, stretched, smiled. This was right. This was her. Yes.

Maka turned on the radio, settled onto the bed. She plumped up the pillows, smoothed down the bedspread.

"Over here's more comfortable than that chair — "

Tahuri moved over, the calico of her slacks meeting the many bright colours of the quilt. She slid her drink along the floor; the diamond ring clipped against its rim. Reminding her. With smallest finger and clever thumb, she prised it off; metal and precious stone clinked then plunged into the glass. She wiped her hand behind her left knee, then shifted towards Maka.

Nothing happened. They just looked at each other, just sat there. Nothing happened. Then, it did.

Guantanamera. Silky lyrics spiralled around the room. Tahuri sank her face into the curve of Maka's shoulder, pressing her into the wall. Maka lifted her chin, drew down, both hands spread across Tahuri's back, one set of fingers coiled around the fraying braid. She wrenched it; Tahuri's head turned, lips reaching the corner of Maka's curling mouth. They kissed, disentangled, kissed again. Drank in each other's breath, tongues describing teeth and tasting gums sweetslick with lemonade. Wrists turned, seeking cool skin beneath fabric: Tahuri's shirt began to ride over itself. She squirmed it back on, grasping the narrow metal nub of Maka's zipper. Running all the way down her spine; a mild tug, the red dress came apart. Maka slipped her lower body out of its skirt, keeping the front against herself, the upper arms still looped in the sleeves. She avoided Tahuri's eyes; the bedcovers were everywhere, tangled around their legs. Maka lowered her voice.

"You can undress me if you take your own off first, Huri."

Down came the perfect hipster pants, off went the T-shirt. The powder blue bikini pants stayed on.

Hands wound into her hair again; her head went down. Biting, she took the red dress with her jaw, and peeled it away. She was laughing, she was swooning, too. Maka's brassiere was strapless; unhooked, it tumbled away, presenting a smooth dusky swell of satin skin, and springy, textured nipples. Maka released the plait, manoeuvreing Tahuri across her. They clung together for a while, mute, exploring. Black nylon briefs slid around Tahuri's left wrist; her fingers delved, waited, delved again. Moisture limned her nails; heat drew in. She caught the elastic, rolled them down. Maka lifted her bum slightly; they came off. Tahuri kept hers on, sliding her lower body between the other woman's thighs, positioning herself, knowing where, knowing how.

Her fingers resumed their rhythm; her hips pressed down, pushing. Long and slow and easy, she began to move, Maka's fullness, Maka's darkness, rising to meet her.

The bed was narrow: single for sure. Sweat damp, they stretched and rearranged; Tahuri was getting a bit of a grip on herself. Her underpants had gone; she lolled beneath the sheet, hauled one corner over, suddenly realized something else.

With Maka, like this, she was the pale one, the hairy one. Her skin — Maka's skin — seemed to glow. All of a sudden Tahuri felt shy — in that eerie light, she looked pink. Pink! Pink like a *pakeha*, like a fresh boiled *koura*, painfully pink like a pig. Like Master Blue Eyes. Except this time it was her. Shit, she didn't want to think of him, not at that moment. But she was so pink. So pale. So hairy. So — yuck, next to Maka.

Whose colour was enhanced, luminous. Hues of subtle burgundy. Folds and texture, fragrant, dark. Secret. And so few sticky hairs and stuff — just the gleam of passion, the nectar immediate, there. She opened her eyes; they were huge, shining.

"How's the lemonade, Huri?"

Tahuri nearly choked. She thought she was asleep. She decided to be smart.

"That's not the drink I want," she joked as she heaved herself up.

Maka's response came from way deep down inside.

"Cheeky. We'll have to see about that one. Anyway, girl, what else do you do with yourself?"

She hauled herself into a sitting position, put a pillow behind her neck, and made herself comfortable. She really wanted to know.

Tahuri reached across the bedding and found Maka's glass. She drained the lemonade bottle into it, and took a swig herself. She passed it over, propped herself against the wall, and linked one arm loose around Maka's large, long, upraised leg.

"I'm going to Auckland in the New Year," she confided.

"Yeah? Auckland? I'm off to Aussie myself," Maka sighed. "As soon as I get the cash together, I'm gone, good-bye Aotearoa..."

"How come?" the younger woman interrupted. "What for?"

"There's not much going for a girl like me here, Huri — not even in Auckland. Up there I'd be stuck in the same rut, you know. Making beds, and doing dishes and waitressing, when what I really want to do is reception work. Front of house stuff, you know, meeting the public, answering the phones, smile, smile, smile, doing the bookings and clerical work, stuff like that. But I've learned already, oh, have I ever, that's it's just beds and dishes for the likes of me girl. Unless I get away, over to Surfers. They say they train you there, on the job, like, you know — and they say they like the dark, exotic look — "

Tahuri knew, all right. Master Blue Eyes and his family had lived near Surfers before moving to Rotorua — his father had often mentioned the South Seas theme in their big hotels. How alluring it was, with the right looking native women at reception. Maka would fit in — they'd like her dark, exotic look, for sure.

"You'll be a winner," Tahuri grinned. She knew.

"And you? What's in Auckland?"

"University," Tahuri felt something funny happening; the diamond ring under the bed pierced her mind's eye. She slid herself against Maka's shoulder, so they snuggled together, worming back into bed, lengthways, side by side. "I'm going to university, to get a law degree or a commerce degree or something. Probably law. I want to do something useful for our people — "

"Then what the hell are you doing with that *pakeha*?" Her voice was harsh. Tahuri's mind went blank. She was aware of her nakedness. Her pinkness. She was trapped under the whiteness of the sheet, against the darkness of her lover's body. She didn't know what to say. She blurted.

"He takes me to nice places and he gave me a diamond ring and I get to see interesting things and to eat food like filet mignon and baked alaska and I drink real french wine and meet people like the mayor and they are interested in me too and they talk about books and films and paintings and I like it Maka, I do. Maybe I'm being pulled along by my *pakeha* blood, you know? My Mum's father was a *pakeha*, but he took off before I was born and yet everyone says I look just like him even though my brothers don't. But I do. Maybe that's it, that's why I really like that kind of stuff, *pakeha* stuff, even though — "

"Even though it's turning you into a *pakeha*," hissed Maka. "Oh shit, let's go to sleep now, Huri. I've got to work early in the morning. Four American tour buses coming in before breakfast. *E moe, e kare*, it's late, too late, for this — "

And she kissed her on the earlobe, turned her face away, and fell asleep.

Glossary

koura fresh water crayfish, scampi
Kuikui Grandma
kuia elderly woman
pakeha white-skinned foreigner, caucasian. Originally meant a person with bad body odour!
E moe, e kare Let's go to sleep, dear
The other Maori phrases are translated immediately in the text itself.

Mercedes Baines

Mulatto Woman
a honey beige wrapper

Mulatto woman Mulatto woman
Brown tones sepia tones
shades summer / winter any season
Mulatto woman Mulatto woman
Where is home
Where is home
Where is home
Mulatto woman Mulatto woman
Are you white — No
Are you black — No
Well you could be black if you wanted to be black you
could pass for black if you acted more black but you
cannot pass for white.
Hey... I'm white
Hey I'm white
Hey I'm white
I could be just give me a chance I'll oppress everyone
and deny my racism because it does not exist in Canada
we are far too nice and besides real Canadians are
white ask anybody who is not from here they will tell
you.
So where are you from?
Mulatto woman Mulatto woman
Honey beige in the shade.

Sheila Batacharya, Claire Huang Kinsley, Lezlie Lee Kam, Gitanjali Saxena, Lisa Valencia-Svensson, and Anne Vespry

Mixed Race Women's Group — *Dialogue One*

LISA: ... I get mistaken for Native North American, South American, Chinese, Japanese, South East Asian, South Asian, a mixture from the Caribbean, Italian and Jewish.

LEZLIE: I hadn't been asked any of those questions until I came to Toronto. I remember the first time I was asked what I was. I was on the subway and this woman said "Are you from Burma?" Burma!? But people mostly think I'm Filipina, I could be Latin American. I've gotten that. I never get Chinese, I get "Some kind of Indian." They're not sure what kind and if it's native, I have been mistaken for Micmac when I'm down east or in Thunder Bay. Most people are totally confused. I used to be confused too, about what I'm supposed to be in their eyes.

GITANJALI: That reminds me of a poem that Jamila Ismail wrote, she's mistaken for all these things in all kinds of different places. She includes not just her racial identity but her political self as well. At the American border they took her for a Communist. All these different places they mistake her for who she really is. It's hard for us to find out. I think that's why identity is so important. I often say I'm sick and tired of all this identity stuff, but we just don't have that reflected enough, how can we construct that? There's no basis to build your life because there's so many assumptions going on around you. You don't know quite how to respond. I grew up not knowing how to respond to those kind of assumptions, because I didn't know where I was in the middle of it.

SHEILA: I wouldn't know how to respond to those types of things, I would always feel ashamed. When I would get asked where I was from, and people always ask you but then they don't wait for you to tell them. They just go ahead and tell you "No, no let me guess" and it becomes this big thing. So... Spanish, Italian, South American, Mayan, those are the ones I remember most. And then, recently, when I moved to Toronto, I keep getting mistaken for being white, like, with a tan.

LEZLIE: Well do you think it has to do with where you are born and grow up? Rosemary Brown wrote about this, the difference it meant for her, for her grandchildren growing up in a predominantly white society and she and her family growing up in Jamaica in a predominantly black society. That she had more sense of self, growing up in Jamaica. Growing up in Trinidad, where I was surrounded by people who looked like me, also gave me a strong sense of "self," and so it doesn't bother me when people ask me where I am from. The only time it ever bothered me was in Trinidad when I had to put down on my school certificate what my nationality or my race was and they put down "mixed," and my friend who was next to me got Black. And then my other friend got Chinese and I went home and I said well what is mixed, and my father said, "Well when you don't fit into any of those categories." So, in Trinidad you have those, you're either Black, Indian, white, or mixed. So, by the time I came up here, it didn't bother me. It still doesn't when people ask me where I'm from. I met a Japanese woman the other day and she said, "Are you a mixture of Japanese and something?" I feel, though, when I hear women who were born here in a predominantly white society, I find that you tend to have more confusion or it bothers you more when you are asked that, because it is sort of getting right to the core of who you are.

CLAIRE: I have a good friend who was working in a store and a woman came up to her and said I'm looking for so-and-so and she said, that's me. And the woman said well, no, they told me downstairs that so-and-so was black and she said, well, I'm black. And this woman, she didn't say, "Oh, sorry, my mistake." She didn't even say "Really, you are?" which would have been bad enough. She said "No you're not."

GITANJALI: I have problems with constructing mixed race in the first place. I'm going to add to the complication (laughter). I applied to go on this weekend the other day, and it had these categories like Native American, Asian, Black, Caribbean and there was mixed race.

SHEILA: At least they had it.

GITANJALI: Yes that was good, because part of the weekend was to discuss these issues. But I didn't check off that box. I checked off South Asian, and behind that box I wrote "Indo-German," because for me mixed race is not a community. It's not a cultural community and it's not a racial community, because we all come from completely diverse racial groups. How can we construct a real community that's based on history and on culture. For me, I draw my cultural identity from my ancestors, my Indian ancestors and my German ancestors. In terms of mixed race people that I meet, I can understand the issues what they might be facing when facing their own communities, I can empathize but I can't identify with that.
It's not a cultural community...
It's more of a situational community...

LEZLIE: It's come up to help other people not have to deal with all of our different backgrounds and where they come from. It is like how the government put out the term "Visible Minorities" so we all became visible minorities. Now the trendy term is mixed race, so now we talk about how do we identify. I used to say I was a mixed race woman, then

I stopped because that didn't feel comfortable, because who understood what that meant? Then I said I was a Brown Trini Dyke and it still didn't mean anything to me because there's so many brown women, and I had to put Trini in because it's important that people know where I come from. So now I say I'm a Callaloo Dyke. If you want to know what callaloo means you have to ask me. Callaloo means you're a mixed race woman from Trinidad. That's how I identify now, and if you can't deal with that, then...
(laughter)
I'm trying to take it back... my identity. Who I am!
(laughter)

LISA: You were talking earlier, Gita, about how there was not a mixed race community, nor could there be, and I was just thinking that in the white feminist community there is so much theory, that broad category "Women of Colour" has enough trouble fitting into their theory. But we, fuck up their theory like nothing. If they were to know my life, all their theory would fly out the window.

ANNE: For me, I went through periods of thinking I have to identify with one or the other or I really have to identify with both, and then realizing no... In some ways I'm Trinidadian the way Lezlie is Indian, I like the food, I like the music, there are bits that I can relate to from stories that my father has told, but I cannot lay any claim to that culture. At the same time there are bits that I like about my Scots heritage, I'm learning to play the bagpipes, but I cannot lay claim to Scots culture, it is not my culture. Culturally, the only culture I somewhat identify with is the lesbian and gay community.... When you're talking about trying to create a community out of lots of different life experiences, that is a prime example. But I've gone from feeling that I have to be part of one or the other racial or cultural community to feeling relaxed that no, I can empathize with bits of people's experience in the Black community or bits of people's experience in white culture, but I don't have any vast desire to say "This is my place. I belong here." Now this is who I am, and I can exist as neither instead of both. This may change, but I'm fairly happy now. Like Pat Parker. She was dealing more with sexual as well as racial politic, and said that some times she went out as a Black radical, sometimes as a feminist, sometimes as a lesbian, and her idea of a successful revolution, would be one after which she could take all her selves wherever she was going, and have all her selves welcome.

GITANJALI: One thing that I think is very important to say before we finish is how often organizing around mixed race falls into the one white parent, one parent of colour thing. I don't like aligning myself with that. In India there are the Anglo Indians, who are a class above Indians and below white people, and I don't want to put myself in that place. The dialogue always seems to centre on being white and not white. Automatically you're setting yourself up to create and feed into a hierarchy. I have a problem with the way this is put together.

CLAIRE: I think often people assume that mixed race means one white parent. It reminds me of that conference Sheila mentioned in an earlier conversation where one guy said that people should not identify as mixed race because they were just trying to use their white privilege, completely disregarding the fact that there were some people at the mixed-race table who did not have any white ancestry.

SHEILA: And presuming that was why we were coming together, to talk about our white parent. Instead of realizing that we had other issues around being of mixed race that are shared with people who do not have a white parent.

Michele Paulse

Commingled

WITHIN THE CONTEXT OF WRITING THIS, FOR A BEGINNING point my memory flashes to the lawn of my parents' house in Crawford, Cape Town, South Africa. A young girl, I stand near the dark grey painted *stoep*[1], dwarfed by an expansive blue sky and neighbouring houses, insecure about myself because I am insecure about my ability to overcome the idea that my colour defines me and that I do not conform to that definition.

Due to the politics of South Africa at the time of my birth, I was classified as "Cape Coloured[2]." This classification was to define who and what I was, and was to become. It also meant I was socially and politically disadvantaged to someone classified as white[3] but advantaged to someone classified as African[4]. In Canada, during my teenhood, I learned that in South Africa the social construction of a racial separation among all South Africans, but especially between people classified African and 'Coloured,' weakened and divided the anti-*apartheid* movement. Due to the manifestation of complex social, political, and economic conditions, many mixed race people identified with white people and perceived themselves as superior to and different from Africans.

Because of this very clear example of how artificial separation not only created *apartheid* but maintained it, I participate uneasily in this anthology because in some respect, it can be perceived to be part of a process in the development of a separate space for women of mixed race. Though I understand the value of sharing life stories and experiences with women most like ourselves, I am against the idea of legitimizing our presence as a separate organizing voice. At the same time, I know how difficult it can be to legitimize our voice among the people with whom we might identify.

Women who consider themselves feminists tend to think they escape the thought patterns of society at large; though we often mirror those same biases. The history of colonialism and present day practices of racism has made racial identity a major issue for people of African ancestry. However, it has also encouraged us to participate in distinctions among ourselves based on colour and physical characteristics.

Identity politics has been heightened by the need to have a representative voice. How representative are mixed race women seen to be? How legitimate are we seen to be among those with whom we identify? Our mixedness is often the unspoken of who we are and what we add to our people. In other words, because of the sense of "purity" which underlies the politics of racial identity, my white German and Scottish ancestry can be used to deny me my African ancestry, my African can be used to deny me my Indian[5], and my Indian, my Malay[6]. The politics of identity insists that I choose only one and ignore my others.

Race is a complex issue and because we have yet to speak frankly about mixed race, women of colour[7] have yet to deal with the biases and assumptions learned through the pervasive thought of society at large and the institutions with which we deal. Because perceptions of mixed race have not been spoken about openly, biases, assumptions, and emotions can interfere and impede the political work at hand.

Though an uneasy participant, I do because in December 1993, I attended a group for women of mixed race and found the experience fulfilling. I realized, indeed, there are others out there whose sense of self is affected by social attitudes that are rooted in the colonialist idea that inter-racial relationships are immoral and as the offspring of those relationships, we often experience a lack of acceptance by either or any of the people with whom we can identify. The group of mixed race women revived memories and unanswered questions.

I come to this anthology with my memory of an experience and some thoughts. My thoughts are mindful of the context in which I write: as a woman of racially different ancestors whose family emigrated from South Africa, I am constantly aware of the profound affect that perceptions of differences among people can have. In the social and political climate of Canada, disrespect for those differences will be to the detriment of us all. Though I limit most of my thoughts to my white and black lineage, they are not my only lineage[8]. I also recognize many women are of other ancestry. I begin my thoughts with questions.

By coming together on these pages, are we declaring our desire — our need — for our own space? Is this space legitimate? What has provoked this development? Are we undermining, depleting, and weakening the ranks of women of colour? How legitimate can a space for women of mixed race be? When you get right down to it, are we not simply bastards? What right do bastards have to anything? If we are coming together because of a self-defined psychological need, what are the reasons which lay at its root? Has living in a complex social and political state of alienation produced this condition? Is this rendering negative?

Up until September 1983, I lived in Vancouver. Aside from the predominantly white population, the city had a sizeable First Nations population and people originally from the Asian continent. During the years I lived there, I saw and interacted with few Black people. During my teens, as a member of the Canadian Armed Reserve Forces, I travelled to New Brunswick, Nova Scotia, and Ontario. One summer, while enroute to Canadian Forces Base, Borden, I passed through the Toronto International Airport. I was struck by the number of Black people in the airport and though it had been years since I had been in Cape Town, their presence made me feel as though I were there. Years later, when I decided to leave my parents' home, I moved to Toronto.

Attracted to feminism, and wanting to meet other lesbians and

Black women, I joined women's groups and organizations. In 1986, while organizing for International Women's Day (IWD), I disagreed with the opinion of a women of colour caucus, and so angered by the manner in which the caucus decision was reached, I revealed my dissension to the organization at large. That act, and my disagreement with caucus which essentially became agreement with white women, led to an attempted isolation of me. During the days that followed, various rumours circulated about my family and the ill-founded political alliance of people of my colour in South Africa.

My apparent collusion with white women was significant because I am mixed and because ill-founded alliance with white people is part of the historical guilt of a people mixed with the white race. Although all people have been betrayed by their own, because of the history of colonialism, any perception of betrayal is particularly profound for people mixed with white.

Historically, white people have chosen people mixed with the white race, particularly those among us who resemble whiteness the most, to guard their systems in countries they have colonized. Among those of us of African ancestry, this has cultivated an historical mistrust among ourselves which our present day consciousness often cannot escape. As a result, the more white features we have, the more alienated we are made to be from our African ancestry. Among Black women, the less "Black" we appear, the more suspicious we are of each other. The amount of kink we have in our hair somehow legitimizes our right to claim Blackness and participate legitimately in the fight for liberation. As a mixed race woman, 1986 highlighted this and other complexities of race for me. It was extremely difficult to accept not only could my colour be used against me by white people but women of colour, too, would perpetuate this colonialist tactic. Though white women likely took advantage of the chasm, I was most aware of the dynamics that occurred between me and other women of colour, particularly Black women in the organization.

During my teenhood, because of my brownness, I identified with

Black people. Though I took it for granted that I would identify with Black people, my birth classification as someone of the "Coloured race" permeated my consciousness and for many years I considered myself Brown, not mixed race. Both my parents are Brown and both my paternal grandparents, the only grandparents I knew, were also Brown.

Since I was conscious only of my Black and white ancestry and clearly was not white, in seeking to place myself with a group of people, in Canada, I identified with Black people. In my effort to maintain my South African identity, I also wanted to be recognized as South African. Yet, I was repeatedly confronted with the reality that my colour and other physical features and ideas about what *is* South African and Black frequently prevented me from being identified as either. In fact, I was often mistaken to be a First Nations, an Indian, or an Hawaiian woman and this mistaken identity was made by those who were and were not of those people. Despite my self-identification as Black, people asked me what I was mixed with. I disliked the question because I thought of myself as Black or Brown *not* as mixed. However, because the question was continually asked, in my adulthood, I began to think about my mixed ancestry.

Our identity as mixed race women occurs in the context of a racist, classist, and sexist society which places greater value on people who are fully able-bodied and young. Our personal experiences often parallel the experiences of women with whom we identify. Yet, because of the way in which skin colour and physical characteristics are socially graded, despite these parallel experiences, the mixed race experience is seen as different. However, this perceived difference does not place it outside of the experience of racism. When we foster discussion as to who is the most racially oppressed, we encourage the colonialist tactic of divide and conquer.

As a result of the gradation of colour, mixed race women can experience greater access to social rewards which is further based on our class, culture, standard of English, and ability. These characteristics further shape our experiences, consciousness, and ideas. Without a doubt, racism advantages the lighter skinned, the straighter and finer haired and so on. This is one of master's tools which is used to build the master's house[9]. Within the context of my blackness, because of the way in which colour and characteristics are measured, I might be seen as less threatening than someone who is darker skinned and whose physical features resemble those which are characteristically stereotyped to describe Black people. I know that because of the way in which colour, physical characteristics, culture, language and so on are measured, I can be socially advantaged to other women. I also know that lighter skinned women can be advantaged over me. The similarities between South Africa and Canada never cease to amaze me. Because it is easy to lose sight of this form of social privileging and begin to take things for granted, I constantly remind myself of the kind of society in which I live and where I may be placed, at any one time, in relation to other people. It is reckless to be complacent about whatever privileges we may be accorded, and to not address systemic barriers of which race is only one.

I experience a beginning point every time I enter a space in which there are people who wonder with what I am "mixed." Trivial testimony is sought. It is trivial because it is not meaningful. It is information collected to categorize things — me, others like me. Though there exist stereotypes of people of all races and cultures, negative stereotypes are often attributed to people of colour. Because of this, I know if I reveal my lineage, I run the risk of having the perception of my behaviour and vocalized thought interpreted by someone who may hold ideas about the races of the people who form my lineage.

Depending on who is trying to suss me out, any behaviour on my part that causes negative reaction, for whatever reason, may be attributed to my Indian, Malay, African, Scottish, or German blood and I may, therefore, be perceived to be genetically at fault. This and other attitudes has often made me feel uncertain about myself and has contributed to feelings of shame about being of mixed race.

During my teens, in the 1970s, in Vancouver, I became aware of and ashamed about my Indian ancestry because I internalized the racism of the racist names I was called. My experience in 1986 made me uncertain about my understanding that my African ancestry and identity with Black people was mine to claim. Remarks made to me, over the past few years, for a time, made me ashamed about my white (German and Scottish) ancestry. Though I have put most of this stuff behind me, I wish neither I nor anyone else would have to deal with it. I know the shame I sometimes still feel is borne of racism. The attitudes I and others have are influenced by our histories and continuing experiences with colonialism and imperialism. These pervasive attitudes influence how mixed race people perceive themselves and are perceived by others. The shame I sometimes experience is shame learned from people who hate the idea of a black person fucking a white person; a Malay fucking a German, an African a Scot, an Indian a German. The colour of my skin shows that the line was crossed. Someone fucked someone who should not have been fucked. When people ask what is my mixture, they are trying to find out who those persons were. My origins do not haunt me. Attitudes about my origins do.

When I told a friend I was going to a group for women of mixed race, she asked me what I was *trying to do*. Her response confirmed the perception that our coming together is seen as subversive. Aside from the unexpected excitement I felt the next day from having been in the group, during the meeting, I was struck by the disjunction and hesitancy among us. One of the women said she had never before experienced such hesitance in a group. I could not help but think our unspoken fears about subversiveness created the hesitancy and anxiety and these were borne of our assumptions that women with whom we would otherwise identify would ridicule us for getting together. It is assumed that when women of mixed race get together we undermine women of colour as a whole. I had the sense, that night, we could not yet trust each other with our personal stories because they were guarded by the memory of rejection and isolation by those with whom we identify. To what extent has the possibility of not knowing of our mixture until adulthood, or having our mixture treated as an embarrassment or illegitimate, created a self-perception of not knowing who we are and where we belong in a society that emphasizes the need to know both?

Women who wish to share their similar experiences ought to be able to do so but I suggest women do so within the context of being mindful that we are part of a larger body of people under seige and all of us are needed in the struggle. The social construction of race has become a critical political tool and has created an intense emotional dimension to the idea of identity which itself has become significant in North America. Because of the times in which we live, it is dangerous to encourage, in any way, separateness because we feed into the notion of difference that is engineered by racism. Rather than criticize barriers imposed externally, women must be vigilant about ones over which we have control and include our surmount of them as integral to our political work.

Thanks to Rosamund Elwin, Brigitte Head, and Dale Martin for their insight and suggestions.

---

1 Pronounced "stoop," it is a low platform outside a door of a house. In Canada, it is commonly called a porch.

2 This meant I was born on the Cape Province and belonged to the 'Coloured,' meaning "mixed" race. For more information on the implications of racial classification in South Africa, please refer to books written on the subject.

3 Under appartheid the official term was originally "European" which was supposed to reinforce the notion of superiority and colonialism. "European" was later changed to "white" which was meant to maintain ideas of racial superiority.

4 Under apartheid the official term was originally "Native." It was later changed to "Bantu" and then changed again to"Plurals." With all due respect to their different groups of people, Black South Africans call themselves Africans.

5 In South Africa, Indian is often used to refer to people who are from or are descendants of people who were from India.

6 In South Africa, Malay is often used to refer to the descendants of people who were taken to South Africa as indentured labour from what is today called Indonesia by the Dutch East India Company.

7 I know this term is problematic. I use it here to mean all women who might see themselves within its definition.

8 My lineage includes Indian and Malay ancestry.

9 The idea for this sentence is based on the ideas of and terms used by Audre Lorde in *Sister Outsider*, 1984.

Lara Doan

for the first 20 years of my life i did not know my biological roots. i was told by you that i was mixed, i was mulatto, i was light skinned. you're not really **black** i was told. you're not white either. you're half-black.

nigger

i was twelve when i first remember being called a nigger. you're a nigger he screamed at me. his face full of rage and disgust... his arm pressing me against a row of lockers blocking my escape.

reaching high school you
called me coloured. i had
to be coloured you said. i
had curly hair and big lips
my skin was not lily white.
but part of me had to be
white for my head was
covered with loose curls.
i was told that i was lucky
that i was not really black.
i was coloured. i was perfect to compare the golden
tans of friends who just
came back from two
weeks in the florida sun.

once
my
friend
gave
me an
island.
i must
be
from
there
she
ex-
claimed
most

vehemently look at your skin... look at
your hair.

Lisa Suhair Majaj
Boundaries, Borders, Horizons

So much goes along with us
on the border of vision,
"street arabs,"
orphans when we have no names
to bring them before our eyes.
David Williams[1]

Beyond this world there are twenty other worlds
Naomi Shihab Nye[2]

Recognized Futures

Turning to you, my name —
this necklace of gold, these letters
in script I cannot read,
this part of myself I long
to recognize — falls forward
into my mouth.

You call my daily name, Lisa,
the name I've finally declared
my own, claiming a heritage

half mine: corn fields golden
in ripening haze, green music
of crickets, summer light sloping
to dusk on the Iowa farm.

This other name fills my mouth,
a taste faintly metallic, blunt
edges around which my tongue
moves tentatively: Suhair,
an old-fashioned name, little star
in the night. The second girl,
small light on a distanced horizon.

Throughout childhood this rending split:
continents moving slowly apart,
rift widening beneath taut limbs.
A contested name, a constant
longing, evening star rising mute
through the Palestine night.
Tongue cleft by impossible languages,
fragments of narrative fractured
to loss, homelands splintered
beyond bridgeless rivers,
oceans of salt.

From these fragments I feel
a stirring, almost imperceptible.
In the morning light these torn
lives merge: a name on your lips,
on mine, softly murmured,
mutely scripted, both real
and familiar, till I cannot
distinguish between your voice

and my silence, my words
and this wordless knowledge,

morning star rising
through lightening sky,
some music I can't quite
hear, a distant melody,
flute-like, nai³ through
the olives, a cardinal calling,
some possible language
all our tongues can sing.

Boundaries: Arab/American

ONE EVENING A NUMBER OF YEARS AGO, AT A WORKSHOP ON racism, I became aware — in one of those moments of realization which is not a definitive falling into place, but rather a slow groundswell of understanding — of the ways in which I experience my identity as not merely complex, but rather as an uninterpretable excess.

Workshop participants, all women from the academic community, were asked to group ourselves in the centre of the room. As the facilitator called out a series of categories, we crossed to one side of the room or the other, according to our self-identification: white or person of colour, heterosexual or lesbian/bisexual, middle/upper class or working class, born in the U.S. or in another country, at least one college-educated parent or parents with no higher education, English as a native language or a second language. Although I am used to thinking of myself in terms of marginality and difference, I found myself, time after time, on the mainstream side of the room. White (as I called myself for lack of a more appropriate category), heterosexual, middle class, born in the U.S. to a college-educated parent, native speaker of English, I seemed to be part of America's presumed majority.

I learned a great deal that night about how much I take for granted those aspects of my life which locate me in a privileged category. It is a lesson of which I remain acutely conscious, and for which I am grateful. But looking across the room at the cluster of women representing what American society understands as "other," I was disconcerted by the lack of fit between the definitions offered that evening and my personal reality. Born in the U.S., I have nonetheless lived much of my life outside it, in Jordan and Lebanon. My father was college-educated and middle class, but Palestinian — hardly an identity suggestive of inclusion in mainstream American society. I considered myself white: my olive-tinged skin, while an asset in terms of acquiring a ready tan, did not seem a dramatic marker of difference. But I have received enough comments on my skin tone to make me aware that this is not entirely a neutral issue. (And as I have learned the history of colonialism in the Arab world, I have come to understand the ways in which even light-skinned Arabs are people of colour.) Native speaker of English, I nonetheless grew up alienated from the linguistic medium — Arabic — which swirled around me, living a life in some ways as marginal as that of a non-English speaker in the United States. Although I do not think of myself as having an accent, I have more than once been assumed to be foreign; I speak with an intonation acquired perhaps from the British-inflected Jordanian English, or from years of the careful enunciation one adopts when addressing non-native speakers. I have been the target of various forms of harassment specifically linked to my Arab identity, from hostile comments to threatening phone calls, racist mail, and destruction of property. I have feared physical assault when wearing something which identifies me as an Arab. And so, standing on the majority side of the room that evening, observing the discrepancy between the facts of my life and the available categories of inclusion and exclusion, I could not help but wonder whether these categories are not insufficient, or insufficiently nuanced.

I recognize in this response my reluctance, here in this country which is so large, and which often seems — however inaccurately — so homogenous, to relinquish a sense of my own difference. When I arrived in the United States for graduate school in 1982, I felt oddly invisible. Walking down the crowded streets of Ann Arbor, Michigan I became aware, with a mixture of relief and unease, that no one was looking at me, trying to talk to me, or making comments under their breath. Years of living in Jordan and Lebanon, where my physical appearance, my style of dressing, my manner of walking had all coded me as foreign, had accustomed me to being the object of attention, curiosity, sometimes harassment. Although in Amman and Beirut I had tried to make myself as inconspicuous as possible — walking close to walls, never meeting anyone's eyes — I always knew that people noted, assessed, commented on my presence. Even as I disliked and resented this attention, I grew to expect it. As a girl and woman with little self-confidence, the external gaze, intrusive as it was, perhaps offered the solace of definition: I am seen, therefore I exist. Without that gaze would I still know who I am?

The idea of such dependence upon external definition disturbs me now. I would like to say that I longed not to be defined by the gaze of the other, but to look out upon the world through eyes rooted in the boundaries of my own identity. But it is true that for much of my life I thought if I looked long enough I would find someone to tell me who I am. Turning to the world for some reflection of myself, however, I found only distortion. Perhaps it was asking too much of that younger self of mine, overwhelmed by a sense of my identity's invalidity no matter which culture I entered, to learn the necessary art of self-definition.

And if I had achieved that skill, would I have merely learned more quickly the cost of difference? Being American in the Arab world set me apart in ways I found profoundly disturbing. But I found out soon enough that being Arab in the United States — worse, being Palestinian — offers little in the way of reassurance. My hopeful belief that moving to the United States would be a homecoming was quickly shaken. Once I claimed a past, spoke my history, told my name, the walls of incomprehension and hostility rose, brick by brick: un-funny "ethnic" jokes, jibes about terrorists and *kalashnikovs*, about veiled women and camels; or worse, the awkward silences, the hasty shifts to other subjects. Searching for reflections of my Arab self in American culture I found only unrecognizable stereotypes. In the face of such incomprehension, such misrepresentation, I could say nothing.

But I have grown weary of my silence and paranoia; my fear that if I wear a Palestine emblem, a *kafiyyeh*,[4] use my few words of Arabic, say my name or where I am from, I will open myself to suspicion or hatred. I am tired of being afraid to speak who I am: American and Palestinian, not merely half of one thing and half of another, but both at once — and in that inexplicable melding which occurs when two cultures come together, not quite either, so that neither American nor Arab find themselves fully reflected in me, nor I in them. Perhaps it should not have surprised me to cross and recross that room of divisions and find myself nowhere.

I was born in 1960, in the small farming community of Hawarden, on Iowa's western border. My mother, Jean Caroline Stoltenberg, in whose home town I was born, was American, of German descent. From her I take my facial structure and features, the colour of my hair, and more: an awkward shyness, a certain naivete, but also a capacity for survival and adaptation which exceeds my own expectations. I learned from her the value of both pragmatism and a sense of humour. She liked to say that she was of farming stock, plain but sturdy. Twenty-three years in Jordan did not greatly alter her midwestern style; she met the unfamiliar with the same resolution and forthrightness with which she turned to her daily tasks. Despite her willing adjustment to Middle Eastern life, she never quite relinquished her longing for the seasonal landscapes of her Iowa childhood — the green lushness of summer, the white drifts of winter. Although I experienced her primarily against a Jordanian backdrop, my memories of her evoke midwestern images and echoes: fragrant platters of beef and potatoes, golden cornfields beneath wide, sultry skies the strident music of crickets singing at dusk.

My father, Isa Joudeh Majaj, a Palestinian of the generation which had reached young adulthood by the time of Israel's creation from the land of Palestine, was born in Bir Zeit, in what is now the occupied West Bank. From him I take the olive tinge to my skin, the shape of my hands and nose, the texture of my hair, and perhaps my tendency toward inarticulate and contradictory emotion. From him, too, I take a certain stubbornness, and what he used to call "Palestinian determination." Named Isa, Arabic for Jesus, by his widowed mother in fulfilment of a vow, my father grew from childhood to adolescence in Jerusalem, that city where so many histories intersect. Although distanced from each other by geographical origin, culture and more, my parents held in common their respect for the earth and for the people who till it. Never quite reconciled to his urban life, my father spoke longingly of the groves of orange and olive trees, the tomato plants and squash vines by which Palestinian farmers live. He could identify the crop of a distant field by its merest wisp of green, had learned the secrets of grafting, knew when to plant and when to harvest. His strong attachment to the earth — an emotion I have come to recognize among Palestinians — made me understand his dispossession as a particular violence. I associate his life with loss and bitterness, but also with a life-bearing rootedness reminiscent of those olive trees in Jerusalem which date back to the time of Christ, or of jasmine flowering from vines twisted thick as tree trunks.

After a youth punctuated by the devastating events leading up to Israel's creation in 1948, during which he fought against the British and saw relatives lose both homes and lives, my father worked his way to the United States for a college education. In Sioux City, Iowa he attended Morningside College, shovelling mounds of hamburger in the stockyards during schoolbreaks. At a YMCA dance he met my mother, a quiet young woman working as a secretary in a legal firm. A year later the two were married.

I do not know what drew my parents together. My father may have seen and valued in my mother both the shy pliancy cultivated by girls of her generation and the resilience learned in a farming family. Though he seemed to take her strength for granted, he assumed she would mould herself to his delineation. My mother, who by her own account had grown-up imbued with visions of true romance, may have seen in my father an exemplar of the tall dark stranger. At their wedding she vowed to both love and obey. My parents' marriage, complex from its outset, promised the richness of cultural interaction, but bore as well the fruit of much cultural contradiction. It is the complexity and contradictions of their relationship which I have inherited, and which mediate my interactions in the societies, Arab and American, which I claim as birthright, but experience all too often as alienation.

When I was born, my mother claimed me in a gesture which in later years I understood to have been quite remarkable. The birth of my older sister three years previously had disappointed my father in his desire for a son and the title "Abu-Tarek," father of Tarek. Forced by the demands of his work to be absent before my own birth, he refused to choose a girl's name before he left — hoping, no doubt, that this second child would be a boy, as the first one had not been. I was born, and my mother called me Lisa Ann. Perhaps she had resolved that this second child would have an American name, as the first one had not. But my father asserted his will over my identity from many thousands of miles away. Upon learning of my birth, he sent a telegram congratulating my mother on the arrival of Suhair Suzanne — Suhair, an Arabic name meaning "little star in the night," and Suzanne, an Americanization of the Arabic name Sausan — in what he may have thought would be a cultural compromise. By this time my mother must have had me home, Lisa Ann firmly inscribed in the hospital records. But this did not deter my father, always a stubborn man. On his return I was baptized Suhair Suzanne. In the one picture I possess of the event, I am cradled plumply in the arms of my aunt, indifferent to the saga of fractured identity about to ensue.

My mother, however, must have been stronger-willed than anyone expected. She acquiesced to the baptism, but her dutiful letters to the relatives in Jordan relate news of baby Lisa Suhair, with 'Lisa' crossed out by her own pen. This marvellously subversive gesture allowed my mother to appear to abide by my father's wishes while still wedging her own claims in. And somehow her persistence won out. My earliest memories are of myself as Lisa: birthday cards, baby books, all confirm it. Even my father only called me Suhair to tease me. But if my mother claimed victory in the colloquial, his was the legal victory. Both passport and birth certificate identified me as Suhair Suzanne, presaging a schism of worlds which would widen steadily as I grew.

When my sister and I were still very young, my parents moved first to Lebanon, then to Jordan. My father had had much difficulty finding work in the midwestern United States; people were suspicious of foreigners, and frequently anti-Semitic, and he was often assumed to be a Jew. Moving to the west coast did not greatly improve his opportunities. Finally, however, he was hired by a moving and packing firm which sent him to Beirut. Realizing the absence of such companies in Jordan, and wanting to stay in the Middle East, my father borrowed enough money to start a small packing firm in Amman, where his mother and brother then lived. By my fourth birthday we were settled in the small stone house in what is now thought of as "old" Amman where we lived for the next twenty years.

Despite the semblance of rootedness this move to Jordan seemed to provide, my childhood was permeated by the ambience of exile. If to my mother "home" was thousands of miles away, beyond the Atlantic, to my father it was tantalizingly close, yet maddeningly unattainable — just across the Jordan River. My early years were marked by a constant sense of displacement, the unsettling quality of which determined much of my personal ambivalence and sense of confusion, as well as a certain flexibility I have come to value. I learned at an early age that there is always more than one way of doing things, but that this increased awareness of cultural relativity often means a more complicated, and painful, existence. I learned to live as if in a transitional state, waiting always for the time that we would go to Palestine, to the United States, to a place where I would belong. But trips to Iowa and to Jerusalem taught me that once I got there, "home" slipped away inexplicably, materializing again just beyond reach. If a sense of rootedness was what gave life meaning, as my parents' individual efforts to ward off alienation implied, this meaning seemed able to assume full import only in the imagination.

The world of my growing-up years consisted of intersecting cultural spheres which often harmonized, but more frequently; particularly as my sister and I grew older, clashed. Home provided, naturally enough, the site of both the greatest cultural intermingling and the most intense contradiction. My mother worked, despite my father's objections, at the American Community School in Amman from the time I entered kindergarten until several years before her death in 1986. The job provided for my sister's and my own tuition, and offered my mother daily interaction with other American women, many of whom had also married Arab men. Though in later years she began to articulate the independence she had muted for years, for most of her married life she acquiesced to a hierarchical structuring of the familial codes. Although the prime agent of my sister's and my own socialization, in general my mother transmitted to us those lessons of my father's choosing. But my father's failure to fully explain his assumptions often resulted in a gap in the translation from Arab to American. Thus, only after I had been away at college for some time did I explicitly learn that I should never go out except in large groups — a rule at the heart of which was a ban upon interactions with men. But such expectations hardly needed to be spelled out. My restricted upbringing and my own desire to maintain familial harmony had resulted in such an effective internalization of my father's expectations, most of which had to do with the maintenance of honour, that I lived them out almost unconsciously. Indeed, these expectations reverberated so strongly that even while attending graduate school in the United States, sure both of the need to direct my own life and of the innocence of the things I wanted to do, I recoiled from each of my "transgressions" with guilt and dread.

Looking back on our family life from the perspective of a painfully won feminism, the gender dynamics pervading our household seem unambiguously problematic. In addressing them, however, I find myself becoming defensive, wanting to be true to my feminist principles but wanting also to preserve my deep-rooted family loyalties, however conflicted. I had learned to understand my relationship to others through the medium of Arab cultural norms filtered through an uneven Americanization. My childhood was permeated by the lesson, incessantly reinforced, that family is not just vital to self, but is so inherent that family and self are in a sense one and the same. I am more familiar than I would choose to be with the constrictions implicit in such celebration of family ties. Moreover, I now see the gendered patterns of such definitions: Arab men, although they too must define themselves in relation to the family, are nonetheless encouraged, even required, to develop an assertiveness and individuality actively discouraged in Arab women. But the mesh of familial expectations stressed in Arab culture provided a sense of security not readily apparent in my experience of American relationships, with their nuances of a cultural emphasis on individualism. However restrictively articulated, the stable definitions of self available in my childhood context held a certain appeal for me, caught as I was in a confusion of cultures.

I have come to understand the constrictions which governed my life not as an innate characteristic of Arab culture, but as a particular, and gendered, product of cross-cultural interactions. In my experience, male children of mixed marriages are often able to claim both the rights of Arab men and an indefinable freedom usually attributed to Western identity. Although the cultural mix imposes its burdens, a boy's situatedness between "Arab" and "American" is not debilitating. But for girls, relegated to the mother's sphere, the implications of a Western identity in an Arab context can be so problematic that claustrophobic familial restrictions are often the result. Although modesty is required of all girls, those with American blood are at particular risk and must be doubly protected, so that there is neither opportunity nor basis for gossip.

As a child, however, I was aware only that being Arab, even in part, mandated a profound rejection of any self-definition which contradicted the claims of familial bonds. When I wished, as an adult, to marry a non-Arab man against my father's wishes, and engaged in a bitter, painful attempt to do so without irrevocably severing family ties, some friends seemed unable to understand why I would not rebel simply and cleanly, claiming my life and my feminist principles on my own terms. But to do so would have meant the abrogation not just of emotional connections, but of my very identity. The cultural conflict which so often delineates Arab American experience makes it extremely difficult for those of us caught between cultures to challenge restrictive cultural codes. Without the security of knowing who one is, of being able to first lay full claim to the identity one rejects, rebellion becomes precarious and difficult.

Although I lived in an Arabic-speaking country, in my private world English was the main language of communication. My Arab relatives, who had all, except for my grandmother, learned English at school, wished to make my mother welcome by speaking her language, and wished as well to practise their skills in English — the use of which, in a residue of colonialism, still constitutes a mark of status in Jordan. Though I learned "kitchen Arabic" quite early, and could speak with my grandmother on an elementary level, I never became proficient in the language which should have been mine from childhood. This lack resulted in my isolation from the culture in which I lived. I was unable to follow conversations in family gatherings when people did not speak English, as they often did not. I could not understand Arabic television shows or news broadcasts, was unable to speak to storekeepers or passersby, or to develop friendships with Arab children. As a result I remained trapped in a cultural insularity — articulated through the American school, American church, and American friends constituting my world — which now mortifies me. My father's habit of speaking only English at home played a large part in this deficiency; it seems never to have occurred to him that my sister and I would not pick up Arabic. Perhaps he thought that language skills ran in the blood. Indeed, during my college years he once sent me an article in Arabic, and was surprised and dismayed at my inability to read it: he had expected me to be literate in his language.

These linguistic deficiencies, though partly self-willed, have come to haunt me. I mourned with particular potency when my grandmother died shortly after I had started studying Arabic for the specific purpose of communicating with her more meaningfully. As a child I had received occasional Arabic lessons from a relative at home and during special lunch-hour classes at school. During my teens and early twenties, embarrassed by the limitations of monolingualism, I had taken various courses in spoken and written Arabic. Despite my efforts, however, I had retained little of what I learned, and my father, perhaps taking my knowledge for granted, had offered little reinforcement. During bursts of enthusiasm or guilt I would ask him to speak Arabic to me on a daily basis. But such resolutions rarely lasted. He was too busy and too impatient for my faltering efforts, and I must have harboured more internal resistance to learning Arabic than I then realized.

Similarly, my father seemed to believe that knowledge of Palestinian history was a blood inheritance. I therefore had only my personal experience of events such as the Six Day War, or Black September, and a basic awareness of key dates — 1948, 1967, 1970, 1973 — to guide me through this history which so defined my father's life, and my own.[5] Only when challenged by my college peers in Lebanon did I begin to educate myself about my Palestinian background, a task which assumed more urgency when I moved to the United States. Indeed, in a pattern which continues to repeat itself, I have come to understand myself primarily in oppositional contexts: in Jordan I learn the ways in which I am American, while in the United States I discover the ways in which I am Arab.

Though my father's cultural codes regulated everything from the length of my hair to the friends I was permitted to visit, the surface texture of my life was indisputably American. I grew up reading Mother Goose, singing "Home on the Range," reciting "The Ride of Paul Revere," and drawing pictures of Pilgrims and Indians, Christmas trees and Santa Clauses, Valentines and Easter bunnies. At school I learned the standard colonialist narrative of white Pilgrims settling an empty new land, struggling bravely against savage Indians. (A year in a public grade school in Iowa during Jordan's 1970 civil war showed me that my education had been in some ways exceptional: I found myself ahead of many of my Iowa classmates in reading skills, a fact I attribute to the creativity and skill of my elementary teachers, as well as to my mother's example of incessant reading.) Yet into this world came many Arab elements. My relatives would fill the house with their Palestinian dialect, the men arguing in loud voices, slamming the *tric trac*[6] stones on the board, while the women chatted on the veranda or in the kitchen. Although my mother took advantage of my father's frequent business trips to serve meatloaf and potatoes, the plain American food she craved, much of the food we ate was Arabic: I grew up on *yakhni* and *mahshi, wara' dawali* and *ma'aloubi*.[7] My father had taught my mother to cook these dishes when they lived in the United States: hungry for the food of his childhood, he was willing to enter the kitchen to teach her the art of rolling grapeleaves or hollowing squash. In Jordan my grandmother took over her culinary education, the two of them communicating through hand gestures and my mother's broken Arabic.

But even food was a marker of both integration and conflict. To my father's dismay, I learned from my mother to hate yoghurt, that staple of Middle Eastern diets: he took this as a form of betrayal. Holidays became arenas for suppressed cultural battles, as my father insisted that my mother prepare time-consuming pots of rolled grapeleaves and stuffed squash in addition to the turkey and mashed potatoes, sweet potatoes and cranberry sauce; or that she dispense with the bread stuffing and substitute an Arabic filling of rice, lamb meat, and pine nuts. For periods of my childhood, having two cultural backgrounds seemed merely to mean more variety from which to choose, like the holiday dinners with two complete menus on the table I learned to like both cuisines, and to this day crave the potent garlic, the distinctive cinnamon and allspice of the Arabic dishes I rarely, for lack of time, make. But early on I learned too that cultures, like flavours, often clash. And my sister and I, occupying through our very existence the point of tension where my mother's and father's worlds met, often provided the ground for this conflict.

Moving through childhood between the insular worlds of school and home, I remained constantly aware of the ways in which I was different. My relatively light skin and hair, while failing to grant me entrance to the blond, blue-eyed company of "real" Americans, set me apart from my Arab neighbours. There must have been some difference about me more elusive than that, however, for despite the fact that I knew Arabs with skin or hair lighter than my own, when I walked down the street I would hear the murmurs: *ajnabi,* foreigner. Even my body language marked me. When I was in my teens an Arab man once told me he would recognize my walk from blocks away. "You don't walk like an Arab girl," he said. "You take long steps; there's a bounce to your stride."

Instead of taking offence at what was in fact a criticism of my lack of "femininity," I hopefully interpreted this description to mean that perhaps I was, after all, American, that identity I had spent my childhood trying to claim. I still clung to some shred of that old longing to be as confidently unambiguous as the diplomat kids who rode the Embassy bus, their lunch boxes filled with commissary treats — Hershey bars, Reeses Cups, Oreos — that we "locals" could never obtain. I wanted an American life like the ones I read about in the books I helped my mother unpack for the school library each year, the odour of glue and paper — that indefinable aroma of newness — filling me with longing. I wanted an American father who would come home for dinner at 6 pm, allow me to sleep over at friends' houses, speak unaccented English and never misuse a colloquialism; who would be other than what he indisputably was — a Palestinian. As a child I convinced myself that we lived in Jordan by mistake, and that soon we would return to the United States, where I would become my true self: American, whole. I wanted to believe that my confusion and fragmentation were merely temporary.

Meanwhile, I searched for someone to explain me to myself. I knew that Arabs — my relatives as much as neighbours and shopkeepers and strangers — thought me foreign, that "real" Americans thought me foreign as well. I knew, too, the subtle hierarchies implicit in these assessments. At school the social order was clear: Embassy Americans, then non-Embassy Americans, and finally those of us with mixed blood, whose claim to the insular world of overseas Americans was at best partial. At the interdenominational church we attended, my mother and sister and I fielded the solicitude of missionaries who never quite believed that my father was not Moslem. When, after exhausting the resources of the American school, I transferred to a Jordanian high school offering courses in English, I learned that there too I was an outsider. My father's name didn't change the fact that I couldn't speak Arabic, lacked the cultural subtleties into which an Arab girl would have been socialized, and as an American female had automatically suspect morals.

I see now how orientalist representations of the Arab world find echoes in occidentalist perceptions of the West. When I walked down the streets of Amman I was categorized as foreign, female; an object of attention, curiosity, sometimes harassment. The insidious touch of young men's hands on my body pursued me, their eyes taunting me in mock innocence when I whirled to confront them. My appearance alone in public, and my foreignness, seemed to suggest sexual availability; whispers of *charmoota*, prostitute, echoed in my burning ears. Once, when a young man crowded me against a wall, brushing my hips with his hand as he passed, I cried out wildly and swung my bag at him. But he advanced threateningly toward me, shouting angrily at my effrontery. If I had spoken Arabic to him he might have retreated in shame. Because I did not he must have seen me simply as a foreign woman, flaunting a sexuality unmediated by the protection of men, the uncles and brothers and cousins whom an Arab woman would be assumed to have.

Despite such experiences, early in my teens I claimed walking as a mark of my individuality. Determined to assert my difference, since I could not eradicate it, I walked everywhere, consciously lengthening my stride and walking with a freedom of motion I longed to extend to the rest of my life. Walking offered a means both of setting myself off from and of confronting the Arab culture which I felt threatened to overwhelm me. I wanted to insist that I was "other" than these people whose language I barely spoke, even though they were my relatives. I wanted to insist that I was American — as was, for that matter, my father. Lacking an understanding of his history, I remained oblivious to his awareness of his American citizenship as a bitter acquiescence to the realities of international politics and the denial of Palestinian identity. Instead, I clung to markers of our mutual Americanness. Didn't we cross the bridge to the West Bank with the foreigners, in air-conditioned comfort, instead of on the suffocatingly hot "Arab" side, where Palestinians returning to the Occupied Territories were required to strip naked and send their shoes and suitcases to be X-rayed? Weren't my parents invited to the Embassy parties? Didn't we go to the Fourth of July picnics and Christmas bazaars? Weren't we as good as other Americans?

While my father shared my anger at being marginalized in the American community, he did not appreciate my attempts to reject his heritage. Despite his esteem for certain aspects of American culture — his fondness of small midwestern towns, his fascination with techno- logical gadgetry, his admiration of the American work ethic — as I grew older he grew ever more disapproving of my efforts to identify as an American. Although he had left much of my sister's and my own upbringing to my mother, he had assumed that we would arrive at adolescence as model Arab girls: when we did not he was puzzled and

72

annoyed. As walking became a measure of my independence, it became as well a measure of our conflict of wills. He did not like my "wandering in the streets"; it was not "becoming," and it threatened his own honour. I stole away for walks, therefore, during the drowsy hours after the heavy midday meal when most people, my father included, were either at work or at siesta. Walking in the early afternoon, especially during the summer months, accentuated my difference from the Jordanian culture I had determined to resist. A young woman walking quickly and alone through still, hot streets, past drowsy guards and bored shop-keepers, presented an anomaly: Arab girls, I had been told both subtly and explicitly, did not do such things — a fact which pleased me.

As my sister and I entered the "dangerous age," when our reputations were increasingly at stake and a wrong move would brand us as "loose," my father grew more and more rigid in his efforts to regulate our self-definitions. Our options in life were spelled out in terms of whom we would be permitted to marry. A Palestinian Christian, I knew, was the preferred choice. But even a Palestinian Moslem, my father said — though I did not quite believe him, conscious of the crucial significance of religious distinctions in the Middle East — would be better than a Jordanian (I think of Black September, the days spent below window level, the nights of guns and mortars, my grandmother's house burned after soldiers learned of my cousins' political affiliations, the horror of Palestinian families massacred in their homes by the Jordanian army, and I begin to understand). To marry an American, or Britisher, or Canadian was out of the question. Westerners, I heard repeatedly, had no morals, no respect for family, no sense of honour — an opinion which seemed to derive in part from observations of real cultural differences between Arabs and Westerners, in part from the weekly episodes of *Peyton Place* and other English-language programs aired on Jordan television. (I have been asked by Arabs whether Americans really get divorced six or seven times, refuse to care for their elderly parents, and are all wealthy. And I have been asked by Americans whether Arabs really ride camels to work, all live in tents, and have never seen planes or hospitals.) Though I now appreciate the difficult balance my father sought to sustain between his identity as a Christian Palestinian in Moslem Jordan, the American characteristics he had embraced after years in the U.S., and the cultural requirements of Jordanian society, at the time I experienced his expectations as unreasonable and contradictory. Most difficult to accept was the implicit portrayal of my mother's American identity as a misfortune for which we all, she included, had to compensate. On constant trial to prove my virtue, held to a far stricter standard of behaviour than my Arab cousins, I both resented and felt compelled to undertake the ongoing task of proving that I wasn't, in fact, American.

In my experience cultural marginality has been among the most painful of alienations. My childhood desire, often desperate, was not so much to be a particular nationality, to be American or Arab, but to be wholly one thing or another: to be something that I and the rest of the world could understand, categorize, label, predict. It never occurred to me that I could identify myself not as half of one thing and half of another, nor even be required to choose, but could lay full claim to both identities: could be not impoverished but enriched by complexity. Although I spent years struggling to define my personal politics of location, I remained situated somewhere between Arab and American cultures — never quite rooted in either, always constrained by both. My sense of liminality grew as I became more aware of the rigid nature of definitions: Arab culture simultaneously claimed and excluded me, while the American identity I longed for retreated inexorably from my grasp.

Upon arriving in the United States to attend my last year of high school at a boarding school in Pittsfield, Massachusetts — a move precipitated by the lack of English language twelfth grade studies in Jordan, and the fortuitous offer of a scholarship — I thought I might at last be simply an American among Americans. But I found that here too I am "other." One of many new students who entered the school from other countries that year, I felt resented, an intruder upon the closed atmosphere of a small graduating class I spent a lonely year, finding few friends except among other "foreign" students. Applying to American colleges that winter, I greeted my acceptances to east coast schools with anticipation. But when my father announced that I would attend the American University of Beirut in the fall of 1978 — a pronouncement it did not occur to me to question — I felt, amid my anger and disappointment, a certain sense of relief at the prospect of returning to an environment where my difference would at least provide the solace of familiarity.

My college experience, however, proved anything but comforting. My father's implicit assumption that political and cultural knowledge could be acquired through osmosis, the failure of my schools to educate me about the Middle East, and the influence of my mother's political indifference — a result, in part, of her exclusion from political discussions by language and gender restrictions — had led to my emergence into young adulthood singularly unaware either of my political context or of Middle Eastern history. Lebanon's civil war had erupted in the spring of 1976, during my sister's own first year of college in Beirut. After her safe return home I had talked self-importantly to my classmates about Phalangist militias, roadblocks, and gunbattles. But I understood little about the conflict except that, like all wars, it was terrible and confusing. I thought of Beirut not as the cosmopolitan playground of its pre-war fame, nor yet as the hell of random violence it came later to symbolize, but rather as a vague setting for the possibilities of cultural and personal experimentation I teased from my sister's enigmatic tales of college life. Long renowned as the "crossroads of east and west," Beirut presented itself as a locus where I might finally begin to untangle the knotted strands of my identity.

Instead, my experiences there exacerbated my identity conflicts. Although accustomed to negotiating otherness, I was unprepared for the exigencies imposed by Beirut's wartime environment. I quickly learned that few identities, whether national, religious, ethnic, political, or ideological, claimed neutrality in Lebanon. The war devastating the country had split Beirut into a Christian eastern sector and a Moslem western sector, filled the country with Syrian forces, aligned Palestinians with Moslem Lebanese and the Lebanese left, and affiliated Israel with the Christian right. A long history of extensive foreign aid and unquestioning political alliance inevitably associated the U.S. with Israel. To be Christian, Palestinian and American thus meant being understood in highly politicized, and contradictory, terms. On my second day at A.U.B. a new acquaintance advised me to remove my various emblems of affiliation: the gold cross, the Palestine map necklace, the black and white *keffiyeh*, the American patch on my windbreaker, the Jordanian logo on my sweatshirt. In Beirut, she informed me, safety lay in anonymity. This initiation to college life was almost as disconcerting as the bombs which sent me scurrying to huddle in the dormitory basement night after night my first week there, or the matter-of-fact advice of the American consul — who rose as he spoke to open windows, rattling with reverberations, so they would not break — that I avoid going off campus unless absolutely necessary, and keep a two-week supply of canned food in my room at all times.

Despite my intrinsic shyness, anonymity proved difficult to achieve. The Palestinian students I met on campus quickly identified me as Palestinian, marvelling at my lack of political knowledge or sense of identity. Their own involvement, whether teaching children in the refugee camps to read or participating in political groups, was so intrinsic to their lives that they could not understand my disengagement. Some of my Lebanese Christian acquaintances looked askance, in the highly charged sectarian atmosphere of wartime Beirut, at my friendships with Moslems, encouraging me in church-related activities with an enthusiasm I only later understood to have been politically as well as religiously inspired. I pleaded ignorance in most political discussions, which usually occurred in Arabic anyway. But my American identity and its implications were inescapable. Watching from my dormitory window as crowds of shouting people burned the U.S. flag in front of the embassy, I realized there was little I could say to assuage the anger at American mishandling of Middle Eastern complexities. The unbearable sound of Israeli jets bombing the Palestinian sector of West Beirut ravaged me with the knowledge of my unwilling complicity, through the American tax dollars my family paid each year, in the destruction of Palestinian lives, and emphasized as well the precariousness of my own safety.

My desperate attempt to flee Beirut in the spring of 1982 shortly before its besiegement by the Israeli army accentuated the irony of my mixed identity. Each possible escape route, whether through Israeli lines or Syrian checkpoints, held more or less risk depending on whether I would be considered a Palestinian or an American. Eventually I managed to join a convoy of students jammed onto open trucks for the trip to Jounieh, the East Beirut seaport, where transportation could be arranged to Cyprus. This alternative seemed preferable to the seat in a Syria-bound car offered by an American acquaintance I had met only once before. (The road to Syria was bombed by Israeli jets the day that car left Beirut, killing fifty-seven people, including four foreigners. I never learned what happened to the person who so generously offered me a ride.)

In Jounieh we spent several difficult days camped out on the floor of a hotel run by A.U.B. graduates, listening to static-filled radio reports of Lebanon's destruction, and watching the horizon billow with black smoke by day and flare with explosions by night. Finally we crowded onto the open deck of a cargo ship which had been guaranteed safe passage by the Israeli forces controlling the area. But an hour or so out of port, after dark had fallen, the sudden spotlight of an Israeli gunboat froze us in its glare. Soldiers boarded the ship, seized our passports and several Palestinian students, and rerouted us, as we eventually learned, to Haifa, Israel. When we docked in Haifa the next day, exhausted from the shipboard conditions, the scarcity of food and water, and our unremitting fear, Israeli soldiers brought bread, cheese, and cucumbers on board in wooden crates while television cameras rolled. Viewers must have thought we were desperate refugees whom the Israelis had saved: although I was hungry, the food stuck in my throat. British and American citizens were given the opportunity to disembark at Haifa, but I refused this offer, claiming my kinship with the Arabs on board. Consumed by shame at American acquiescence to Israeli actions, I longed to throw my American passport overboard. Yet my discomfort changed neither the fact nor the privilege of my American identity: I was interrogated briefly, then dismissed, while soldiers grilled Arab students for hours.

My arrival in the United States for graduate school several months later in some ways encapsulated my desire to flee such politicization of my identity. Although the invasion had forestalled both final exams and commencement ceremonies, A.U.B. professors and administrators cooperated in ensuring that seniors in good academic standing would graduate. Thus the untimely conclusion of my college career did not preclude my plans of attending graduate school in the United States — plans to which my father, his desire to keep me close to home rivalled by his belief in the importance of higher education, had acquiesced. Despite my intense discomfort with America's role in the Middle East and my own identity conflicts, I felt a certain relief at returning to an environment where I hoped, yet again, to belong.

But in Ann Arbor, Michigan I plunged deep into culture shock. Even when I had learned to divest myself of the linguistic and cultural mannerisms which made people eye me strangely — my tendency to utter the Lebanese "yiiiii" as an articulation of surprise, my absent-minded use of Arabic expressions, my awkward confusion about the appropriate physical gestures accompanying greetings and partings — I moved as if on ice, my footing precarious. The broad sidewalks and neatly trimmed lawns, campus grounds spilling without walls into the town, women and men walking down the streets in shorts and tank tops, all suggested a world which I seemed to have entered by mistake. My nights of violent dreams, for all their surrealism, seemed more grounded in reality than grocery stores vast enough to lose oneself in, endless aisles of food under humming florescent lights, shopping malls with winding mazes of corridors and lights, processed air and music, swirling seas of faces out of which bits of colour would surface, only to sink again. Trying to articulate, against this backdrop, the splintered images that filled my memory and consciousness seemed impossible: words lay weighted on my tongue. Instead, I admonished myself that my task was to succeed in the world of American academia. I reserved my obsession with Lebanon and Palestine for stolen moments with the international pages of the *New York Times*, and set out once again to claim what I still thought was mine — my American identity.

Although my high-school experience had diminished my hopes of an American homecoming, it seemed, at first, possible to pass. I learned to draw as little attention as possible to my name, my family, my background. I made no Arab friends at all, and joined no organizations where I might meet Arabs. Though so distraught about the events in Lebanon that I briefly enroled in a mini-course on the invasion, I soon dropped out, fearing the kind of revelation and emotional energy the course demanded. Lacking the confidence and fluency necessary to challenge the hostility with which I found Middle Eastern topics typically addressed, I learned to be wary of political discussions. A few days after my arrival in the U.S., a man asked me pointedly why I wore a map of Israel around my neck. I replied, truthfully, that it was a map of historic Palestine. When he retorted, clearly wanting to draw me into debate, "It's the same thing," I avoided further discussion, shrinking deep into myself. Palestine markers were obviously not neutral here; how could I have thought they would be? But I had not expected my American context to require the discretion necessary in war-time Beirut.

Michelle Cliff writes, in *Claiming an Identity They Taught Me to Despise*, "Passing demands a desire to become invisible. A ghost-life. An ignorance of connections."[8] While the incidents which first made me afraid to reveal myself in the United States were minor — pointed questions, sidelong glances, awkward silences — they were enough to thrust me firmly back into a desire for invisibility. I sought anonymity, as if trying to erode the connections which had brought me, juncture by juncture, to where and who I was, the product of histories I could no more undo than I could undo my bone structure.

"Passing demands quiet," writes Cliff "And from that quiet — silence."[9] I have learned to understand silence as something insidious. Lost between the contradictory demands of the worlds I moved between and their confusion of cultural codes, embarrassed by my lack of fluency in Arabic, intimidated by men and boys on the street and by schoolmates who excluded or taunted me, I had learned silence as a tool of survival; I honed it still further in my American context. What I did not then realize was that silence, with time, atrophies the voice — a loss with such grave consequences that it is a form of dispossession. Silence made it possible for me to blend into my surroundings, chameleon-like; it enabled me to absorb without self-revelation what I needed to know. But its implications were disastrous. At the University of Michigan I sat silently through classes, rode silently on the bus to my dormitory where I spoke to almost no one, went silently to the library where I struggled with a weighted fear I could not define. Silence wrapped itself around my limbs like cotton wool, wound itself into my ears and eyes, filled my mouth and muffled my throat.

I do not know at what point I began to choke, a dread of suffocations welling inside me like a sponge in water. Perhaps there was never a single incident, just a slow deposition of sediment over time. Until one day, retching, I spat out some unnameable substance. And attempted to speak.

By this time I was beginning to claim the tools of feminism. In my college years in Beirut I had picked up a second-hand copy of Betty Freidan's *The Feminine Mystique*. Startled by the wave of recognition it evoked, I had taken it home to my mother, who sat up reading it all one night, underlining passages in fierce acknowledgement. My later graduate school exposure to academic feminism provided the analytical training and the affirmation of voice which I had been lacking, pushing me to understand that most primary, if now cliched, of feminist principles: that the personal is political. Although I was later to discover its cultural insensibilities, American feminism enabled me to begin interrogating the entanglement of gender and culture in a search for my own definitions.

My increasing anger at the portrayal of the Middle East in the United States, and a slowly developing confidence in my own political and cultural knowledge, came together with this burgeoning feminism to make possible an articulation which, although tentative, was more empowering than anything I had experienced before. I had begun to realize that our familial conflicts had their origins not in an innate Arab propensity toward the oppression of women, but in the complexity of my parents' culturally inflected understandings of gender roles. While much in my experience had tempted me to reject Arab culture as misogynist, my growing awareness of the ways in which my experiences represented not Arab culture per se, but a conflicted interaction between Arab and American, led me to explore my Palestinian background for positive symbols — not just nationalistic but gendered — on which to draw for identification and strength.

I think of the Arab women in my personal history. Tata Olga, my grandmother, who raised three boys and buried two girls, and raised two grandchildren as well after their mother, her oldest son's young wife, was killed at a Jerusalem bus stop in 1948 by a Jewish terrorist group's bomb. Widowed when her youngest child, my father, was still an infant, she refused to remarry, maintaining a fierce independence of which my relatives still speak with awe. Im-Ibrahim, the comfortingly wide-breasted Palestinian woman from a refugee camp who cleaned houses to support her family, hiding her pay to ensure that her husband didn't squander it. Even when she no longer helped my mother with housework she would come to visit, telling fortunes in the grounds of the coffee we sipped together. I loved to listen to her stories in the simple Arabic which she adopted for my benefit, and which I sometimes understood. Aunt Hanneh, my father's cousin who never married: a dynamic and accomplished woman who went to college and graduate school in the United States, directed several libraries in Jordan, and cared for her ill mother for years. Retired now, she oversees the welfare of her extended family across several continents, remaining active as well in church and community affairs. Aunt Betty, the Lebanese wife of my father's favourite cousin: a skilled nurse, she headed a Jerusalem hospital ward for years, raised four children, gracefully met the social requirements of her husband's busy political and medical career, and now directs a centre for disabled children. Though balancing full-time work and innumerable family and community obligations, she still manages to produce a four-course meal at an hour's notice.

I see in these women the same strengths I saw in my mother: intelligence, tenacity, resilience, the maintenance of good humour despite often overwhelming difficulties. In these women, moreover, I see a certain recognition of their own worth — a recognition which seems in part the result of their cultural self-confidence. Secure in their identity as Arab women, they could challenge the interpretations and limitations placed on their prescribed gender roles without losing the cultural ground beneath their feet. This enabled them to assert themselves in ways that my mother, continually negotiating the conflicting demands of her Arab context and her own midwestern background, could not.

In my own struggle for self-assertion and articulation, my attempt to mould contradiction, I too have been caught in this tension between Arab and American cultures. American feminism offered me the possibility of personal articulation, of creating independent definitions in ways that had not always seemed possible in the Middle East. But it was the representation and misrepresentation of the Arab world in the United States which first compelled me to speak. There are ways in which Palestinian women escape the typical stereotypes of Arab women — exotic, sensualized, victimized — only to be laden with the more male-coded, or perhaps merely generic, images of irrational, fanatic terrorists and impoverished, backward refugees. Sweeping statements about Palestinian terrorism, about the Middle East as a chaotic realm outside the boundaries of rational Western comprehension, about the Arab world's backwardness and lack of civilization evoked silent protest in me long before I could articulate a response. I would smile faintly at jokes while inwardly seething, too unsure of myself, then, to reply — my silence in part an ironic legacy of my experience as an American woman in Jordan. I became acutely aware of the deep ignorance, prejudice, and fear pervading the responses of otherwise well-educated and well-intentioned people to the place which represented my childhood, the place I had finally begun to call home.

And at some point I began to feel anger. At the jokes about *kalashnikovs* in my backpack and grenades in my purse, about setting off security alarms in airports. At the woman who exclaimed in sheer amazement when my mother spoke of her Palestinian husband. "But why did you marry a terrorist?" At an acquaintance's blank face when I mentioned Arab feminism, as if the words "Arab" and "feminism" could not be contained in the same breath. At the looks of incredulity at my references to Arab women novelists, Arab women scholars, Arab women scientists. At the comments that it must be dangerous to live in Jordan "because of all the terrorism." At the implicit dismissal of my explanations that Iranians are not Arabs, that Allah is simply the Arabic word for God. At the college professor who did not believe that Arabs could be Christians. At the insidious query of a scholar to whom I had spoken of my research on Arab Americans as to why I wasn't working on 19th- century kidnappings of Americans by Arabs — as if the subjects were related. At the knowledge that when I posted announcements of Arab cultural events on campus they would be torn down moments later. At the look of shock and dismay, quickly masked, on the face of a new acquaintance just learning of my Palestinian background. At the startled response of a woman who, having assumed my Arab name to be my spouse's, made clear her surprise that I would have chosen to keep an Arab name. At the conversations in which I am forced to explain that Palestinians do indeed exist; that they claim a long history in

Palestine. At the tense, strained silences which punctuate all too many of my interactions with others.

And with the anger has come fear of the unknown person in my apartment building who intercepted packages I had ordered from an Arab American organization, strewing their contents, defaced with obscenities, at my door. Of the hostility of airport security personnel once they know my destination or origin point: the overly-thorough searches, the insistent questions. During the Gulf War, the escalation of both fear and its causes: The anonymous person who dialed my home after I was interviewed by the local paper, shouting "Death to Palestinians!" The unsigned, racist mail. The mysterious hit-and-run driver who smashed my car — a Palestine emblem clearly visible through the window — parked on a quiet residential street. The frightening reports of Arab Americans threatened, harassed, beaten; of homes violated, property destroyed. The Iranian man pulled out of his car and beaten so badly, for the crime of merely being *thought* to be Arab in America, that he underwent six hours of brain surgery and remains disabled. If to be an American woman in the Middle East may mean being viewed through the lens of exaggerated sexuality, to be Palestinian in the United States too often means being objectified into a twisted mask of hatred and violence. The feminist message that the personal is political becomes caricatured in such responses: the personal becomes only political, the individual reduced to an unrecognizeable stereotype stripped of human potential.

During the Gulf War I became more aware than ever that to position myself as an Arab American, specifically a Palestinian American, meant setting myself outside of the boundaries that define "real" Americans. On the first day of the war a radio commentator proclaimed, "In war there are no hyphenated Americans, just Americans and non-Americans." It is a familiar, and chilling, sentiment: Japanese Americans in particular can speak to its implications. But what is to become of those of us in-between, those of us who are neither "just" Americans, nor "just" non-Americans? I could say that I opposed the Gulf War as a human being first, as an American second, and only third as a Palestinian. But in fact my identities cannot be so neatly divided. I am never just an American, any more than I am just a Palestinian. Yet I am not therefore any less of an American, or less of a Palestinian. This constitutes, perhaps, the indefinable boundary separating me from those who identify wholly with a singular cultural identity. Many Americans who opposed the war were willing to join in calls for peace until the day the war began, when they retreated from public protest — as if their dissent had been merely theoretical, or the actual fact of war made opposition impossible. The yellow ribbon flurry among peace activists demonstrated just how much tension is embodied in the identity "American," how fragile it is assumed to be; as if national identity can only be sustained through absolute unanimity, through the principle — typically ascribed to tribal Arab systems — of defending one's own group irrespective of truth or justice.

It is true that I responded with anger to the rush to war before exhausting diplomatic methods, to the double standards implicit in the readiness to oppose with force the invasion of Kuwait, but not other invasions or breaches of international law. I was dismayed by the suggestion, implicit in public response to the aerial bombing of Iraq, that loss of human life, whether civilian or military, is acceptable in order to maintain American hegemony and strategic interests. I wanted the United States to be worthy, for once, of its own ideals. The violent hatred of the pro-war demonstrators screaming of blood and patriotism frightened me. If the desire for peace, for justice, for the preservation of life can be termed un-American, than perhaps I do not wish to claim this identity as my own.

But in the end what choice do I have? I am by birth and citizenship American and the fact is that I watched the war on a colour television screen thousands of miles away from the people who huddled in bombshelters that did not always save their lives. And so despite my reluctance and shame I must take responsibility for that identity. Yet, I am Palestinian too and neither can I assume the neutrality of that identity. As I was rarely given the choice in the Middle East to claim or not claim my American identity so I am not often given the choice in my American context to be or not to be Palestinian. At most I can attempt to pass, suppressing my identity and resorting to silence. And when this strategy fails — or when I reject it — then I am forced to take responsibility for Palestinian identity too, for its legacy of dispossession and oppression, but also of a desperation sometimes culminating in violence. And, in claiming this history, I come to a fuller understanding of the contradictions, the excesses, which spill over the neat boundaries within which I am often expected to, and sometimes long to, reside.

I continue to discover new facets of myself in contexts where my anger and fear are reflected back at me in the eyes of others. I have been pushed to deeper understanding of myself as both Palestinian and American in discussion with those positioned as my opposites: Jewish Americans. Building upon a common interest in the Middle East — albeit one differently situated and informed — upon our similarity as Americans yet difference as Arabs and Jews, such discussions demonstrate the possibility of tracing paths of communication through the chasms of history. These interchanges have both heightened my sense of difference and emphasized the fluidity of the boundaries which separate us. Asked, or challenged, to explain my perspectives, I have been forced to confront my own ignorance and to explore the facts behind my internalized beliefs. As a result I have become more grounded in my Palestinian identity. But the possibilities of developing ties across what once seemed an unbridgeable divide, suggest that the boundaries which separate self and other are finally constructed and so may be reconstructed. Upon receiving a vitriolically anti-Semitic letter during the Gulf War from a stranger who apparently thought that I would share his sentiments, I felt assaulted: my sense of violation at those ugly assumptions remains.

Yet, I discover myself, as well, in contexts of sameness longing to explore those parts of myself I had been able to articulate only oppositionally. I turned to Middle Eastern groups seeking not just opportunities for activism, but also friendship with other Arabs. To experience one's identity as continual exile is both stimulating and tiring: it may facilitate what Edward Said describes as "originality of vision,"[10] but it leads, as well, to a profound longing for the amelioration of loss, for the simple note of belonging. There is an undeniable pleasure in being able to take for granted cultural inflections, nuances of social behaviour, habits of mind. Like all who long to find their own reflection, I respond with particular intensity to individuals who radiate an indefinable mixture of Arab and American: who possess a passion about Palestinian issues a tangible emotional engagement with the Middle East, but whose demeanour suggests as well a refraction of Arab cultural codes through an American lens. Although I now recognize the strengths upon which Arab women draw and have learned the history of Arab feminism, my first introduction to the vision and possibility which feminism offers was through American voices. I retain an undeniable loyalty to that early introduction. But the words of Palestinian American writer Naomi Shihab Nye, who speaks of the "rapturous homecoming"; that recognition of heritage she experienced upon first meeting other Arab American writers resonate deeply: "The gravities of ancestry, the camaraderie of familiar images, even a certain slant of humour were bonds that seemed to connect us."[11] It has taken personal loss — in particular, the deaths of both my parents — to bring me to a fuller understanding of these connections in my own life. Haunted by the image of my father's fresh grave beside my mother's headstone, and by my growing understanding of the difficulties my parents had weathered in their lives together, I realized that I could no longer tolerate the schism of identity implicit in my divided names. Out of an increasingly rooted sense of myself as child of *both* parents, as well as a desire to live out my feminist principles, I decided to relinquish my husband's name — adopted in a gesture of resistance to my father's rejection of our marriage — and to change my name legally to Lisa Suhair Majaj, in a reclamation of familial history on my own terms.

But this gesture, however personally meaningful, has not erased the tensions implicit in my tangled identity. Although, this spring, I will exchange my amended passport for a new one bearing the name of my choosing, when I travel to the Middle East I will still need to explain to Jordanian officials, to whom I once feared to reveal my Palestinian identity, why I am not an Arab national. Upon crossing the Jordan River into occupied Palestine, I will still be separated from my fellow Western citizens and taken to one side for strip searching and questioning by Israeli soldiers who, whether they humiliate me or treat me with cold courtesy, will make it clear that my U.S. passport means little in the face of my Arab heritage. Here in the United States I no longer resort to spelling when stating my legal first name, nor worry about whether to use Lisa or Suhair in a given situation. But the memory of being more thoroughly grilled by U.S. airport officials than my Greek Cypriot husband, a so-called "alien resident" whose "foreignness" is more apparent than my own, remains. And the multiple mailings I still receive — addressed to Suhair Suzanne Majaj, Suhair Majaj Alexandrou, Lisa Majaj Alexandrou, Lisa Suhair Majaj — remind me on a daily basis of the many definitions of self which accompany me.

The profundity of the loss I experienced at my parents' deaths; at the foreclosing of their attempts to negotiate difference in their lives together, compels me to claim and validate their legacy: the fragmented mosaic, the interwoven fabric, of my life. I look in the mirror and recognize their mingled features in my own; I lift my hair and note the curl, the colour bequeathed by their mixed genes. My skin, lighter now since my years away from the strong sun of Jordan and Lebanon, retains the faint tinge of olive which set me apart from my white-skinned playmates, even in babyhood. Tata Olga, my Palestinian grandmother, used to lament my propensity to stay in the sun. "You'll never find a husband, dark like this," she would scold, speaking the words of internalized racism and sexism. But I search now for colour in my life. On the shelf above my desk I keep a card depicting a small Maldivian girl whose richly-hued skin, deep brown eyes, and dark unkempt hair compel me with their beauty. The Lebanese American poet who gave me this card recently adopted a vibrant Guatemalan child; the girl in the picture reminds me of his daughter. She reminds me, as well, of a group of Maldivian students from A.U.B. whose embracing presence and steady endurance during our exodus from Lebanon, sustained and comforted me. And she brings to mind all the small girls growing up in a world where women are less valued than men; dark skin less valued than light skin; poor people less valued than wealthy people; non-Western cultures less valued than Western cultures.

She reminds me, too, that it is through a willing encounter with difference that we come to a fuller realization of ourselves. I possess no representative photograph of a Palestinian American, no non-personal touchstone of my mixed heritage. And despite my longing for such tokens, perhaps they are unnecessary. Although I remain acutely aware of the importance of communal symbols in affirming individual and group consciousness, I find glimmers of myself in people I do not recognize, in faces which share with mine only questions. No closed circle of family or tribe or culture reflects from the Maldivian girl's eyes. She looks slightly away from the camera her gaze directed wistfully at something just over my left shoulder, something, I cannot see and which she may not be able to claim. The card identifies her as Laila from a Maldive fishing family, noting that Maldivians are a mix of Arabs, Singhalese and Malaysian: there are, after all, some connections between us. But I cannot intercept her gaze. Laila looks steadily beyond me, light planing her pensive face. Whatever she sees remains unspoken. I look at her often remembering how much I do not know.

Like my parents, I am grounded in both history and alienation. But if it is true that we are ideologically determined, it is also true that our choices allow us a measure of resistance against the larger patterns which map us; a measure of self-creation. Constructed and reconstructed, always historically situated, identities embody the demarcation of possibilities at particular junctures. I claim the identity "Arab American" not as a heritage passed from generation to generation, but rather as an ongoing negotiation of difference. My parents articulated their relationship oppositionally, assumptions colliding as they confronted each other's cultural boundaries. Child of their contradictions, I seek to transform that conflict into a constant motion testing the lines that encircle and embrace me, protect and imprison me. I am caught within a web: lines fade and reappear, forming intricate patterns, a maze. I live at borders which are always overdetermined, constantly shifting. Gripped by the logic of translation, I still long to find my reflection on either side of the cultural divide. But the infinitely more complex web of music beckons, speaking beyond translation. Who can say how this will end?

Claims

> I am not soft, hennaed hands
> a seduction of coral lips;
> not the enticement of jasmine musk
> through a tent flap at night;
> not a swirl of sequined hips,
> a glint of eyes unveiled.
> I am neither harem's promise
> nor desire's fulfilment.
>
> I am not a shapeless peasant
> trailing children like flies;
> not a second wife, concubine,
> kitchen drudge, house slave;
> not foul-smelling, moth-eaten, primitive
> tent-dweller, grass-eater, rag-wearer.
> I am neither a victim
> nor an anachronism.
>
> I am not a camel jockey, sand nigger, terrorist
> oil-rich, bloodthirsty, fiendish;

not a pawn of politicians,
nor a fanatic seeking violent heaven.
I am neither the mirror of your hatred and fear,
nor the reflection of your pity and scorn.
I have learned the world's histories,
and mine are among them.
My hands are open and empty:
the weapon you place in them is your own.

I am the woman remembering jasmine,
bougainvillaea against chipped white stone.
I am the labouring farmwife
whose cracked hands claim this soil.
I am the writer whose blacked-out words
are birds' wings, razored and shorn.
I am the lost one who flees
and the lost one returning;
I am the dream,
and the stillness and the keen of mourning.
I am the wheat stalk, and I am
the olive. I am plowed fields young
with the music of crickets,
I am ancient earth struggling
to bear history's fruit.
I am the shift of soil
where green thrusts through
and I am the furrow
embracing the seed again.
I am many rivulets watering
a tree, and I am the tree.
I am opposite banks of a river
and I am the bridge.
I am light shimmering

off water at night
and I am the dark sheen
which swallows the moon whole.

***

I am neither the end of the world
nor the beginning.

---

1. From "A Tree by the Water/Saltatory Process," in *Travelling Mercies*, by Lebanese American poet David Williams (Cambridge: Alice James Books, 1993).

2. Poem title in a selection of Naomi Shihab Nye's poetry entitled "Twenty Other Worlds," in *Texas Poets in Concerts: A Quartet* (Denton: University of North Texas Press, 1990; Texas Poets Series No. 2). Nye is a Palestinian American writer.

3. *Nai:* Arabic flute

4. Arab headress traditionally worn by men, now often used as a scarf by women.

5. The state of Israel was established in 1948, dispossessing 750,000 Palestinians, more than 80% of the Arab inhabitants of what became Israel. The Six Day War of 1967 resulted in Israel's seizure of land from Jordan, Egypt and Syria. During Black September of 1970 the Jordanian army killed thousands of Palestinians; militants who were not killed or captured fled to Lebanon. In 1973 war broke out between Israel, Egypt, Syria and Iraq.

6. Colloquial term for backgammon.

7. *Yakhni:* stew, typically made from any of a variety of vegetables, and lamb meat, and served over rice. *Mahshi:* vegetables, especially squash or eggplant, hollowed and stuffed with a filling of rice, lamb meat, and spices. *Wara' dawali:* grapeleaves rolled around a filling of rice, lamb meat and spices *Ma'aloubi:*literally, "upside down" — a dish of rice, lamb, onion, and cauliflower or eggplant, cooked in a large pot and up-ended onto a tray for serving.

8. Michelle Cliff, *Claiming an Identity They Taught Me to Despise* (Watertown: M. PersephonePress, 1980), p.5.

9. Cliff, p. 6.

10. Edward Said, "Reflections on Exile," *Out There: Marginalization and Contemporary Cultures.* Russell Ferguson, Martha Gever, Trinh T Minh-ha and Cornel West, eds., (New York: The New Museum of Contemporary Art, and Cambridge and London, England: The MIT Press, 1990), p.366.

11. Naomi Shihab Nye "The Gravities of Ancestry," *Grapeleaves: A Century of Arab American Poetry*, Gregory Orfalea and Sharif Elmusa, eds., (Salt Lake City: Univ of Utah Press, 1988), p.266.

But You Don't Look Like a ...

faces,
body,
hair

Lisa Jensen

(one more time now:)

WHAT NATIONALITY ARE YOU?
Canadian
BUT WHAT BACKGROUND DO YOU HAVE?
a B.A.
WELL, WHERE ARE YOUR PARENTS FROM?
(Sigh then quickly for want of a better response):
My mom's Japanese and my dad's Danish
JAPANESE EH? THAT'S AN INTERESTING COMBINATION
Yes.
WELL, IT'S CERTAINLY VERY BEAUTIFUL. I KNEW THERE
WAS SOMETHING...

O thank you thank you thank you kind white sir for your compliment.
Ever so glad to know I'm "something". I can see why you find "it"/me
a beautiful combination, I can see that I'm not quite white, enough to
be "exotic" but not so dark as to offend your colonialist sensitivities.
You know, my hair's dark though my eyes are round but not too round,
something... Besides, being Oriental is in these days.
Now how's this for a better response:

> *My parents are from their parents, where*
> *are your parents from?*
> *How much money do you have?*
> *What size shoe do you wear?*
> *Do you use Grecian formula?*
> *Is that your natural breath odour?*

96

Ijosé

Two Halves — One Whole
(excerpts from a journey through life's differences)

PART I

oyinbo pepe
if you eat-ti pepe
you go yellow
more more
oyinbo saluti
goody morni sa
are you beans?

IT MUST HAVE BEEN THIS LITTLE SONG THE OTHER CHILDREN SANG that made her realize the difference. The difference everyone else saw. This little song and loud shouts of "Yellow Banana!" Their energetic similarly thin bodies like darker shades of those heavenly chocolates her mother buys her in one of those little bribes known to children of regularly absent mothers in those mothers' times of maternal guilt to replace the several unavoidable-what-can-I-do? absences here and there.

It could have been this little song that made her rock — rocking herself gently into the night, on the bed\with her knees drawn to her chin and held together, reciting nursery rhymes taught in schools and read from bright colours print-smelling books over and over — rocking and reciting.

Until she passes onto the journey of sleep, dreaming dreams of several other little sisters and brothers, maybe just one or two; small and children just like her; and they have faces full of smiles and discoveries and they have found a garden, very pretty and bright with lots of flowers and mangoes, and they all hurry to the garden so they can spend lots of time there, and flowers, and laugh and tell each other stuff; and sometimes one of them would go to pee just by the side; but when it is her turn, she always wakes up because her mother said if she wants to pee in her dream it is because she really wants to pee.

So she wakes up.

It could have been knowing the other children thought of her as physically weaker made her thin little girl's body contract with fear of physical hurt; as in that time when a boy ran secretly from behind her and hit her so hard on her back just below her nape it made her cry angry tears because it hurt and because she did not know who did it. And her back began to feel like an open venue for attack. And it frightened her so she hardly left the walls of the house she spent holidays in. As in those times when loud little boys and not so little boys and strangely muscular little girls and not so little girls would say to her:

"You tink say you special... one day I go beat you — you africa oyinbo."

As in those times when she'd agree to run some errands for her mother... grocery stores that seemed too far away — far too too far away but mother said not to worry it is just next door. But it was never JUST next door. No. And the other children would throw stones. Sometimes sand. Red sand. Red lumpy sand. At her. Simply because she is part this and part that; and thereby diluted. Meek. A halfcaste who would probably cry like a baby; a halfcaste. Available for teasing; for bullying.

It must have been that like all children who wish to seek out a different land for themselves, she made for herself images and day dreams and ribbons of bright blue, yellow, red, purple wrapping herself in waves of vibrance and colours during those trying holidays when she came home after months in the boarding school, for Christmas; always alone, she talked alone and ever reluctant to be exposed to name-calling and that little song, she stayed within the gates of her home and played alone even when some of the other children came to her house — asking if they could come play with her. And when they did (including some repentant ones who don't call her names anymore), she found it is more fun to play with her friends from that secret land who reside on the walls and ceilings with happy and sad faces only she can see.

Her mother kept saying the other children admired her and that they really liked her. They like her hair; they want to play with her; be her friends; laugh and talk with her and see how she lives... That was why they gave her such trouble; so she should try to be nice to them even if they call her names; afterall, it is because they liked her so that they sing for her just so she could at least say something to them; so she should be nice and invite them in to come play with her dollies and crayons and watercolours. She thought this was probably true... but it was still very lonely to be called names; it was still very lonely to have sand thrown at you; to have other children get excited whenever they saw you; like you were something new... And those times when her mother would invite some of the other children in, they always acted strange with her, not like they were between themselves, and they would treat her in a special arm-length way, maybe because they considered her an "oyinbo-girl" who probably thinks differently and has no idea of the rules of the games they'd like to play. And as if they had decided among themselves what to do, they would eat up all the sweets and goodies offered, and leave the house just as silently as when they came in. This was also the case when she had twice stopped — actually stopped — amidst darts and loud cries of "yellow banana!" and "africa-oyinbo" hoping maybe they would realize she is just like them and get bored and tired of seeing her. They had come over; took forever to say a word to her; and went home with play stuff they asked if they could keep.

It must have been that little song that made holidays spent in her mother's ancient city so much of a living terror she would count the days left to go back to the boarding school, where she was not different and no one sang names. That little song that made going across the country on long holidays to see her father, a big treat — there the other children do not run after her and call her names and throw sand and maybe stones. No one called her an "agric fowl." Weak agric fowls who are not as strong as house-fowls; who have to be fed specially and superficially, fertilizers and stuff house-fowls would puke on; meek agric fowls who are not street-wise and do not know how to fend for themselves. The other children. The ones who did not have to go to a boarding school; who stayed with their mothers and whose mothers stayed with them, all the time; not a few months each year. The other children who had several other little brothers and sisters to play with and share dinner with; eat together with and call her names with. Whose father lived in the same house and was not from a foreign place they know nothing of, and no one seem to like. Even her mother prays she would grow tall because there is a chance the other blood in her might make her not as tall as *she* wants. The other children whose fathers slept in the same room with their mothers. The ones who never had to make yearly wonderful trips across the country up where it is windy and dry and very hot in the afternoons to go see a silent father who would smile gently at them and ruffle their hair and take them for a drive and buy them biscuits they like but would never call their names... maybe because the name had nothing to do with him and was not in his language and was not given by him and does not identify with him... so he would simply refer to her as 'baby,' always 'baby.'

So let it be their faces, their clapping singing shouting laughing face-making faces that closed her up. Closed her within the walls of her imagination and living dreams... dreams of visions of colours and lights and still sound waves that enter gently into her thinking while she lies under the bed away from cool pillows of comfort as if hiding — hugging rocking her little girl's body against her little girl's body. So let it be their faces — their faces — and not the silence that tore her in the house in the city up north and the harrowing words that grew within the walls of the house down south — words the mother spat out that drove her in desperate need for a little more sign of his love... a child's pain that made a little child sleep with her mouth turned upside down...

So let it be memories of their animated eager faces running up a little closer to at least touch something of her and maybe get to pull her hair. Hair that fascinated them in its length, its shining blackness plaited in silent heavy four plaits; or two huge drooling sister plaits; or several quick small plaits coming down rapidly all over her small face like curly black shiny snakes with the tail end rooted in her skull... as she tries not to run... but walk steadily... maybe a little faster... because if she runs from their shouts and names they would think she is afraid and become bolder... call her even more, an agric fowl... frightened halfcaste with water for bones — maybe smart in school, probably is... but still a weak oyinbo with frying pan bottom and everlasting lipstick... small Oke here fit beat am proper proper and show im fine fine halfcaste yellow bread and butter face real pepe...

PART II

"NEXT... June Cheung!"

The woman who had bent to call this name into the quiet-looking mike behind the glass counter protecting the government officials from the claws of the big white room of mostly newcomers is looking past June as she approaches in definite strides in the way one does to answer to a name they recognize as theirs after having been waiting or hoping to hear it soon. The woman looks towards June and begins to say in a high pitched nasal voice that was both authoritative and near-snappy,

"Sorry m'am but you'll have to..."

"I am June Cheung."

She looks closely now at June, her face blatantly displaying that she is not convinced. A slight frown of suspicion queried quite audibly at her brows for some seconds. Her face seemed to say: NO, YOU'RE NOT (And I Can Tell)!

101

"You are June Cheung?" she repeats, sounding like she is half expecting June to deny it — and hopefully turn around and go back to the waiting section and wait for her proper name to be called instead of deliberately creating this confusion and fuss by answering a name so obviously not hers...

Now there is nothing wrong with this name; especially not here in Toronto with a large Chinese community. The problem is that in Canada, June is BLACK — anonymously black — not even African; definitely not "half this and half that"; not "africa-oyinbo" as she would be fondly teased in her home country. June's mind flashes back to her home, and she thinks: "Thank goodness, at least here it is merely an issue of colour." Back in her home country, it was a mixed case of dramatic intrigue and near bafflement when people met her and immediately assume she is half "somewhere in Europe" and naturally perceive and refer to her as a mulatto and a "halfcaste." And when they learn she is half Chinese, they almost cannot contain their surprised interest, their face spreading in delighted curiosity: obviously they find her genetic combination simply incredible as they reason that Chinese people are not known for marrying out of their lineage, not to think of marrying out of China — and most especially not for allowing their daughters to marry men from other cultures (at least not Africa!). People in her home country always assume it is her mother who is the Chinese one. And so, when they come across her last name, it becomes a slightly different issue of how come one of their own country women had the guts (and "whoreness") to have a baby by — not even a European which is still bad enough for a woman to do — but a CHINESE MAN! A Chinaman! What did she see in him? What attracted her to him? They decide it could be nothing but money and material wealth. The people in her home country were always quick to assume she probably does not know her father, who also does not know he has an African/Chinese child and that her mother is apparently one of those crazy promiscuous women who decide to make babies with visiting foreigners. Sometimes some more inquisitive ones would flatly ask her if she knows her father without thinking they might be rude and crudely prying — and when they learn she does and also lives with him, their amazement seems to know no end. These instances were always tediously trying for her. They would tell her, "At least you're lucky you don't look really Chinese." And they considered it a compliment. Or some would say, "You know you do look somewhat Chinese." And it becomes a sad thing: after all she does not have a straight nose like she most definitely would have had, had she been half European; afterall she is not tall because Chinese people are not known for height (and God help her that her future children be at least tall).

However, in Canada, this attitude regarding her looks is completely the reverse: for some who think she looks somewhat 'Chinese,' it becomes an added plus; while others who think she looks more black than Chinese, look almost disappointed and their facial expression seems to imply that she has been denied some vital exotic statistics for her report card — or menu.

While her mind was still on the trail of looks, June quietly recalls how the men back home always paid her so much attention and profess to be in love with her (without even knowing her person). But it never did anything for her and gave her almost no feminine-vanity pride — at least not after her first year in undergrad school when she passed a group of "guys" walking just so behind her — near enough for her to hear one of them saying he heard Chinese girls have vertical"virginals" and all other girls horizontal. And they all went silent as she felt the air behind her heavy and loud with curiosity because it was obvious she had heard. They all must have wondered what she had: a diagonal one maybe.

The woman behind the glass counter that seemed to say KEEP AWAY is asking her for identification papers, some immigration document she says — although June knew she had most if not all of the same documents — in her possession — that has her picture on it. She put meaningful emphasis on the word "picture" in such a pointed way that it was hard to imagine that in a professional dealing, she could get anymore hostile than she already was. June obediently fingers through her red paper file to sort out the relevant documents required and handed them over through a square cut in the glass. As she does so, she looks steadily at the woman to restrain herself from telling the woman what she could do with her crisp hostility, and as she does so, she passively acknowledges how gravity seemed to be calling and pulling at the woman's mouth, chin, shoulders, breasts. The only thing that gravity seemed unable to call or pull was her nose, which stood away from the inevitable lure, alone and aggressively tipped in the air. The woman had an incredibly thin stiff upper lip which barely moved when she spoke and gave the funny feeling that her voice was coming from somewhere other than herself. This stiff upper lip took all the attention from her pale grey eyes which June was trying furtively to focus on and which gave nothing but frost and fog. The peculiar movement of the woman's lips gave the impression of barely being opened and her words seemed forced out of some other outlet, and this made June feel she has seen them before now. Maybe at other past times when she had encountered similar reactions to her name or when she had found herself, not knowing fully the directions of the city, at such crispy clean places that her very presence seemed to produce the same effect or movement of lips. Since her reception on arrival at the Pearson Airport, she had become familiar with the "whiteness" of things. The white-washing and whiteness quite crude and loud at some times, and subtle and deadly at others. She had come to observe that white-washed minds see themselves as normal and also rightful owners protecting their own, and anyone with a darker skintone or "colour" is duly treated with suspicion and guardedness.

As far as the white eyes of the woman were concerned, June is a black woman claiming a Chinese name for reasons not too clear. And her well-bred instincts for precaution are properly alarmed. And to make matters more obscure, this black person is also a newcomer and you never know with these newcomers and their clever gimmicks: fake names, fake IDs, fake passports... the list never ends. And as if it weren't bad enough, this one is from that country the U.S. media and state reports have appropriately warned the international community about...

She throws June one more accusing look heavy with bare tolerance as if to make her point clear and received. She then turns a slight angle just so to her left and begins to expertly petition the silent computer backing the wall closest to her, to perform what it is supposed to and expose this impostor at her games. But the computer, after what seemed to be a long time, obviously had no comments because the woman heaved a sigh and looked away from the machine to the wall to her left, as her eyes calmly scanned a black and white poster of two men, of African and Asian descent respectively, smiling in a half embrace. And the poster read: "Let A New Canadian Know How Friendly We Old Canadians Really Are."

She looks away with the air of someone forced to give in and succumb to inexplicable laws that leave her bound to give food and shelter to liars and imposters at the door.

"Could you SPELL your last name."

"C H E U N G."

"Date of birth."

"22nd June, 1970."

"That's all for now," she stiffly declares, still looking as though she is not quite satisfied. "You'll get our response in the mail." Her tone was such that June would not have been surprised if she said, "You will get our warrant for arrest in the mail and we will bloody well throw you back where you come from unwanted newcomer you!"

Ngaire Blankenburg

Don't say
"you know, if you
hadn't told me
I'd never have known
that you had
black blood"
I'm not flattered
to have passed

Blue

It was a blue-uue summer,
hot like a chili pepper
hot like a salsa
hot like I didn't want to put my feet
down on the burning ground
stretching for a glass of coo-ol water
steaming up the tap space
reachin' for a Blue —
blue summer.

sweatin' off my fingertips, reaching
to put some air through
my frizzy curls/dancing to a heat tune
all on their own,
scornfully singing an anti-straightener song.

My hair and I were kind of tired of
cold voices asking us what we were
what we are
what we were trying to be
tapping out a beat and rhythm and
sweet music
sweet
fresh and
rock and roll
rap
funk-a-delic
summer music.
We, my hair and I, dancing
faster than sweat streaming or
water running
spoke louder than a drum.

"nothing..." we said
feeling the burning in our feet
"and EVERYTHING."

blue, mmmm
there's no blue in this summer.

Joanne Arnott

Mutt's Memoir

THE SUMMER I WAS FIFTEEN, MY YOUNGER SISTER AND I HAD A great adventure. We visited our mother. We left Manitoba by train, and two weeks later she accompanied us on our return. Not to stay, of course, but to visit the others. Together we boarded the plane, and soon a flight attendant was leaning over us. The flight attendant asked my sister what she'd like for lunch, giving two options. She asked my mother the same question, in the same words, and I sat back, formulating my own decision. Then it was my turn. She smiled in a genuine way, and proceeded to address me in French. I was stunned — even drawn to the edge of panic.

For years my siblings had teased me that I was adopted. Finally I had to ask my father if it was true, he snorted, and said no. The father of my girlhood friend helped to define me, though I didn't understand him then. "Heinz 57," he called me. "Mutt."

One winter day I was strolling across my aunt's livingroom when she swept up and caught my face in her two hands, forcing me to standstill. My father's sister pushed my head back, into the sunlight coming through the window. We were the only ones in the house. She rolled my head this way and that, examining each feature. "There *must* be Indian in us," she said. "There *must* be." On another occasion, in a different season, she stood in the yard discussing me with a neighbour. She sounded embarassed. She laughed. "Nigger in the woodpile somewhere, eh?" she said. More laughter.

The litany my mother taught me was thus: French, Belgian, Scottish, Irish. French Belgian Scottish Irish. FrenchBelgianScottishIrish. French... "We may *speak* English, but we are *not* English." Those old colonial resentments carrying on.

The shadow litany that accumulated went like this: Old Black Joe, Indian Joe, Mexican Joe, Any Old Joe. Old Black Joe Indian Joe Mexican Joe Any Old Joe. Old Black Joe... There I was in my early teens, reading about slavery, watching Bugs Bunny in the afternoon, forging an identity. There is definitely something missing here, or something huge, present and unnamed.

Lois Robertson-Douglass
No Nation Gal

No nation gal is weh yuh
come from! My lawd!
A weh yuh get dat deh head a hair
gal a so yuh skin fair!
Missis, go back a yuh yard

When sun lick yuh, yuh turn
colour like green lizard...
eheh! yuh almost fava one a we
when likkle colour creep in yuh face!

But is a damn disgrace...
Because as cold wedda and cool breeze blow!
yuh start to fava English man
Gal! Meh no know!!

But wait deh likkle!
is yuh bredda dat!
But a so him pretty
Him skin kine a Black!

No nation gal!
Come yah mek yuh and me talk
Call yuh bredda
Mek me and him walk!

Marilyn Elain Carmen
The Issue of Skin Colour

My son was small at the time, maybe about five. We were riding the city bus. He looked at me. Then he looked at the woman sitting next to me. Then he looked at me again. Again at the woman. Then he said, "Mommy you almost made it. Mommy you're almost white."

EVERYTIME MY AUNT TELLS THIS STORY, A STORY THAT SHE relates with pride, she breaks into laughter. I really cannot blame her. It ain't easy being black. Not then. Not now.

Her father, my grandfather, worked his way up from being a Georgia sharecropper to owning a farm and then to moving to Harrisburg, Pennsylvania where he was to buy a home for his family. This, to my aunt, provides justification for her belief that she is better than those "po' black niggas that ain't got a pot to piss in."

Our family bloodline, on my mother's side, is very mixed, which accounts for my mother and aunt's near-white complexion.

"Ugly black nigga"

"Liver-lipped hussy"

"Flat-nose just like a nigga"

"Black and ugly like her daddy"

These are a few of the names I was called as a child by my mother and aunt, who by that time were both mentally ill. With a skin-tone darker than theirs, I became an easy target for them to vent hostilities.

I'll never forget one day when I was finally tall enough to reach the mirror in the hallway of our home, I smiled and said to myself "I have a pretty smile. I'm not ugly at all."

My mother died when I was eleven, and after she died, I went to live with my father and stepmother. My stepmother is a brown- skinned woman, the darkest of three sisters.

So now the situation was reversed. Instead of being "not good enough" because I was the darkest of the family, I was "not good enough" because I was the lightest of the family.

It never occurred to me that the mean and unjust treatment I received from her was based on my skin colouring until about ten years ago. We were arguing. "You're crazy just like your mother," she said to me. "And if you keep putting that cream on your face you'll soon be white."

Claire Huang Kinsley

Questions People Have Asked Me. Questions I Have Asked Myself.

To start with, I don't know what I look like.

I'm not complaining. There are plenty of worse fates. But still, how odd — to look at yourself in the mirror, to see the face you know best of any face in the world, and to ask yourself, "What do I look like?" and to not really know.

———————————

Question #1. What do I look like?

"You don't look very Chinese."

"You don't look Chinese at all."

"Your mother's Chinese? Really?"

"Well, now that you mention it, I can sort of see it..."

"Are you Vietnamese? Chinese?"

"I thought maybe you were part Inuit."

"Are you the young lady with the Oriental features and the very nice haircut?"

"You don't look Chinese. You look Canadian."

"Interesante... tipo chino, pero con pecas."

"I can kind of tell, but only because of your eyes."

"You have Chinese hair."

"I want to speak to the staffperson I saw last time. I think maybe she was Filipino or something."

"You don't look Asian at all."

"I could tell you were mixed as soon as I laid eyes on you. I'm from Trinidad, we're used to that."

"Your mother's Chinese? Really?"

"Really?"

"Really?"

Do you mind me asking what your ethnic background is?

———————

Question #2. Do you mind me asking what your ethnic background is?

"I'm half Chinese."

And the other half?

You know. Regular. Normal.

A friend of mine knows a little boy who, on being asked this question, said, "I'm part Jewish and part plain."

Another variation, which served me well in elementary school in Montreal: "Ma mère est chinoise et mon père est américain."

In fact, *both* my parents were American. My mother was born in Guangdong; her mother was Fukienese, and her father Cantonese. They moved to California when she was a small child, and she grew up there. My father was born in Vermont, and that's where he grew up. His mother was Irish American and his father mostly, I think, English American.

Question #3. Your mother's Chinese? Really?

Yes.

Question #4. Your father's white? Really?

This question doesn't belong in this piece. No one has ever asked me this.

———————

My parents met at a student Mass at the University of Rochester; they got into a discussion after the service about Eastern Orthodox liturgy, of all things. They got married about a year after they met and moved to Montreal, and my sisters and I were born there. There are three of us, three Chinese/Irish/English Canadian children; I'm the middle one. The U.S. Supreme Court ruling that states could not outlaw interracial marriages was handed down in 1967, the year that I was born.

———————

My mother, my uncle and my grandmother, shortly before they left China

My grandfather

My aunt, my grandparents and my father, at home

My parents, my grandmother, my sisters and me. I'm inbetween my younger and older sister

Question #5. What do they see? And why?

Sometimes when people aren't perceptive enough to notice something, they take for granted that it isn't there.

People often assume that I'm white (nothing but white). That, I think, is an understandable mistake. What gets to me, though, is if, after finding out that their assumption was wrong, they nevertheless figure that it was inevitable. That anybody in their place would have thought the same thing. That this assumption was entirely a result of the way *I look,* and nothing to do with the way *they see.*

Too often, people don't stop to ask themselves how their own experience may influence what they see. I was once trying to talk about this whole thing to a white acquaintance of mine, and she said, "I don't usually notice what race people are so much as other things, like the way they talk, the way they express themselves." And, you know, I didn't say this then, but I'll say it now: *Maybe you don't notice because you've never had to notice. How often have you ever scanned a roomful of faces in the hope of spotting people who might, just might, have the same racial background as you? When you see another white person in the subway or the supermarket, do you ever feel a tug, an impulse to go up to that person and say, "Are you white? You are? What's it been like for you? And when that white person gets off the subway or disappears behind a stack of paper towels (without you having had the nerve to say a thing), do you ever feel slightly wistful as you watch them go?*

Question #6. What's your racial background?

I'm Eurasian.

Question #7. Are you Asian?

Yes.

Question #8.

This question lurks. Deep down. Wait a minute — I need to dredge it up. Ah, there it is.

Question #8. Who the hell do you think you're kidding, white girl?

_____

_____

Why should I answer this question? I don't have anything to prove. I am what I am. I... I can't even *remember* not knowing how to use chopsticks. And I'm going to learn more Cantonese soon. And people have told me I have nice Chinese handwriting. And people *have* accepted me. They've *welcomed* me. I'm a member of ALOT[1]. I was a member of the Asian American Alliance in college. I went to meetings. I did theatre skits. I was a *keynote speaker* at the Sixth Biennial Midwest Asian Pacific American Student Conference. I do belong. I do. I *do*.

Question #9. Don't I?

_____

At the *fifth* Asian student conference, my friend Ed Lee and I decided to go to the conference banquet. When we got there, the student at the door asked me, "Do you have a reservation?"

"Uh, no," I said. "Were we supposed to?"

"I'm sorry," she said, very politely, "but non-Asian students need to have a reservation."

I work at a community information centre. We do information and referral, and help people fill out forms, things like that. One day we had a rather nasty incident where a woman said that she didn't want one of our volunteers to do her income tax because he was Chinese. (He was actually Vietnamese, but what did she know?) When we were discussing the incident later, one of my co-workers said, "You know, Claire, I've never told you this before, but another one of our clients once said that she would rather you not be the one to serve her because you're Chinese."

Question #10. How did you feel when you heard that?

A bit upset, but not seriously. The way I look has typically shielded me from overt expressions of bigotry, so I didn't come into the situation with the same buildup of anger that another person of colour without access to that kind of privilege might have felt.

Question #10. How did you feel when you heard that?

Well... I was glad, in an ironic way, that at least she had noticed I was Chinese.

Question #10. How did you feel when you heard that?

I just told you.

Question #10. How did you feel when you heard that?

It's none of your business.

Question #10. How did you —

I was pleased. Okay? I was pleased that I had been a target of racism. The REAL kind, the blatant kind, the kind that regular people mean when they say "racism." I was pleased because this was proof that I really was a woman of colour, no matter what anyone said. I had my credentials. I had my badge. I counted.

Did you have to ask? Does the whole world have to know this? What are they going to think?

———————

Question #11. What are they going to think?

That's up to them. Give them a space and let them write it in for themselves.

———————

I'm standing around in a theatre, chatting, waiting for an improv workshop to begin. A white woman in the group makes a racist comment about Chinese people. Which I'm not going to repeat.

She says it lightheartedly; it's supposed to be funny. I don't think she knows I'm Chinese. I don't think she would have said it if she'd known.

Question #12. WHAT did she say?

You heard.

Question #13. How DARE she say that?

She dared.

Question #14. What should I do?

I got stuck on this question. I felt sick.

Consider, for comparison purposes, two other scenarios.

SCENARIO A: I'm standing around, chatting. Someone makes a racist comment about Native people. Or says something derogatory about fat people. Or tells an anti-Semitic joke.

Question #14. a) What should I do?

Call them on it.

Question #15. Do I have the guts to?

I might, or I might be a coward. An uncomfortable choice, but a pretty straightforward one.

SCENARIO B: I'm standing around, chatting. Everyone there knows my racial background. Someone makes a racist comment about Chinese people.

Question #14. b) What should I do?

I *could* call them on it. But I may choose not to. In that kind of situation, I've often felt, "If you can say what you just said in front of me, knowing what you know, then either you're too obtuse to realize how this hurts me or you just don't care, and I'm not even going to *try* to educate you. Why the hell should I?"

Back to the chat in the theatre. Lights, camera, action. Racist comment.

Question #14. What should I do?

Call her on it? (Scenario A)

But I shouldn't have to. I'm the one being hurt here. Why the hell should I have to educate her? (Scenario B)

But she doesn't know I'm Chinese. If I don't say anything, it looks like a white person not saying anything. I'd be complicit. Passing. Betraying my community.

But that's not fair. I shouldn't have to do the teaching about this. Where am I supposed to start? "Um, excuse me, but did you know that what you just said made me feel like I'd been punched in the stomach?"

But if I don't —

But how can I...?

But...

But...

I got stuck. I felt sick. I said nothing.

———————————

The phone rings. A member of an overwhelmingly white women's organization, to which I belong, would like to talk to me about a discussion on racism and heterosexism which another member and I are organizing.

"I'd really like it," she says, "if you could do it in a way that would make people feel good about being in the organization."

Question #12. WHAT did she say?

You heard.

The conversation goes on. She would like to know what we are planning to discuss.

"... and so," I say, "we'd like to talk about what the experiences of women of colour have been in these workshops we offer."

"What information will you be basing this on?"

"Well," I say cautiously, "I can talk about my own experience when I first took these workshops..."

"Yes," she says briskly, "but you can't generalize from your own experience."

Question #16. What IS this?

Question #17. Does she think I don't know that?

Question #18. (I can't help wondering, I simply can't help it) Would she have said just what she said, in just that tone of voice, if I had been darker-skinned?

I don't know.

———————

Question #19. Do I exist?

A year or so before, I had attended a workshop offered by this organization on images of women in advertising. To the best of my knowledge I was the only woman of colour in the room, unless there were other mixed-race women there whom I hadn't spotted. I made a point, during the discussion, of talking about images of women of colour, and Asian women in particular, because that's what I was particularly interested in. At the end of the discussion, when the workshop facilitator was summing up, she touched briefly on the issue of racism in advertising, and the way she touched on it was by deploring the harmful effect it had on the way "we" perceived "other races"! I was stunned. It was like, "other than *who?* Hello? Do I exist?"

Did she know I was Eurasian? I don't know. I thought she knew my name — and there I was yakking away about Asian women this, Asian women that — I mean, you'd think these things would be *clues,* even if she wasn't particularly experienced at observing variations on the epicanthal fold of the eyelid and whatnot. So, did she not know, or was it just easy for her to forget? I don't know.

But, you know, even if she was convinced everyone in the room was white, still, to talk about the effect of racism only in those terms — its effect on "our" perception of "them" — like, who's the centre of the universe here?

Question #20. Who is the centre of the universe?

I read a lot when I was a child. I read when I was supposed to be getting dressed in the morning. I read walking along the sidewalk, and almost, but not quite, when crossing the street. I read curled up on the sofa, for hours at a time. And most of these books I was reading were about white kids.

Now, many of these were really good books — some were quite wonderful books, actually, which I still re-read now and then — but that's not the point. The point, in terms of my own identity, is that in comparison there were very few books out there about Chinese or other Asian kids, especially books that didn't portray them as exotic and "other." And there were virtually *no* books about children of mixed race.

And I think my sense of identity was very weird. I mean, I *knew* I was of mixed race ("I'm half Chinese," remember?) and there were aspects of Chinese culture in our house that I more or less took for granted, but I think in many ways, on a less conscious level, I tended to think of myself as a little white kid — a white kid with brown braids, like Laura Ingalls or somebody. I drew pictures of white kids. I wrote stories about white kids. I played make-believe games about white kids. And this seemed normal to me.

Mind you, this kind of experience is not unique to children who have some white ancestry. And it could be said that having the culture of *half* one's ancestors, at least, overflowing from the bookshelf, is more than a lot of kids have. It could also be said that having the *option* of thinking of oneself somehow as white, and getting away with it, as it were — having within one's reach the sense of normalcy, of belonging, of existing that this brings — is a privilege many kids do not have. And both these things are very true. But if you say these things, you also have to ask, *at what cost* does this identification come?

I still don't feel I have a complete answer to that. But I do know that it messes with your mind.

Take a relatively trivial example:

Question #1. (Reprise)

On the whole, when I was younger, I liked my face, as I saw it in the mirror. You usually see your face in the mirror from pretty much the same angle and that's what you get used to. But then sometimes when

I saw photos of myself, I would think I looked kind of peculiar in them. And I usually thought of it as, "well, I'm not very photogenic." Or "that wasn't a very good photo of me." It was only much later — in my early twenties, I think — that I came to realize that much of what I thought of as odd-looking about my face, that the camera had caught, was what was Asian about it.

And the interesting thing is that if you'd asked me, I'd never have said that I didn't want to look Asian. In fact, I have Eurasian cousins who look more obviously Asian than I do, and I used to think it would be neat to look like them. But those photos of me — I just thought they were funny-looking. Which made me realize how very subtle internalized racism can be. And how can you undo that stuff when you don't even know it's there?

I'm loitering in Chinatown, looking at fruit. The store owner and a customer are chatting in Cantonese. I listen, wistfully. I have no idea what they are talking about. The sharp-cut syllables rise and fall.

"Gau sup sam," says the customer. Ninety-three. It's the only word I've understood in the whole conversation, but I feel as though I've been given a present.

I pick out some apples. The store owner puts them in a bag. "Thank you," I say, in English. "Thank you" is one of the few things I know how to say in Cantonese, but I never have the nerve to say it.

Question #9. (Reprise)

I remember a conversation with Tommy Woon. Tommy was the Asian American Counsellor/Coordinator at Oberlin College and the staff liaison to the Asian American Alliance.

Did this conversation ever literally take place? Or did what we had to say actually come out more gradually, in the course of several conversations?

My memory has distilled it down to this one exchange.

I had been wondering about taking part in a student theatre project about being Asian American, and I said to Tommy, "The thing is, I don't feel as though I've really lived the... the Asian American experience." (Whatever I thought that was.)

Tommy kind of looked at me. And he said, "But, Claire, *you are* Asian American. So whatever experience you have lived, *that is* the Asian American experience."

I have never forgotten that.

"I'm sorry, but non-Asian students need to have a reservation."

What did I say? What did I stammer? I don't remember clearly. What I do remember is that Ed Lee — good old Ed! — put his arm around me and said firmly, "This woman is VERY Asian."

And we did go to the banquet. And the food was great.

Epilogue

Question #21. What would they have thought?

I am awed by the mere existence of the past.

I stare into museum cases at small objects ("Terra-cotta bowl, 250 — 200 B.C." "Pine box, ca. 1340") and think to myself, "Somebody made this. Who? What did they look like? How old were they? What did they think about while they made it? What did they do with it once it was made?"

And what fills me with wonder is that there are answers to these questions, even though I'll never know them. Each of those whittle marks on the box was made by a motion of a real human hand, belonging to a real human being. They're dead now ("How long did they live? What did they die of?" My breath leaves steam marks on the glass case) but still they existed, they made that box.

I sit in a corner of my room and try to imagine my ancestors. Ancestors, blood ancestors, form a root pattern that is fascinating in its symmetry — you had two parents, exactly two, and so did each one of them. And the thing about ancestors is, you know that they existed. There are no gaps in the pattern. There are only so many generations back that you can find out anything about them, and yet you know that far beyond that, farther and farther into the past, they were there, they really lived, these people who had children who had children who had descendants who had you.

Pick a moment in the past, randomly. Any century, any date, whatever calendar you know best. Let's say, for example, April 27, 1639 (Gregorian calendar). Let's say the moment in that day is when the sun rose on the eastern tip of this continent. Fix that moment in your mind. And wonder: how many of the people alive right then were your ancestors, and what was each one of them doing at that moment?

In these moods, I am awestruck by the fact that my ancestors — my mother's ancestors and my father's — lived on completely different continents, thousands of miles apart, spoke virtually unrelated languages, lived in radically different cultures, for thousands of years — and yet all of these ancestors, have, in a sense, come together in me. Me and my sisters.

Here are photographs of my grandmothers' parents.

My mother's mother's parents, who died when she was a small child, lived in the city of Fuzhou, Fujian province. Her father was a merchant; her mother had been a lady's maid before she became his concubine, or secondary wife.

My father's mother's parents had a small dairy farm in Lowell, Vermont. Both of them were children of Irish Catholics who had emigrated to the United States from the western part of Ireland.

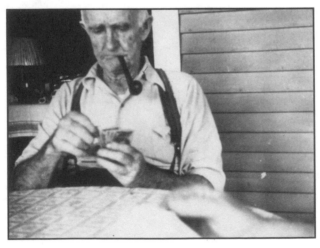

131

Pick a day before my grandmothers were born — let's say sometime in 1900. Pick a day when the weather was good, in both Lowell and Fuzhou.

If I had been able, that day, to tap my great-grandparents on the shoulder, and say, "Stop what you're doing for a minute. It'll keep. Come with me for a second. Look at the horizon. Look past it — look farther. Look as far as you can. See that continent there? See that other couple? They're looking at you too. Wave.

Why? Because your grandchildren are going to marry each other..."

...what would they have thought?

---

[1] ALOT refers to a group called Asian Lesbians of Toronto.

Gitanjali Saxena

Second Generation; Once Removed

interview excerpts

What is your nationality?

I don't know

I wish I had a dollar for every time someone asked me that question.

What is your nationality?

Maybe it's just an obsession.

Yeah, maybe it's you!

What is your nationality?

My mother's Zebra and my father's a Martian.

So, what is your nationality? Is it a secret?

Gita, facing camera, reaches to TV and changes channel.

female voice-over

And now for something completely different. Yes, this is a different message. In fact, this message is so different that it won't sound at all like any message previously heard. This different message definitely differs in most aspects from most others, with different tonal quality, different speech patterns and totally different meaning or lack thereof. If any difficulty is experienced in differentiating this different message and other not-so-different messages, well it doesn't matter anyway, as long as you get a different message of your own.

texts on screen:

MHTV
mixed heritage tele-visions presents:

SECOND GENERATION; ONCE REMOVED

text from "Ramayana[1]"
Oh Gold and Silver found wild are better than coins tamely won.

slow scan of Gita

distorted, layered sound
Es ist wie es ist.
Ek, do, thin, char, panch, che, sat, ath, nau, das.
One, two, three, four, five, six, seven, eight.

text from "Ramayana"
treasures found on a hunt
are as good as
the pleasures of fancy in heaven

close-up of face with superimposed water
Est ist wie es ist

image of Goddess from performance by Gita
Gita's voice-over
My father is from Bombay, India and my mother is from Hamburg, Germany.

image of birds

older Indian male voice-over
...usually don't accept this... yes. Even perhaps I might not have accepted it that way. But we belong to an old orthodox tradition.

Gita's voice-over
They had a traditional wedding in India.

older Indian male voice-over
...but I think the main thing is that you should get someone's love — means parents, mothers, fathers — that will be a healthy thing.

Gita's voice-over
Then I was born in a small town in Germany.

text from "Ramayana"
where i have been there
is no light from any sun.

image of Gita eating

Gita's voice-over
We moved to Canada when I was two. My first language was German but I don't speak it well now. As a child I had no idea that my parents' interracial marriage was at all unusual or different. I just considered people to be who they are. It wasn't until I started going to grade school that I started encountering the attitude that this was something that was really an unusual thing. When I was around six years old, my parents were divorced and the courts gave custody to my mother, so I grew up mainly as a German Canadian and went to a German school on Saturday and visited my German relatives every few years.

Usually when I heard people referring to Indian people, it was usually in some really negative way.

image of birds
I think in this process, I denied who I was.

image of a Goddess
There were Indian people in my school. I would talk to them but I was always sort of secretly ashamed of them and I didn't want to hang around them too much because then I would be associated with them. When people asked me what my nationality was, I would tell them that I was German. But, they didn't believe me, of course, because my features didn't look very German. I wished I had blond hair with blue eyes like my cousins. I didn't have an extended Indian family, you know, people who could be role models for my Indian side.

text from "Ramayana"
we have no moon nor stars,
no lightings like these
much less any of this Fire.

close-up of face and water

older Indian male voice-over
Hmmm... very nice so
You have inherited the qualities of both.

female voice-over
I was in the back of a taxi and we were whipping down some street in New York City and the cab driver proceeded to tell us some story and actually he wasn't telling a story, he was butting into our conversation and he kept on saying, where are you from? where are you from?

"Half Breed," poem by Nicole Tanguay

female voice-over   2 sets of arms
     reach across
2 different cultures
     to give birth to
2 different entities

half breed =
half devil =
metis, mestiza, hupa

male voice-over   combo
2 in one =

female voice-over   discrimination amongst
2 different cultures

male voice-over   torn in
2 not fitting in
where do I reach to?

female voice-over   I fight I struggle
to keep identities

male voice-over   I fight I struggle to keep
2 feet planted in

female voice-over   one self

text from "Ramayana"
Mother Earth laughed
yet these kings,
these mortal puppets
are willing to admit
they own me.

image of Goddess

older Indian male voice-over
I want to see you settled in anyway with some young man who is a little
older than you, a little more educated than you, a little more earning
than you because a little superiority of husband in these things make
you a good wife.

text on screen
I quake;
the cities of men downfall

text from "Ramayana"
friends are impermanent
wife and children are unreal
the world is untrue,
and sorrow is a lie

Gita's face is manipulated by hands

older Indian male voice-over
Das...
That is just a story, just a story.
In seventy to eighty per cent of marriages, there is no domination,
they live very nicely, comfortably, enjoying equally all the things.

layered sound with cackles
and make you a good wife
usually it happens...
ninety/eighty differences means if a husband is good in something
ninety per cent good
sie ist hübsch
sie ist hübsch

text from "Ramayana"

image of hands modelling clay within larger image

voice-over
Eyes look back through
Skull-bone and stony set face.
They are veiled now
Safe from harm.

But am I really living?
I have two oceans of tears
When coming across the ocean, there are two
oceans of fears
fears of the half cast.

text from "Ramayana"
do not let the ways of the
world dismay your heart,
Being a warrior

close-up of face from image of Goddess

voice-over
Half-breed, half-wit
I've been much mistaken
I've been much mistaken; I've mistaken myself
for everything
but me.
I've received from both sides,
the best and the worst.

text from "Ramayana"
For i will play in your despite,
and i will make the wrongs all right

close-up of hand and moving up arm from image of Goddess

voice-over
There is a war being waged in my blood.

image of water
Sometimes it flows so coldly

image of Goddess
still and silent
like ice
as the journey across the ocean of tears is made
my eyes are washed clean again.

text from "Ramayana"
for i will do what pleases me.

image of ducks on lake

older Indian male voice over
Hmm... very nice so. You have inherited the qualities of both.

Gita's voice-over
Even though the lies I learned are often subtle and hard to find, as they
are unearthed, in the chasm,
ever becoming apparent between us. I stand and wait at the shore edge,
I wait, I pray, I hope,
maybe you will discover your own lies.
Underneath the differences of flesh, we are the same.

single word or phrase on screen at one time
that
which makes
you
sick
when harnessed
can
be
that
which
makes
you well.

text from "Ramayana"
i'm still myself, i'm me
here is the true,
have no fear.

close-up of mask from image of Goddess

layered sound
one, two, three, four, five, six, seven, eight, nine, ...
eins, zuei, drei, vier, fünf, sechs, sieben, acht, neun, ...

text from "Ramayana"
this is for you
for you are dear
to me, i'm still myself

close-up of paper on water

older Indian male voice
Eastern theory says, there is very big contradiction. In love, you don't
fall, you rise.

female voice-over

...and then I said that I was mostly from Canada and he said, well what are you? and I said I was a combo-girl and I never have said that term before in my life, it just came out of my mouth, 'cause I just wanted to schlep this guy off, just say something to stop him from butting into our

image of goose

conversation because we were trying to figure out where we were going to go to eat, or whatever. So, I said I was a combo-girl, without thinking about it. He goes, a combo-girl? So, I guess it did sound a bit strange. He goes, where is a combo-girl from? I guess he meant originally because I had said I lived in Canada. And I said combo-girls come from all over and I was one of them.

image of Goddess

It was really weird because he did say... he didn't think it meant it was a combination of things, he thought it a race or something, I don't know, it was really funny and,... that was that!

---

[1] The "Ramayana" is a classic Hindu text.

CREDITS
"a different message"
written and spoken by: Erin Clarke

"Half Breed" written by: Nicole Tanguay
spoken by: David Findlay
Gita Saxena

"mirror girl"
written and spoken by: Gita Saxena

quotes from "Ramayana"
translated by: Shardaji

camera: Camilla Clarizio, Gita Saxena, Jenny Keith

graphics: Gita Saxena

sound recording: Uwe Zedler, Gita Saxena

mix: Gita Saxena

voices: Gita Saxena, Shardaji, Laura Coramai, Uwe Zwedler hands:

extra hands: Suzanne Fortin, Nadine Arpin

thanks: Uwe Zedler, Malika Mendez, Laura Coramai, Mr. Sharda, Brigitte
Rabazo, David Findlay, Bradley Bell, Peter S. Calvert, Todd Graham, Peter
Gmehling, George Docherty, Paul Dempsey, Pratibha Parmar, Midi Onodera,
Nicole Tanguay, Nila Gupta, Milagros Paredes, Stephanie Martin, Katie
Thomas

a video poem
arranged, written, performed,
directed, selected, and everything else by:
Gita Saxena

My Name is Peaches...

objectification
exoticization

Mercedes Baines

Bus Fucking

IT IS NOT A COMPLIMENT TO SAY HE IS STARING BECAUSE I AM attractive. It is not a compliment. I see the rolling eye balls. I feel the emotion... it is not benign. I hear the stereotypes about my sexuality, my birthplace, my otherness drip from his eyes like crocodile tears.

It is simplistic to say... well just decide...
define yourself...
create your own
re-ality
When each day I push through the sea of white eyes staring at
me on the bus
as if I were some strange fruit
as if my vulva was hanging outside of my skirt whispering exotic
welcomes.

I return his stare.

He looks down
or thinks I am coming on to him
as if my skin and my sex were an invitation
to random bus fucking.

Where Are You From? A Broken Record

So... uh... where are you from?

A white young lusty man asks hoping for a delicious exotic entree.
I look around knowing he is asking me but I'm still surprised
the record plays on
He has not asked my white women friends / only me.

Assumption: Plain white wrappers come from nowhere but here
but plain brown wrappers must be from someplace else / Not from
here definite — ly
Not from here.

Where are you from?
Why — I ask / do you want a taste of the exotic? To fuck another
other?
Does it make you feel...

*Well you look like you could be from Trinidad, Spain, France not
from here, South America, not from here def-in-ate-ly not from here.*

He smiles hopeful thinking he's impressed me... the record plays
on and on.
I am from here — actually.
Oh — he says truly disappointed. It was not the answer he was
looking for. He did not ask the right question.
The right question would be: Why is your skin the shade it is? Why
is your hair the texture it is? Why are your lips and hips full / your
eyes brown?

There is not a simple answer — I do not fit in a simple box.
It depends on the day
The colour I feel.

Today I am Black and beautiful with my heart full of song and my
hips full of music. She is in my walk, my loud laugh and my anger
when it speaks.

Yesterday I was white
Tribes of Irish French Danish
Methodical, inward spirit meditate, white light staring at my brown
self laughing loud.

Tomorrow I will be red — heartbeat to drum — walking on a long
journey.
I remember what it was like when the earth did not have an owner.
I remember our people when we would have also laughed loud
I remember when Black skin did not need explanation.

Do you see my face trans   form with each invocation?
Ask me where I am from?
I am from here
and everywhere
I am multinational/United Nations/United in one body
Bloodlines intermixed/travelling centuries
To create me
A Millennia of inter racial fucking
I am from here — especially here.

Michele Chai

Resistance

Don't mamaguy me   because I am sick of towing   your guilt ridden
burden   your imaginary colourless world that pleads for equality
While your insides rank with racism /   How can you be so blind   to
the good intentions that constantly tie me to your children by apron
strings   half-assed promises of bread and roses   of part-time jobs   in
sweat shops   of assimilation   appropriation   exploitation
that rape me   of   my   i d e n t i t y.

Don't mamaguy me   because I am tired of explaining   WHO I
AM /   WHERE   I   COME   FROM /   HOW   I   REACH
HERE /   Tired of repeating myself   Sick to my stomach of   YOU
DON'T LOOK BLACK /   YOU SURE YOU'RE FROM TRINIDAD /   YOUR
ENGLISH SURE IS GOOD FOR SOMEONE WHO WHO COMES FROM THERE.

Please   don't bother me.   No longer   can I   be   polite
to   YOU'RE NOT AT ALL LIKE THOSE OTHER IMMIGRANTS /
        SOMETIMES I FORGET YOU'RE CHINESE BLACK PORTUGESE /
HANGING OUT WITH YOU MAKES ME FEEL LESS WHITE -   etc. etc.
I am sick of being tokenized   so don't patronize me.   I have lost
gumption   FOR YOUR GOOD INTENTIONS   have silenced and
oppressed me for too long   and I am fighting back.

S.R.W.

What is a "Sister"?

Funny thing
You don't come to me like a sister, he said.
His skin was oiled navy blue, brown
his eyes were waxed with resentment.

My skin is dark and I'm standing here,
So how else would I come to you.

What's funnier,
Is that I've never seen you with a dark-skinned woman.

Barbara Malanka

Noblewomen In Exile

i hover on the perimeter of a loosely formed circle
a spectator of tears
an audience to hollowed anguished voices
voices that echo
reverberating in my hollow places within

in silent reflection i observe
women's faces
pain etched in darkened brows
tugs the corners of eyes
welled with tears
flashing with fright

i gaze at my coppery arms
at the pale band on my wrist
that has not been kissed by the warmth of the sun
and am reminded that i will never enjoy
the free exercise of white privilege

so i scrub
scrub until the blood mingles with tears
but i can not erase
the stain on my skin
on my soul

with a sneer they exclaim
i'm what you get
when you put
cream
in the coffee
a humiliating reminder
of the master's midnight visits

high yeller
a prize to the men
a threat to the women

what you frett'n for girl?
you got good hair
you can pass
you don't even sound like us

the circle tightens
in hushed voices
we expose our scars
share our wounds
wounds inflicted by those
we had hoped to trust
hoped would embrace us as their own

before us is set a great banquet
a bountiful harvest of our labours
eyes lowered in fear we come to the table
but the food we are permitted to partake of
sours in our swollen bellies

what is there that is truly mine?
will i wander
forever scarching for that place i belong?
as i watch *them* parade
the artifacts
of a birthright
i feel unworthy to claim

who are we?
the ones who dance between worlds
tossed in the windstream
that slips between the clouds
noblewomen in exile

Stephanie Martin

Is true what dem seh bout colrd pussy?

hey
is it really true what they say about colored pussy
come on now
dont be trying to act like you dont know what i am talking about
— excerpted from "is it true what they say about colored pussy"
by Hattie Gosset, 1982, *Heresies,* No. 15, "Racism is the Issue"

o all you, white and black who eroticize mi light brown skin, who
see me as different but never angry, who checking fi a hot pussy
under dat deh skin, who see me as politically non-threatening
because mi blackness nuh apparent as real
back off, mi tyad[1]
to dem all who define me as it suit dem interest, as anodda black sistah
in solidarity, as a lover, or as a light skin ooman who cyaan be trusted
tru[2] mi have no race fi defend
mi seh, kirout[3], define unnu[4] self
as a mix race gal ah me fi say who mi is

colored pussies are yet un-named energies whose powerful lighting up
the world is beyond all known measure.
— excerpted from "is it true what they say about colored pussy"
by Hattie Gosset, 1982, *Heresies,* No. 15, "Racism is the Issue"

---

1 tyad tired
2 tru because
3 kirout clear off, get lost
4 unnu you all

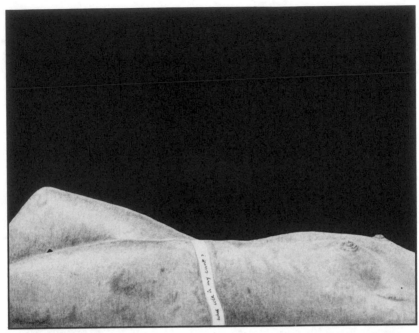

what colr is my cunt   (Acrylic and graphite on canvas - 48" x 60", 1987)

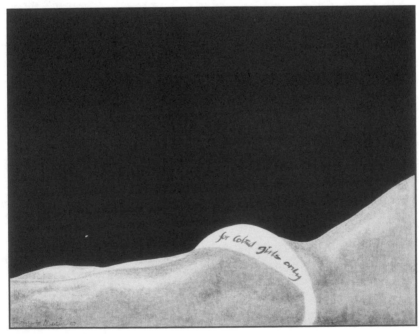

for colrd girls only (Acrylic and graphite on canvas - 48" x 60", 1987)

Michelle La Flamme
Yo White Boy

Yo white boy, Ya, you, are you talking to me?
Asking about my eth-nic-ity?
Wanna know where I am from?
Wondering why I am brown?
Wondering if I will live up to your idea of the exotic, the erotic,
Black, brown-skinned beauty with a grin?

Yo white boy, ya, you, are you talkin' to me?
Aunt Jemima, now ain't she sweet?
She's smiling through a vale of tears
Tears of syrup on your shirt
Poc-a-hon-tas in a Blood-stained buckskin mini-skirt...
Just for you, Ya just for you.

Yo white Boy
Ya, you, are you talking to me?
From your perception of SUPERIORITY?
Equating my darkness with sinful sexuality!

Yo White Boy
Ya, you, are you talking to me?
Hoping I'll feel shame for my silent pain,
Taking on the blame for my people's degradation?

Yo White Boy
Believing in God and trying to make me,
believe that GOD wants ME to be free!!

Yo White Boy
I don't buy your religion —
separating me from ALL MY RELATIONS

Yo white boy
Army fatigues and Nintendo games, can't you see?
I can't connect with playing "KILL THE OTHERS"
'cause the others are
the others are Me!!

Yo white Boy
Ya, you, are you listenin' ta me
I don't sell my sex for money,
it's your domination fantasy, that's not me!!

Yo White Boy
Ya, you, you talking to me,
Yer "Dry and Abstract" Point of View,
Is not what my mind is in to.

Yo white boy
Ya You!! Now I am talking to you —
Discover what the colour of your skin means?
Discover what wasn't written into history's scenes.

Y'know, like the thousands of my ancestors killed,
raped
beaten   tortured
oppressed   hung
hunted
mutilated
shamed   tormented
and assaulted by *your* ancestors.
AND are still suffering under white, corporate, Eurocentric, racist
structures based in dehumanization and racial segregation.

Believe it!!

Yo white boy
Ya you, I'm still talking to you,
You were taught the Master Role,
I was taught to live under your control,
Sym-bio-tic   re-lat-ion-ship!!
Until I refused to submit,

Yo White Boy Yo White Boy, Were you talking *to* me?
Or were you talking *down to* me?
Not only are you white in a society that says that WHITE IS RIGHT!!
you are also a male, a pale male...
and ah...speaking of degradation of the FEMALE...

Still wanna know where I am from and why I am brown
or is the story too heavy for you to hang around?

Carol Camper

Genetic Appropriation
A Response to a White Liberal Fad

* Broadcast, in slightly altered form, as commentary during Black History Month 1993 programming on CKLN 88.1 FM radio, Toronto

THE MICHIGAN WOMYN'S MUSIC FESTIVAL IS A WEEK-LONG camping festivalwhich yearly draws over 7,000 women and children from all over the United States, Canada and the world. Most of the women at the festival are middle-class White lesbians.

In 1991 I attended the entire festival for the first time and noticed that there were many white women in attendance who had their Black children with them. There were also white women with children from other people of colour backgrounds; some adopted, some not. I saw only three Black women there with young children and at least four times as many white women with Black children. As I continued to observe these families, I became aware of an increasing uneasiness within myself.

As a mother, I know that giving birth to a child and mothering it, is the closest thing in this society to "owning" another human being. There are other types of "ownership," such as husband of wife, father of child, pimp of prostitute etc. But these are not acceptable to feminists or liberals. The ownership of children by their mothers is rarely challenged. Mothers control, shape and influence children as no one else ever will. In the context of racism and colonialism, the mothering of a Black child by a white mother might not be all that benign.

I am a Black woman of mixed race. My natural father is white and my natural mother is Black. I was adopted and raised by white, working class parents (I say White, however, my adoptive father was actually Metis, though he never admitted this and I always thought he was white). So, like these children at Michigan, I was raised by a white mother.

I have my own feelings about being "owned" that comes out of the controlled, abusive atmosphere of my home. Race, plus being kept culturally isolated contributed to me feeling like a "specimen" while the abuse confirmed my status as chattel. I find that many of the mixed race young adults that I encounter have been raised outside the Black community as I was and that their struggle around identity is sometimes a painful, difficult one.

Since the vast majority of 'Michigoers' are lesbians, it's safe to assume that so are most of these mothers. When lesbians become pregnant, it is rarely because they have developed a relationship with a man (unless it was prior to coming out). It may be that they have conceived through alternative insemination, a one-night stand or via a gay male friend who may co-parent. In any case, conception has not occurred because of the emotional and sexual alliance of a white woman and a Black man. This also may be the case with straight women who want a Black child. Some of these women are specifically selecting a Black man to impregnate them. Why? I have no concern about a woman conceiving without emotional connection to the man. I am concerned when she also has no connection to the community that her child will ultimately belong to.

The Black community knows that white, middle-class women rarely align themselves in any lasting way with Black people. Paths may cross. A "cause" may bring white women our way for a time. But generally, that's it. Working-class white women are more likely to align with Blacks because there is the common experience of economic oppression. These women at Michigan were not working class. They were middle-class white women, many of them wearing their Eddie Bauer, Laura Ashley and Birkenstocks, sleeping in Eureka tents. Fashionably down-dressed and rustically housed, they were experiencing their option of temporarily humble circumstances. Their children seemed to be one more trendy accoutrement to the white, upwardly mobile lifestyle. Like the Bouvier or Shar Pei, Black children are the fashionable breed. Having the breed of choice, like the BMW in the driveway, conveys certain things about the owner. Prosperity, status, options in life. But what does having the "right breed" of child mean?

We know that white people often exoticize Black sexuality. Are these women doing more than that? Are they exoticizing their own children? Are they trying to make some statement about race? Is it their naive idea that racial mixing eliminates racism? Is this their answer to some Black ex-lover's accusation of racism? "How could I be racist? My own child is Black!"

This is the same strategy used by white liberals in the 60s and 70s when marrying a Black person was especially trendy. (In the 70s I was married to a white man). Not only did this move imply non-racism, it also guaranteed, for those who wished to rebel, a big response from white parents. And it garnered entry into what was perceived by many whites as an unusual (exotic) culture and lifestyle.

As the days passed at the festival, and my uneasiness grew, I felt the need to speak out about my concern. At first, I felt badly for believing "the worst" about these white women. I felt I had no "proof." I doubted my analysis of what I saw. I was hesitant even to share these observations and feelings with my Black sisters. I thought they would say I was overreacting. One night, the conversation turned to the subject, "Who is a woman of colour?" It seemed that many white women now lay claim to a First Nations or African heritage and wanted to be included in "Women of Colour Only" events occurring at the festival. These were women who did not display any alignment with us in their behaviour; any appearance of anything but whiteness; who had "passed" all their lives. Since it now suited them, they donned the cloak of colour and wanted all the "privileges" that went with it. Some of them admitted to being white in this life but insisted that they had been "of colour" in past lives and should, therefore, qualify. They seemed to actually covet our colour. What better way to "acquire" colour genetically, down to the bone, than to conceive, gestate, birth and raise one of us? White people with money are so very good at acquiring. Even this is apparently not out of their reach.

I finally raised my concerns. To my relief, my sisters had observed the very same things and agreed with my analysis. They too, had misgivings about what all this meant.

I returned to Michigan in 1992 and found that the situation was the same. There were so many more white mothers than Black with children of colour, it was astounding. I almost felt like applauding the first day I saw a Black mother with her Black child. It was my intention to find out more by interviewing some of the white mothers.

I was surprised, one day, to find a note from a white woman who was offering to discuss the fact that she had a Black child. I finally connected with this woman and was pleased to discover that she did not necessarily fit the "type" that I had generally run into. She was middle class like the others, but there were some interesting reasons why she had a Black child. This woman had had a long term relationship with a Black woman. The two of them had considered having a child of mixed race who would reflect the racial mixture of their relationship. The relationship ended for a time and the white woman moved away. Since this had been her first lesbian affair, she had doubts as to whether lesbianism was her true nature and wondered if she should be with a man. She then had a brief fling with a Black man whom she became pregnant by. She was not interested in having a co-parent and he was not really available because he was a sailor. She had the child and then resumed her affair with the Black woman. The white woman had also had white partners in the past, so she seemed not to have a pattern of focusing on Black people only as lovers. She eventually broke up with the Black woman once and for all.

The thing that encouraged me about this woman was her concern for her child's upbringing with regard to race and culture. She lived in a largely white community and was hoping to find work in another city where there was a substantial Black community. She had asked at the festival if there were any activities for children of colour (there weren't any, but the suggestion has since been raised). She also tried to discuss her concerns with other white mothers of Black children and was quite dismayed at their lack of interest and even puzzlement. She gave me hope for her child while also confirming my fears about some of the other children and the mothers who seemed to own them.

I know also, how it feels to be "owned" in the way that white friends have tried to "own" me. This is something I permitted for a time, since I was isolated from other Black people and did have the need to belong, somehow. Eventually, with some of these friends, the belonging went too far. They more than appreciated and supported my dreams, talents and Blackness — they coveted them! I felt how keenly they needed me in their lives to answer some question, prove some point. Some of these people were lovers and so there was a sexual element that heightened the intensity of the ownership. Sometimes I felt exoticized and there was a time in my life that I welcomed this because it made me feel special and desirable in a world that said I was neither. I realized that this desirability came with too high a price. Why is it still so important to own us?

I know how it feels to be a commodity. All people of colour do. A sexual commodity, an economic commodity and, of course, a philosophical commodity. We experience personal appropriation and some of our children have become the objects of genetic appropriation in a way that recalls the sexual interference our foremothers experienced from slavers before they even left African soil. The Black people here had no choice. Babies don't choose their parents, just as African women did not choose to be raped to inject precious white blood into the race. Children from both situations are raised as "house niggers." House niggers are more acceptable, more trustworthy. Easier on the

167

eye. Both are given access to things their darker brothers and sisters are denied; education and economic ease while being denied access to Black family and culture. So many of these children see much more of their white mothers' families than those of their Black fathers. They are separated, stolen from us.

This is genetic appropriation; theft on a grand scale. I don't believe that all interracial relationships are exploitive or that all mixed race children are exploited. I do believe that it's necessary to examine what's going on with these particular white, middle-class, liberal women. Don't they need to hear something from Black people?

We want these children back. They need the opportunity to be a part of the Black community. I'm not against racial mixing. It is a fact which means I exist. I'm saying that white women who are conceiving by Black men with no intention of providing some Black family/ community for the child need to take a good look at what their motives really are. They need to ensure that their children are not being deprived for the sake of being "privileged."

Family Album

Camille Hernandez-Ramdwar

Ngaire Blankenberg

Joanne Arnott and
Harper Arnott Campbell

Doris R. Heggie and daughter

Michi Chase and family

Bernardine Evaristo

Faith Adiele and her aunts - Opu Umuobu Village, Nigeria

Pam Bailey

Mercedes Baines

Michelle LaFlamme with niece Brandi
and nephew Jerome

Gitanjali Saxena

Myriam Chancy
Age 2

Domino
filming the stories of interracial people

Shanti Thakur

Lisa Jensen

A. Nicole Bandy

Diana Abu-Jaber and sister
Suzanne Romana (neé Abu-Jaber)

Deanne Achong

Jaimi Carter

Lorraine and
Wilfred "Inky"
Saunders
August 1948

L—R : Lawna London, Nona Saunders, Daria Saunders,
Lorraine London

Maxine
Hayman
(far right)

Marilyn Dumont

Some More Stories

Annharte

Emilia   I Shoulda Said Something Political

you spoke to me compañera   I chiquita
tiny bit lick paste on label   you chiquita
green tinge pretty banana   wait for ripe
yellow chiquita skin moment   takes more
than Spanish descent i mean   to be decent
descend even the imported banana   gets mushy

hey, hey celtic conquistadora   my ancestry
a search for potatoes   why have a famine
in the first place   I say I ask how about you
where you come from   we have it in common
so far away   do you happen   on a feast often
grab a clean plate   sit down next to
talk to   someone like me   talk turkey

I'm so serious   cute tomato   how you gave
them yourself   had to   had to   so did I
me too, I shared so I did   I share more
did you forget the gold   did you did you
give it away   the gold chain
my friend gave me to wear   gets in the way
when I eat   my fingers   catch it put it
in my mouth   so you passed the ketchup
to them too bad it happens   squashed tomatoes

178

we are   just delicious   they put us on
french fries I gave up potatoes to make poutin
now that's strange   does it have much blood
any barter   taste enough gravy

you sprawl next to me   long legs   log jam
look you harvested timber   you fall
your arms reach across miles   how do you
do that   trick   for agricultural sake
you fondle the cornsilk   kiss up pumpkin vine

your anatomy & mine separate from what belongs
to the Mohawk tobacco trader   asks for a light
gets up to smoke outside   the lodge we see him
give offering of tobacco   pray we watch him
without him to watch us play   entangle
human sculpture should he take notice be bold
scold after doing righteous act   gotta brace
for trouble   entwine legs arms minds
if he comes back without smokes   let's behave
give thanks for lights surprize   spirit sparks

I could lounge summer away our Mohawk warrior
wrote sensuous war poems knows best conduct
a gentle Mohawk war   he fought that way
leaving his lover   lovely example
how queer for you, for me to lay back wonder
the rest of the summer   I lazy ass down
druggy park kept vigil unlike   outhouse poet
behind the treatment centre   kept folks
occupied, safe he loved laughs, and war alike
it occupied my mind   no fierce risky business

stopped my preoccupations   gross everyone out
arouse oppositions   shoulda been the poet
at Oka, sneak up in monk habit   fire words
take the straight forward approach   fire at
choppers   write poetry on walls   waste less
paper, words   maybe Emilia, I apologize

should go to Peru   accompany each other
be safe escorts   for us mixed up together
just us tourists   in blonde California wigs
dark Barbie twins   shining our hair
right shampoo   the Other Path   sheer economy
we set up a stall to sell   big words
to fatten the skull   trepinate paths
poem trouble again   I instead

made myself comfy   lying on a railway track
to blockade national trains   gave support
warriors need more uplift   hard curve balls
pitched   at their athletic supporters
makes me wince and groan ow   my fast lips came
in handy where it should be   the groin
talking   such Indian woman heterophobia

that summer   I just missed it   had to be
there to catch a great conference   needed
the proper lesbian lovemaking   establish
Indian men higher awareness   now
that's revolution   maybe it will happen

in Peru the altitude does it   guaranteed
an identity   that don't split, sexes up

the first time dropped   nothing breaks out
sags, or leaks   the victim in you refuses
everything that happened before   doesn't

want explanations   make it right for others
be a non-statistic   be understood
in the marketplace   let's for once
inside you let that jaguar purr   asleep
she shifts leg but inside growl   deep
I hear it compañera   growl dark like me

Victoria Gonzalez

Nicaragua, Desde Siempre: War fragments from a woman's pen.

Identity as a point of re-departure.
Trinh T. Minh-Ha

"WHAT IS THE TRUTH ABOUT NICARAGUA?" THEY ASK. OR "from your perspective as an insider..." Inside/Outside. Insider/Outsider. As if there were a Nicaraguan truth to be inside or outside of. As if we lived without pain and complexities, as if our lives were all straight lines.

This is a testimony then, mi testimonio pues.

I am not the first and I am not the only one.

Many 19th- and 20th- century Latin American intellectual elites (for example Ruben Dario, Jorge Luis Borges, Claribel Alegria, Marjorie Agosin) have tended to be "Inappropriate Others" through imposed or voluntary exile, or through extended travel to Europe and the U.S. I share with them the pain of migration and a Latin American version of Inappropriate Otherness. Here but still there, there but still here, literally.

As mestizos, we have a long tradition of writing down our interpretations of the realities around us, as both insiders and outsiders, for ourselves and for others. When I visited Spain, unknowingly in the same Cordoba gardens as el Inca Garcilaso had been in, over three hundred years before, I too spent afternoons writing down my thoughts about the Americas. We go back to some of the same painful sources of our mestizaje in our writing.

Sor Juana Ines de la Cruz in 17th- century Mexico, documented through her writing her struggles against patriarchy. Writing was her passion, and yet it was only one of the things she was not allowed to do as a woman.

In the process of writing we document,
create and re-create.
And we also bear witness.

I am a Nicaraguan woman writing. And my story is many women's story.

Europeans (for example Bernal Diaz del Castillo) have — since the conquest — a long tradition of writing "insider" reports on the Americas by visiting our homes and writing descriptions of us and our environment, either to facilitate conquest and colonization, or to help lessen the white man's burdens. We keep in mind that objectification and appropriation have not been mere by-products or lesser evils in any of these processes.

How can I write differently in order not to do the same?

The process of constructing Native America and Latin America as Other, which renders those Latin Americans who live in the U.S. inappropriate Others, was initiated in the Americas by the Spanish conquistadores and is still in effect today. Indeed it is one of the few ways we have in which to communicate on the topic of difference. And we use it still to mystify domination.

How can I write differently in order not to do the same?

I am a product of a second mestizaje, still happening amidst war: Anglo-U.S. mother, Nicaraguan father. Yet this time the India has not betrayed, she has been betrayed inside and by me.

Malintzin/Malinche mexicana
blamed for our bastardization,
when will you cease being betrayed?

The myths continue to blame the darkness in us, continue to blame us as women, continue to blame us as mothers, as daughters, as sisters, as lovers. Do we also betray ourselves and each other at times?

Now in the United States, I realize how in my Nicaraguan extended family thinness and tallness — features which were often valued — were associated with whiteness and the U.S. Perhaps this was because my mother, a white U.S.-American was both tall and thin, blue-eyed and blonde; and because my father was short, fat, and brown-skinned.

Associating whiteness with a particular type of tallness and thinness is very much related to U.S. physical and cultural imperialism in Nicaragua. It is felt through the presence of the many U.S. Marines who have invaded Nicaragua and through the presence of Peace Corps members who were also predominantly white; more recently it is felt through the presence of European and Anglo U.S.-American Internacionalistas. It is also felt, of course, through the invasion of Nicaragua by transnational corporations, global advertising, U.S. fashion, and music.

I now wonder how much of what I still associate with whiteness really is white middle-classness. I still believe many of the myths. Even when I know I cannot afford to make poor and working-class whites invisible, I still often think of whiteness as being middle-class.

In trying to fit in as a teenager in the States, I had my long hair cut and went on one diet after another. It was not only about making a body disappear. It was about making a Nicaraguan woman's body cease to exist as such. My body took up too much space, I thought. It made me stand out even when I was silent and no one could hear my accent.

At least now my long brown hair, no longer long enough to braid, made me less Indian. Had I finally heeded my Nicaraguan aunts' warnings? *"Con ese pelo trenzado, pareces India."* And also the voices of the blond children I babysat for? "You look ugly with your hair like that, you look like an Indian." And yet the long hair had pleased the men. I was not supposed to cut it. It was supposedly "soft" and "wavy" unlike the heavy, straight, and thick black hair of some of my Nicaraguan cousins, and "the wind could breeze through it" unlike that of some of my other cousins who had short tight curls.

Racism always hurts, but sometimes the wounds are deeper.

"Spic" I can laugh at. I can laugh at "Speedy" too. The racism that hurts the most are the questions about belonging, about belonging in the U.S., about taking up too much space, too much land, of taking up too much of their time, of there being too many of us, of not having the right to exist, or the obligation to. *"Somos de la tierra, no somos ilegales"* are the only words I can think of. But the pain still does not go away. "All of us who have Native American heritage belong in the Americas" I say. But they still don't agree. And we can't seem to believe it either.

December, 1983

As I arrive in the United States on my way to Seattle I am questioned repeatedly at the Miami airport by the guard who greets those of us in the U.S. citizens' line. "Are you Nicaraguan?" she asks. And I deny myself three times in order to get in. My U.S. passport has not protected me, nor has my English. My light skin fails me. And though they don't believe I belong here, I am allowed to stay. It took me a while to figure out that I would not have most of my mother's Anglo privileges. But when my Nicaraguan cousins are deported from California they don't have to figure anything out. They already knew they didn't belong. This is not our home.

We have a home elsewhere. Bordered by two oceans that were once only about salt water and fish. We have a home now bombed at its harbours like the British pirates did many years ago. We have the home Rafaela Herrera fought the British back for, the same home Arlen Siu died defending. The home in which we are not allowed to be at home.

Where is one's home in a "civil war"? Where am I ever safe?

War is separation, and separation is painful.

I, relatives and friends have become separated from our land, our homeland, our religion, language, culture, and material goods.

We have also been separated from other people.

I've become separated from other people through death, exile, and imprisonment.
I've become separated through political disagreements among family members and friends.

I've been separated from loved ones by their craziness in response to war.

My tió Celestino suffered in Somoza's jails until his fingers turned blue, responding to the needles under his nails. I caught a glimpse of the colour before he disappeared for a while. Being a socialist was his crime.

My best childhood friend, Brenda, left Nicaragua with her family soon after the Revolution in 1979. She never said goodbye before she left for Costa Rica but she left me a note, inside a small wooden box with the Nicaraguan flag pasted on its lid.

Sonia and Karla never said goodbye either.

Guillermo's mother went crazy after he died. She'd scream his death to anyone in a olive-green uniform. She wanted her son back.

This is the hardest to write about, the separation, the loss, the war which I have experienced, and continue to experience, which I *know,* yet which I also absorb as Other, through Western representations.

I am Other here in the States in as much as Nicaragua is Other. And Nicaragua is Other on the seven o'clock news, in the *New York Times*, in the words of George Bush, in the descriptions given by most white U.S.-American liberals, in the smiling faces of Nicaraguan women sold on postcards, posters, hanging on walls...

I don't want to hear yet another white liberal voice tell me that "Nicaragua will survive." Of course we will survive, of course. Haven't we? For five hundred years almost we have resisted, why would we stop now?

No more romanticization of struggle, *"...porque los heroes no dijeron que morian por la patria, sino que murieron..."* Our heroes did not set out to be martyrs, it just so happened...

My cousin Guillermo was killed on the border with Honduras during the rainy season, and his dead body lay hidden in the mud for days. The Contras also killed my cousin Raquel's father. They tied him with a rope to a truck and dragged his body until the pavement had scraped every bit of life out of him.

This is the pain of separation, of death, which has been distorted by many who speak of it. Who speak of it without having experienced this type of pain themselves.

How can we speak about it differently? How do we change?

My mother sometimes tells me that I am harder on white liberals than on conservatives. But who is the "real" enemy when we all perpetuate so much of this pain?

Ohio, February, 1990

I used to think pain was the worst feeling I knew until last night when I felt fear again as if for the first time. Empty election ballots fill the air with dust. I will be going back to Nicaragua soon. Where is Nicaragua going? The rich rich again, the poor poor again, my own family still mostly middle-class?

Everything else seemed unfamiliar to me in the midst of this fear which opened chains for me and showed me their inner clamps.

Ni-ca-ra-gua! Ni-ca-ra-guaaa!

Woman, woman running on the pavement. No dirt road here. Trampled feet crumbling into broken stones forever.

Ni-ca-ra-gua! Ni-ca-ra-guaaa!!

If I can feel fear like this then I must still be alive.

Ni-ca-ra-gua! Ni-ca-ra-guaaa!

Enumclaw, Washington, December 1984

It's a different kind of fear I feel here. *"Hay que comer ahora porque manana viene la guerra."* If there is food now I must eat it because tomorrow... who knows what might happen tomorrow. Even here. Especially here. I had experienced hunger before I came to the U.S., and desperation too. But not like what I saw in the States. On welfare, in the winter there were no trees around us to cut fruit from. In the fall — a time of harvest — I helped Mrs. Smith make applesauce with the promise of a few jars back in return for my labour. But I never tasted the results. She forgot her promise. In the summer I was reminded only of how everything is property, even food. In the spring there was only mud in Seattle.

At age fourteen, my best friend Ruth tried to commit suicide twice that year but failed. Her mother got married for the fifth time and got divorced again. No way out of welfare. Their whiteness did not ease them out of poverty, neither did her mother's marriage to five white men, or Ruth's 4.0 GPA in high school. Finally religion — fundamentalist Christianity — gave Ruth a family and a sense of belonging that also separated her from me. It was through a letter that Ruth told me she had been bulimic all those years. No fuckin' food in her house and she had to throw up the little bit she ate. In part because she was still hungry and ate more than her share she felt guilty. The food was supposed to be saved for her siblings, both younger and boys. And she was the only hope for marriage to a good man, who could provide. No rich man would want a fat whore. So she kept all her appetites under control.

I wish to feed you woman, in all your hungers.
I wish to feed myself.

Is hunger in the U.S. the same as peace? Are war and peace opposing categories?

This is a woman's war story. A Nicaraguan woman's experience of war. This is my life. But not all of it.

So many stories already written.

He said "you write what you know" and proceeded to write his story. And so he did not write about the fear all men inspired in me. He said "you write what you know" and proceeded to erase me.

Compañero, in your poems, songs, and slogans you call our country *Nicaraguita linda*, and our *revolucioncita chavala*. The earth is also considered female. Defending her is your role. And so protecting our world is an extension of your manly duties.

So often I come in only as your supporting lady. My relationship with the revolution mediated by your male presence. We wouldn't want to encourage any lesbian love in our metaphors would we?

But we know that really the earth is only female in its grammar: *la tierra, la revolución, la Nicaragua...*

La Paz/Peace is not female either.
Women are not inherently peaceful.
Men are not inherently war makers.

Mayra, they called you "La Matona"/ the killer, because you killed so many men during the revolution. But you didn't *want* to kill them, you had to. When were you given a choice? Not when you left your father's beatings and decided to fight back against all your oppressions at once. You joined the guerrillas in the mountains and became a Sandinista at age seventeen. The revolutionary songs you taught me in silence are still with me. Those secret visits back home to Matagalpa trying to avoid the Somoza National guard knowing you were in town, trying to avoid my tio Julio's angry stares. Mayra, my cousin, I fought back for you. I cared.

Nora Astorga is among us. Another killer. Mayra is still alive. And so is Nora. Cancer didn't kill you Nora. The man you killed is dead but not you. You didn't plan to kill him, he kept touching your buttocks, your breasts, you stopped saying no, you finally said yes, set the place, the time, it couldn't be at the office, he came, you didn't come alone, you killed him with all your revolutionary force. Scandal for a woman to have killed a Somocista man in bed. What he did to you: that should have been the scandal. That was the crime.

They still mentioned the incident at your deathbed and in the obituaries. Is it so rare for a woman to have killed a man in self-defence?

There were some men all along who did understand, and stopped the *piropos* on the street. They knew it was wrong to hurt us and themselves. And they didn't believe the myths that Nicaraguan men were more sexist than any others, that it was somehow *cultural*, in our blood. Some stopped. Some changed. Too late for Nora. Although Nora is not dead.

"Amo tus poetas famoso/as y tristes,
"I love your sad and famous poets,

tus muerto /as alegres que se niegan a morir.
"your happy dead who refuse to die."

Tomas Borges

When I was thirteen I became a pacifist and refused to learn how to use a gun. But times have changed since then.

"Children caint play war when they in one,
caint make believe they dying
when they are..."

Ntozake Shange

Children's play disrupted/children's lives destroyed. How many of us were there? At Soledad's birthday party when a sixteen-year-old boy, twice our age, ran into the pinata, got tangled in the cord it hung from as he fled from the Somoza police man running behind him. We were having the party inside Soledad's house, next door to mine, and always left the door to the street open, so that air could come through, so that the sun could shine through, so that life could be shared from the inside out, not death. What ever happened to that boy after the police caught up with him?

The fate of others whose blood, like glass, was also shattered until the rain came and swept it all away. I believe in the power of the rain, which is consistent over time. We were sitting on our doorstep that Sunday afternoon next to Soledad's house when we heard the brakes screech, a door slam, a shot kill. Another Somoza guard getting out of his jeep to kill someone who this time by mistake had crashed into him.

I saw it and I saw the rain wash the blood away until the pavement was once again grey.

Greyness enveloped our lives during those Somoza days as tear gas filled the air and our nostrils, and then as we covered them with red and black handkerchiefs, Sandinista colours, we were given hope again.

The Sandinistas were as familiar as the skin on the tortillas which rises as if it were leavened bread. The Sandinistas were my cousins Mayra, Guillermo, Jose, Marta, Roberto, Lucy. The Sandinistas were sixteen-year-old boys running into pinatas as they fled the Somoza national guard. The Sandinistas were those whose blood was shed on pavements and unknown roads throughout Nicaragua. The Sandinistas continue to be Nora Astorga.

And many of those who left after the revolution were Brendas, Sonias, Karlas... my friends.

I've never known any Nicaraguan who boasted of the number of people s/he'd killed in combat. No man, no woman. Two percent of the population dead since 1978. Deaths which were not about men's egos, at least not about the dead men's egos, or the egos of their immediate killers. Wars and deaths not inherently about masculinity.

I know no Nicaraguan man who enjoyed looking into his reflection as he pulled the trigger. The men I know come back silent after they've killed. In silence they take off the clothes of the men they've killed — there's a shortage of uniforms in this poor country.

They wear them carefully aware of where the bullet pierced the cloth. They wear life carefully aware of death.

During food shortages after the revolution, it's the women and the children who stand in line. Women and children first to know that they've run out of milk at this store, maybe try the store down the street, maybe there'll be milk tomorrow. Maybe not. Maybe not the next day or the next day or the next. Maybe never? That's what it feels like at the time. That's what it's like for many still. That's what it was like for most before the revolution anyway.

The men come home. No food on the table. No food. Sometimes they understand. Sometimes they don't. But who understands 5,000 percent inflation? Who has ever seen this world before?

Many of the old folks, *los viejitos*, die without ever understanding. They can't give the young advice about a world they never knew. But some of them remember Sandino and believe in his cause. They can relate Contra war with U.S. funding to Sandino in his big sombrero. Some even bring out their bibles and preach the good news. They relate their religion to their human cause.

> *Entre Cristianismo y Revolución, no hay contradicción."*
> *"There is no contradiction between Revolution and*
> *Christianity."*

Managua, March, 1983

"We want Peace!" is the other slogan people start chanting as the Pope says Mass, after they have realized he does not understand. His first trip to our home: *"Bienvenido Juan Pablo a estas tierras..."* He arrives the day after a Contra attack. The Sandinistas have arranged for the mothers of the dead to be on the platform with him. They want a prayer for their dead young sons, draped in red and black, in white and blue. He does not hear their request at first and then he forgets. When he is finally reminded of what these Catholic mothers want, he shouts back at us "Silencio!"/"Silence!

All we ever asked for was peace.

Mass is going on, prayers are being said, obedience to the hierarchy of the Catholic Church should be upheld, always. That is his message to the Nicaraguan people after we have waited for him in the Managua sun for nine hours, after we have sung songs for him, after our president Daniel has begged his forgiveness on public television, after he leaves. Silence. Silence does indeed equal death.

That is why I write. And why I go back to Matagalpa in order to move on. Identity as a point of redeparture and revolutionary processes as a goal. Ten years of revolution, 60,000 dead Nicaraguans, and many more alive, none of it forgotten by a generation that only remembers death and hope. That is all I know. That is what I write.

Marilyn Dumont
The Halfbreed Parade

the mystery of the white judges
who sat encircling our two storey schoolhouse,
the one my father "skid" into town with a team of
horses and a
parade of snotty-nosed, home-haircut, patched
halfbreeds
trailing behind this floating prairie structure.
The only thing missing was a mariache band
and a crowd of pilgrims stretching
miles down the gravel road
which offered passage to our grand mansion
of clapboard. So magnificent,
we all slept upstairs
in rows of double beds like cadets
sharing one long sleeping quarters,
while downstairs our sentinel, grandpa Dan stirred
the oatmeal that bubbled at dawn on the air-tight heater
and poured himself another cup of heavy coffee.

The Red & White

god only knows, Mary tried to say these things but
her lips cracked and
words fell out like
mad woman's change

god only knows she tried but
we all thought she was crazy
a little twisted, Mary was
in one of her spins again
who knows who she would twist into it,
like hair in a french braid

god knows Mary tried
to keep us clean and fed, respectable but
all the bleach and soup bones
in the Red & White couldn't keep our
halfbreed hides from showing through.

S.R.W.

For My Sister Rosemary: Just Like Mine

He and his sister had grown up in a small town in B.C.
Where there were no other black people.
They went to live in Trinidad for a while when they
were young
And attended school.
It was the first time his sister had seen anybody that
looked like her.
She played with another little girl down there
And touched her face as she said:
Hair just like mine, lips, eyes, nose and skin just like
mine.
We grew up in isolation too.
But I had a sister.
Hair just like mine,
Lips, eyes, nose and skin just like mine.

Carol Camper, Heather Green, Lezlie Lee Kam, Kim McNeilly, and Stefanie Samuels

Claiming Identity: Mixed Race Black Women Speak

(a radio panel discussion originally broadcast for African Liberation (Black History) Month February, 1993 on CKLN 88.1 FM a community radio station in Toronto, Canada.)

Producer/Host - Carol Camper

Technician   - Faye Collins

CAROL: Welcome to Claiming Identity: Mixed Race Black Women Speak. I'm your host, Carol Camper. African Liberation Month programming continues on CKLN 88.1 FM with this segment exploring the particular struggles and insights of mixed race Black women. In-studio guests will discuss the issues from a multiracial perspective. Where do we stand on racism? Where do we fit? Where is our community? Stay tuned for the entire hour to hear music and thought-provoking commentary. *Genetic Appropriation: A Response To A White Liberal Fad[1]* will be a challenge to many, but isn't that what liberation is all about?

Welcome. Joining me today is Lezlie Lee Kam, a Brown Trini dyke in the business of saving women's lives. We'll let Lezlie expand on that later. Also joining us is Heather Green, who is a Black lesbian feminist and internationalist, born and bred in the Hamilton (Ontario, Canada) area. Kim McNeilly is a multi-disciplinary artist and Stefanie Samuels is an actor.

All of us are mixed race Black women. We come from different experiences, yet we share many things. Not all multiracial people have a white parent. Some of us here today do and some don't. Our discussion will be pertinent to having ancestry from the race currently having dominance in this culture, as well as other issues. And there's a lot of them, believe me. We grew up with all kinds of things especially in this particular setting of North America. Sometimes, where we come from, it wasn't so much of an issue, but it seems to be one here. I'd like to begin by asking each of you to talk about how you define yourselves racially and how other people, like friends, parents or strangers try to define you.

KIM: Well I guess I'll start. I call myself a Black woman. That's not really a question in my mind, but it's a big question for most people that... say, with strangers, people who don't initially recognize me as Black just on sight. And that's Black and white people alike. The people who know me and who care about me, who... you know... I value... they see me as Black because they know how I define myself. But I encounter a lot of ambiguity about my identity just by, the general public. Yeah, so it's a pretty complicated issue.

HEATHER: Well you already heard my intro as to how I identify myself. I consider myself Black, and that's for reasons of colour. I'm from a mixed couple, Black and white, but my features are relatively obvious, and I think both the Black and the white communities would be saying, "She's a Black woman". I also identify myself as Black for political reasons, with respect to the white-dominant culture, and also to unite with people of colour in general and to unite specifically with the Black community in struggling against various forms of oppression.

LEZLIE: I'll jump in now. I'm the Brown Trini dyke who was introduced earlier, and I identify myself as Brown. What's been happening to me within the past three or four years is that, because of my mixed race heritage, I am sort of thought of as maybe South Asian or Indo-Caribbean or East Indian or something like that, around Indian lines. I'm also part Carib Indian, so one of my questions to people is, "Well, what kind of Indian am I? I'm also part Chinese, and then there's a whole bunch of other stuff thrown in. A large part of how I identify is also my nationality, which is Trinidadian. So that also tends to throw people off a lot. I guess I don't fit into anybody's categories or definitions. I'm sort of, again, on the margins.

CAROL: One thing I wanted to ask you, Lezlie, since you're from Trinidad, which is a nation with lots of mixtures of races, is, have you noticed a difference in how, say, for instance, white people respond to you and your identity *here* as opposed to what is usual for you in Trinidad? Is there more questioning here, or more puzzlement?

LEZLIE: Yeah, there's a lot more definition of who I am here. I actually was involved with a White Trini woman, who's listening right now to this show. I was involved with her for a long time. Whenever we went out together, I would be introduced and, you know, I would chat with whomever for a while. And then she'd be introduced. And we both have exactly the same accent, and people would say, "Oh, how quaint! Where are you from?" And, you know, it just shows how white people view you if you're white and you have a non-North American accent. You're quaint or you're different. But, if you're somebody of colour, you're expected to have that kind of accent.

HEATHER: I just wanted to comment on that, because it's interesting. I've been talking with other friends of mine who are also women of colour, and they've been born in Canada, raised in Canada, and they have an accent like mine, which is considered without an accent by Canadian terms. And one of the jokes that... it came out of a rather degrading experience... it's a fact that it comes perpetually out of a degrading experience... is the fact that, when you're communicating with people on the telephone about political issues or about... you know, if you're communicating with white feminists, for example, on the telephone, they've got a perception of you, judging you by your voice, that you are White. And then, when it comes to... you know, you make your arrangements ... you coordinate an event, for example. It comes to the actual event and you meet them. Suddenly, their attitude changes, their behaviour changes, their perception of you changes, and they become very condescending and defensive and, you know, all the possibilities. So one of the running jokes that we have is the fact that we're not audible minorities, but we're visible minorities.

(laughter)

CAROL: I like that... I am a mixed race woman. I consider myself black. I get challenged on that all the time because of the lightness of my skin, or my accent or lack thereof, or whatever. And it is a struggle. And certainly for political reasons, like Heather, I identify myself as Black. But not just political. It's cultural and it seems to be who I am. I grew up in a totally white setting. I was adopted by white people. But it just seems that the main thing that had to do with *me* while I was growing up was my colour or my race. And so that seems the biggest part of me, of shaping who I was, racially, and so that's how I identify. I wanted to get into some stuff about what people call us or how people find out what we are. Now, some of us are more identifiably Black than others, but there's some fairly typical little questions that I know I've been asked in my life, and I wondered if any of those had come up for you. Like, "What are you?" would be one of them.

KIM: "Where are you from?" It doesn't matter if you're born here. I mean, that's part of the problem of being... one of the issues about identity for us, being born in Canada, is that this society is very alienating as it is, especially if you don't identify with the values of society. It's very alienating, you know, when they ask you, "Well, where are you from?" I get asked that question on a regular basis. You don't have back home, you know, like "back in the wherever." Back home for me is Yonge and Eglinton, you know? So, it ends up making you feel you really don't have anywhere that you belong.

CAROL: You're listening to *Claiming Identity: Mixed Race Black Women Speak on CKLN 88.1*... We're talking about how people identify us and the confusion they often have. I think a lot of us have probably experienced some confusion ourselves too, at least in our growing up years. I also want to touch on being exoticized as Black women, especially within the context of being bi- or multiracial. Because of values introduced with the slave trade, light-skinned Black women have been viewed, unfortunately by both whites and Blacks, as more desirable. It has been said that the light-skinned woman is the Black man's blonde. Aside from the sexism of such a statement, the racism inherent in it is painful. Mulatto women, to use the slave term, were seen as tragic, exotic figures caught between two worlds. This was especially true if the woman could pass as white. Yet, they were hot sexual commodities. Historically, mixed race Black people in North America originated from the rape of slave women by their owners. This was widely known and accepted by pro-slavery whites. The children usually remained Black identified and were part of the Black community. Today, there are many light-skinned people whose parents are both Black. In their families, the racial mixing happened generations ago. Although the same colour as many of these Black sisters and brothers, some of the women here today have a white parent and, therefore, a different experience. The supposed increase in racial tolerance, along with increased inter-racial relationships, has created a generation of children who have not always felt a sense of belonging in any community. Focusing on popular culture for the moment, though, how does it feel to see so many mixed women in videos, television and movies these days? Are we represented in an accurate, positive manner? Or, should I rephrase the question and ask if anyone's told you lately that you look just like Lisa Bonet?

(...laughter)

STEFANIE: The "You look just like" fill in the blank... happened to me a lot of times. And it's interesting to note that, while I always considered myself Black, but was very proud at the same time of my own particular bi-racial heritage, it was interesting because, for me, as I think was stated earlier, it was much more of a state of mind. I would walk down the streets with sisters who would kiss their teeth... you know, cut their eyes at the first inter-racial couple that they saw, not really knowing that this was an exact representation of my parents... because of my darker skin. Yet there are so many light-skinned women who do have two Black parents. So I think, for me, what I find interesting is just how I'm able to relate to white people with a certain ease, you know? I never thought twice about having a white mother until my much later teens. It's interesting, because I'm almost ashamed of the images that I see of light-skinned women in popular culture. You look at the tall models. They all have to have "good" hair. They all have to be... you know what I mean... a light-skinned woman. And, for a long time, I was on my way to long, long locks of processed hair. After a while, both because of the resentment and the animosity I felt from within the women's community ... the way sometimes Black women treat each other if there's a light one in the circle. There's some sort of exclusion sometimes, both for personal reasons and because of the way I was representing myself as being the package, the commodity, the best-looking a Black woman can get. Throw in a little caucasian blood, some contact lenses, and some straightened hair. So, what angers me most about the way light-skinned women are represented in the media is the animosity I think it perpetuates within our community.

CAROL: I know I found that people will sometimes focus on my eye colour, for instance, which my mother used to say was hazel. And then I decided green was more glamorous, so I had my passport say they were green to sort of make it "official" that I had green eyes. So I would get into this focus, too, on having unusual eye colour, you know, and all these other things. Because, in those days, that was what seemed to make me special. And I certainly felt like I needed to feel special, because I was up against all this other crap.

STEFANIE: And now it's exoticized. Now people are saying... the fashion industry is saying, "But, we are celebrating Black people. See? Look at these tall, six-foot-two, one hundred and ten pound, black women." And, again, what they are doing is furthering the beauty myth, not representing all Black women. I've commonly referred to myself as having caramel-coffee-coated caucasian features, which has been a plus for me... you know what I mean... in the way that I've been treated by white people.

KIM: What I've become increasingly aware of is how we are treated differently than dark-skinned Black people. So I've come to the conclusion that I have a responsibility. I'm on my toes, you know, to see, am I being given privilege here? Am I being treated differently? And then, to be aware of what role I play, do I take the privilege? Am I aware of it when it's happening? Or do I call people on it when they're doing that?

LEZLIE: Yeah. Just following what Kim is saying, in terms of the women that I mix with — and I usually align with women of colour — and I find that when I'm out with Black women, Black-skinned women, I am treated differently. And I do have the same thing that you do, Kim, you know, to pay attention to the privilege that I'm given, because I'm not "Black." I'm Brown, and I'm exotic, and I'm different. And also, when I was coming out about fifteen years ago, I was usually the only non-white woman going out to the bars. And I was very popular, and I couldn't figure out why. Now I know.
(...laughter)

STEFANIE: You mentioned that you have privilege. I've felt, sometimes, that in groups where I'm with women who have darker skin, there's sometimes a rift if we get to discussing something that's very political. I feel like I'm almost being invalidated because I'm not coming from a total Black experience. That because of my caucasian connection, because I grew up with parents of two different races, that I'm somehow not justified in saying some things that go against the grain.

CAROL: Well, there's lots of stuff coming up in today's panel. I think we would have needed a number of hours to really do justice to all of the things that happened in our lives and in our communities. One of the things I wanted to touch on was our experiences or our relation-ships with the white people in our lives, especially if there's a white parent or white lover. What happens? I knew of a young woman who was mixed race. Her boyfriend was Black, and he left her for a white woman. And, you know, that happens, but my particular thought about her was how would she go to her white mother and confide in her and seek comfort. And would there be a little tension there, or would it even come up? We get exoticized a lot, unfortunately, by the white people in our lives and also by some Black people in our lives, and it ends up being a kind of betrayal. I wondered if any of you had experienced this.

KIM: Well, I've grown to despise this word "exotic." (...noises of affirmation...) It's one of the dirty words in my vocabulary now. I grew up being called exotic by my mother's family. My mother's family is Jewish-Rumanian. And I realized when I became a teenager that I had been called exotic all my life by my relatives. Yeah, there's a lot of problems. At first, I felt okay about my identity. I thought, "Okay, I've got this double oppression in my heritage. I've got the slave trade on one side and the holocaust on the other." But it wasn't until I realized that there were a lot of conflicts around race within my family. My mother's family, of course, was against the marriage and my parents had to date in secrecy for three years before they got married... the whole schtick, you know? And my mother passed away ten years ago, and I sometimes wonder how, if she was still alive today, that would have affected my development into my awareness of and my pride in my Blackness. But, I'm really at odds with her family on these issues, they refuse to see me as Black and they don't want to hear me say it. If I'm with the family and a friend is there and someone asks me, "So what are you? What do you consider yourself?" I'd open my mouth to speak and my grandmother would say, "No, no, no, she's a Mulatto! She's a half-breed! She's this or that." So they really don't want to hear that I identify as Black, and it's... I mean, there's love, of course, because it's family, but around the issue of race, it's very tense.

STEFANIE: There are a lot of similarities in my family's history, as well. My mother came from Ukrainian parents in Manitoba, and her entire family would not attend the wedding, including her two sisters. And, to this day, our family keeps in touch with one of her sisters. Her parents have died, and her other sister... my aunt I've only met once, we're completely estranged from. And in a way, I feel like my whole family has sheltered itself, in that sense, from the outside. Even within the church, we've been going to the same church for about the last seventeen years. In the very early stages, there was always a feeling of everybody wanting to peek in and look at the juicy bits. As a teenager, in the church, I remember getting into a disagreement with one of the pastors and him announcing in front of the entire church that he felt I was having difficulty dealing with the fact that I came from a mixed race background. So, with all of this bombardment, I think my parents, in turn feel protective about that, there have been so many incidents. My mother orders a dress from the store. My father goes to pick it up. They won't give it to him. Things like that. But as far as Black and white, I think my brother and I have always identified ourselves as Black and Mom as being white. And it's interesting. I've always felt that she's sort of been on the outside of things. I've always felt that I wanted to draw her in, because I feel she has abandoned much more her Ukrainian side and our family has adopted many more Jamaican values. She left a Catholic church to go to a Baptist one, etcetera. So it always bothers me when I hear the stereotype, that the person of colour in an inter-racial relationship is always the one that will somehow be oppressed. I find that it's an assumption I've seen opposed too many times.

KIM: Well, I think it's interesting to look at, too, if it's an inter-racial couple that has a child, I think that the child's life would be very different if the mother is the Black one, because we know that it's the mothers who raise children. Generally, that's the case. So, if you have a Black mother raising you, chances are you wouldn't have as much confusion about your racial identity as if you had a white mother raising you. So, I mean, it's not exactly what you are talking about. It's just an interesting thing that I've wondered, you know?

STEFANIE: It's also interesting how now, today — in circles, I guess, that I come in and out of — when I see white people who consider themselves to be sort of a bit on the left politically, socially-conscious, intelligent... to make a choice to become involved with a person of colour [which is the] thing to do. *(...laughter)* On the other side, if it's a person of colour who is, perhaps ... considers themself to be politically, intellectually aware, conscious, evolved, however you want to term it ... for them to then go and have a relationship with a white person, seems very backward. And there just seems to be a lot of pressure from their own community that they will have to encounter. It's interesting just to look at that.

CAROL: I wondered if... just quickly, we're about to wrap up the show... if we could say something about isolation. Lezlie, you talked earlier about being the only woman of colour in an all-white dyke bar, and that. Some of us don't even have the benefit of another sibling to grow up with who's also mixed. Some of us are the only child. Has isolation affected your lives?

HEATHER: I can talk about that. (...*laughter*) Isolation... growing up in a small, very middle-class, very white town in Ontario. I was adopted into a white family, being the only Black member, and I was also the youngest child. And I grew up with that. I went to schools and had friends that were all white. I was the only Black person in all of my classes, the only Black person on all my sports teams, on any occasion to speak of. And so that is extremely confining and it just makes you grow up in one state of mind until you can finally connect with other Black people, talk with them, read about them, start mixing with them, interacting with them. And then suddenly you recognize who you are and what you've been put through for the last how many years of your life. As an individual in an all-white community who is Black, what you are is a novelty. And you're treated with, you know, a lot of fun and "Oh wow, isn't she cute?" and "Can't you play basketball and volleyball well?" and you fit into all their nice stereotypes. And when you start speaking up and asserting yourself and connecting with other Black people, everyone gets scared. My family got scared. My family is very scared to the point where, as I was growing up, the words "Black," "White" and "race" were never mentioned. And so, now, when I say I'm a Black woman, you know, a lot of eyebrows get raised. So, I mean, those are just some of the instances of isolation. And I think those aren't so rare in the Canadian situation.

CAROL: Yes, in Canada, we do like to treat race like an unwelcome relative and just ignore it. We've come to the end of our panel discussion. My guests were Heather Green, Lezlie Lee Kam, Kim McNeilly and Stefanie Samuels. I'd like to thank you all for coming today.

---

1. This article appears in Part Three *My Name is Peaches... objectification, exoticization* on page 163 of this anthology.

Joanne Arnott

Song About

this is a song patterned
after a song sung
for centuries

maybe you recognize it

it is a rhyming song,
but the rhymes are
in another language

maybe you can hear them

it is a song sung
by a native mum
to her babies

maybe you recognize her

she sang it to her baby who
sang it to her baby
who sang it

maybe you remember that

she married nice gaelic men
she married herself
into the white race

maybe you recognize me

she sang it to her baby who
sang it to her baby
in silence

maybe you can hear me

this is a song patterned
after a song sung
to a baby

maybe you recognize it

it is a song about
it is a song about

a sound caught
in a mother's throat

it is a song about
it is a song about
a song caught
in a mother's throat

it is a song about
it is a song about
it is a song about

kim mosa mcneilly

don't mix me up

excerpts from a dub poem
threaded with thoughts
fleetin tween the beats

musical beats
da riddim is sweet
make ya wanna win' ya batty
an' shuffle yo' feet

so you can see
right off the top
where i'm comin from

where i stand
where i locate myself
in this shadey sharade

don't mix me up
don't mean i'm mixed up
though i have been...
used to be........
but i got fixed up

too much mix up mix up

we **laff** kri **pray**
we **weak** we **strong**
fall **down** stand **up**
we **rite** we **rong**
feelin **in** & out a **place**
& that's the — **human race**

you got the horse race
you got the dog race
you got the human race
but this is a rat race
rat race rat race

but now **in** our **case**
it's a **change** of **pace**
meet me at the **racez**
double **trouble 2 face**
this **time** we comin **at** ya
with the — **mix race**

& this ain't no half & half
bleedin heart
cry me a river sob story neither
this mix race-mix me a drink-concoction
knows what time it is

always known the blackness within me
so real so rich so true within me
no question in my soul within me

doncha **see** the **rich**ness
the **full**ness with**in** me
wut's this **1/2** & 1/2 **crap** — cha
moov away **from** me

it's just when i step outside i realize
  step into the world of repetitious repetitious

   repetitious repetitious
   repetitious repetitious

repetitious reminders
  day in day out day in day out
   cooontinuuuuuum ad naauuseuuum

that's when my inwardness
  comes into question....
   me inside in opposition
    in conflict in contradiction

colour
  skin
   deep

     shallow sallow
     pale bright
     sallow pale
     chalky white

   i have this sister of mine
   father vietnamese & irish
   mother pure french

what brought us both together
was our mixed experience

thank you sister for helping me embrace my whole self

ya gotta **play** yo cards **rite**/ in this **mix** up **biz**niz
wen i'm **chat**tin down **hard** with ma **bro**thaz/ ma fine **sis**taz
well i **get** fed **up**/ they look 'pon **me** 1 an**otha**
kinda **tie**-up un**eazy**/ wen ma **tung** lash the **otha** — **side**
wite **man**/ who iz the **fatha** uv ma **motha**

wen i'm **hold**in a dis**kussion** wit da **wite** folks **klan**
say ma **part** — **take** a blak **stan**
they won led **up**/ kik up a **fuss**
they jus don **wan**na ova**stan**

> don't try & tell me what i am
> don't try pullin that tired ol' line on me
> i ain't no half o nothin
> i'm not no race horse for the breedin
> which half is which anyway
> tell me that

i kan take **sidez**/ without d**eny**in any **part** o me
i **will** remain **whole**/ say wut u **will**/ jus **watch** me

> and don't you call me mule
> i ain't no mule-atto
> don't be comparin me
> to no half horse half ass
> and be callin me mule

chop up/ **skram**bl/ shred/ **mash** up & **mix**
i em**body all**/ **not** dismemberd **piecez**/ parts & **bits**

> **some sorry ass creature of the earth**
> **can't reproduce itself mule — huh —**

1\2 kaste/ **1\2** breed / hi **yella**/ okto**roon**
lite/ fair/ **red** skin/ mu**latto**/ qua**droon**

> **take those lyrics — and take a long walk**
> **somewhere far from here — please**

don **mix** me **up**
in yo **mix** up foolish **biz**niz
min' ya **mix**-interpret
& i won ex**plain** wut you mix-**take** iz

don **mix** me **up**
in yo **mix** up foolish**ness**
min' ya **mix** the point mix-**un**dastan
& hey — that's yo **biz**niz

the exotica syndrome... feast your eyes
> *you can look... but don't touch...*
> > *yes i'm a hybrid honey... eat your heart out*

you can take the strokes from all the folks
> *or see it for what it is... a benign sikniz*
> > *in.... the minds.... of most...............*
& ma **blak** folks **kuss**sin/ alwayz **say** the jewz dun
krook 'em
& **jew** kut **blak**/ kuz they **jus** a pak o **hood**lum

so what about us
don't you see us
what about us
you're looking right through us

heeeeeeeellooooooooooooooooo oooouuuut theeeere

white people

they act themselves around us
they don't see us as a threat
they assume we think like them
they don't wear the masks they wear

around black people

we become one dimensional
trying o so hard
to prove our blackness

we internalise our hatred
for white supremacy
we also internalise
white bigotry

whatever it takes
we walk a fine line
am i black enough for ya

& all the **sistaz** got **babiez** / kuz **abor**tionz r im**moral**
well **sum** uv us don **talk** / had an **abor**tion or **2**

& all the **bro**thez **see** me az a **1\2** breed / wanna **breed** me
all the **wite** boyz wanna **try** me for an / exotik **skrew**

alwayz hafta **say** that me **dad**dy's from grenada
no one eva **carez** that ma **mo**tha waz a **jew**

& the **wite** folks **snika** wen i **say** i am an **af**rikan
alwayz feel they **mus** remind me **i'm** kanadian **2**

ru**man**ian grenadian / **what** a kombi**na**tion
they go **on** & **on** with their **ob**jekti**fika**tion

i grew up living a white lie in a white society
        white dollsongschoolfriendsdreamsandtv........
            and of course we can't forget.................
                mommyandherfamily............................

                    tell me black daddy
                    who really raised me

one black man....
    against the wholejewishclan

& to **top** it all **off**
i waz **born** on yom kip**pur**
pesach **cha**nnukah
mish**pucha** ga**lore**

besides we all know moms raise kids
    well some of us had white moms...
        who didn't really know... what to do
            with our hair... for one thing....

i had this mat of knotted hair
disguised as a bun
tied neatly with a bow
on top of my head
my mom finally threw up her hands
and took me to a black salon

the **hair**dressa jus **snipt** it off
wile **kur**sin mom & **me**
& **that** was the **first** day
of my **afro**-sentrici**ty**

mom with all the love in her heart
        mom with all the love in her heart

                full of humour
                full of grace
                clever witty
                smiling face

so should i **keep** on **danc**in
the **kame**leon **dance**
one foot **this** side
one foot **that** side kinda **stance**

i jus wish **some**one would hold **up**
& **give** me a **chance**
so i kould **bridge** the gap with**in** me
& en**hance** the sirkum**stance**

        don't worry about me
        i gotta grip

218

now what about the rest of y'all
i mean
if it ain't happnin
it just ain't happnin

chop up / **skrambl** / shred / **mash** up & **mix**
i em**body all**
not didmemberd **piecez** / parts & **bits**

1\2 kaste / **1\2** breed / hi **yella** / okto**roon**
lite / fair / **red** skin / mu**latto** / qua**droon**

i am **fu**sion
all that **stuff** iz yor con**fus**ion
multi-**fac**etted not **frag**mented
i kover the **spek**trum

i kan take **sidez**
without de**ny**ing any **part** o me
i **will** remain **whole**
say what you **will**
jus **watch** me

i'm a child of the creator
    blesss my saaacred soouul

                    i'm a flower in the garden
                    of many shades and hues
                    i am jambalaya
                    i'm calalou stew

polyrhythmic polyethnic
limitless & universal
praise jah........

jah jah jah jah
jah jah jah jah

i will meet the challenge planted in me

*don **mix** me **up***
*in yo **mix** up foolish **biz** niz*
*min' ya **mix** -interpret*
*& i won ex**plain** wut yo mix-**take** iz*

*don **mix** me **up***
*in yo **mix** up foolish**ness***
*min' ya **mix** the point mix-**un** dastan*
*& **hey** that's yo **biz** niz*

---

don't mix me up is a performance piece, to be played by four women
1) *the mystic:* she recites the italicized parts that stagger across the page and she represents truth
2) *the singer:* she sings the bold italicized parts tabbed at the center of the page and she represents humour
3) *the dub poet:* she rhymes the parts flush left with the bold syllables and she represents experience
4) *the rude girl:* she shouts the tabbed parts in bold type and she represents rage

The Unmasking

betrayals
hard truths

Lorraine Mention

Journal Entry: Thoughts On My "Mother"

January 14/90 7:38 am

TALKING WITH YOU LAST NIGHT WAS LIKE TALKING TO AN acquaintance. You no longer upset me with your distance, your excuses, your false promises. I have accepted who you are, what you are and no longer long for what will never be. A relationship with you.

You spoke of your dog — losing him 2 weeks prior to Christmas. You told me that you have driven everywhere looking for him; you have walked for miles and still you have not found him. With determination in your voice you say you have the hope of combing the area in the spring, desperate to find him. And if you don't, there will always be a bitch giving birth to a baby that you can adopt as your own.

As for your own, have you supplied just one of them the love you so joyfully give your pets? Are we undeserving or are we less than a dog? Perhaps we are monkeys.

Are you a mother? Have you carried a child for nine months? Have you witnessed (if not experienced) the enlargement of your stomach? Have you felt the pains of labour? Did you labour the pains that produced me? My bothers? My sister? Did you look into those dark brown eyes? Did you feel the smoothness of the earth coloured skin as it tremored out through your pink flesh? Had you really known what your love had given birth to?

And yes maybe for a moment you tasted society's rejection; felt the punishment, even suffered the ostracization of your family — this the cost of loving a Black man.

222

Will you ever rise above your self-pity and rationalization of circumstance? Your profound justification? Will you ever stop mourning the dead? Will you take the time out and provide some maternal care? If not to your offspring, then to your second generation?

Yes, how long will the ghost in your closets haunt you? When will there be a time when not even cobwebs will hang collecting the thoughts, the pains, of your yesteryear? When will you be able to replace the skeletons hanging with fresh pleasant memories of life?

If you can reflect on what has taken place or not taken place and the monetary cost that made things possible, or impossible.

If you can look into the mirror and see the monetary cost of change, or better yet bank away the interest.

Can you afford the emotional?

Lorraine Mention

Letter to a Friend

March 18/92

DEAR MARY,
I hope this letter finds you in good health. The children and I are all well. I am writing you because I am still troubled about our last conversation. I feel it necessary to further discuss the "differences" experienced by me, a Black woman, in the feminist movement and moreover, I would like to recollect the "differences" I experienced, and which you watched me experience, as a Black child growing up in London, Ontario.

It grieves me when I hear you say (and I am quoting you from a recent letter), "I always get the impression from you that white people can't understand what it is to be black and it's not their place to even try. It is true that we will never experience being black first hand, but we can understand to a certain degree, especially we women, what it is to experience oppression. And it's important for whites to know the struggle of blacks if we want to end the oppression of blacks" Mary, I find your statement to be vague, insensitive, racist and therefore oppressive.

I would agree that you can not experience being Black first hand, but tell me, can you experience it second hand? And if so, by the examples that I am about to present to you, Mary, then you clearly have failed me as an understanding friend. I ask you, is every woman a feminist? Is every white woman a declared feminist? We both know that the answer to both of these questions is no, therefore one may be able to assume that being a feminist is a choice. Further, one might be able to assume that any well intentioned white liberal-minded woman can choose her, shall we say, cause. The "causes" ranging anywhere from saving the whales, to marching with pro-abortion signs, to being a white feminist.

When you say "we women" experience oppression, I understand this to mean, we white women experience oppression through sexism. What I want you to understand is that we Black women experience sexism in a racist society. One is not without the other. I feel that my experiences are equally grounded in my race as well as my gender. I find my womanhood to be inseparable from my Blackness. I can visually camouflage what is seen as my womanhood and yet I can not do so to my Blackness. I cannot get up in the morning and decide that I don't want to be Black for a day. So, yes, all women suffer from the institution of sexism, (whether acknowledged or not), but only certain women suffer from the affliction of racism and sexism combined.

Mary, we have been the closest of friends since the fourth grade. And as adults the only thing that has separated us at times has been miles. Lately the miles have been used as an excuse for lack of communication and/or separation when in actuality it has been our mind-sets that have separated us. I dare not assume what you are thinking, however, I do know you well enough to know you are avoiding me. Painfully, I am confronting you on this avoidance of me as I value your friendship and I simply cannot let go of the history we have between us. Please know that I love you, and that I am not drawing from my memory to hurt you, but, quite the opposite: I am going to use these threads of my life to hopefully bridge some of your misunderstandings on "what it is to be Black," and hopefully to give you some insight and understanding on what it is like or what is was like to be me.

Do you remember when the kids used to call me "zebra"? Do you know what it meant to be called zebra? Do you know what it felt like? Well I will tell you. It hurt, it more than hurt. It penetrated my very being, it insulted my very existence. It was no secret that my mother was (is) white and my father black, but it was my secret determination to not let the perpetrators of these words know just how much they pained me. It was in secret that I shed my appalled tears about being reduced to the stripes of a mule-like animal. Other names that I have had to endure because of my biological make-up are "half-caste," "halfbreed," "ms. peach," "yellow girl," "mixed gal," "light-skinned mama" and the list goes on. This name calling has gone on both in your community and within mine. All my life I have been burdened with being either too dark or not dark enough.

And my God, when the television show called *The Little Rascals* got popular I was better known as "Buckwheat." As a late teen it was a haunting flashback when Eddy Murphy revived Buckwheat when he was humouring us on *Saturday Night Live*. I failed to feel flattered when I had seemingly been promoted from being called Buckwheat to "jig-a-boo," and/or "jungle-bunny." It is a wonder that my self esteem survived "the cruelty of children." Now that I am an adult and, further, a parent, I can't help but question where those children learned those racial slurs. After all, children are not born racist, they are made racist through learned behaviour, and learned behaviour usually starts at home.

Oh, "racial" and "racist" are some of those forbidden words that we have between us, correct? So I am going to confront those words now Mary. I felt it was a racial "thang" when my playmates thought they were complimenting me when they would touch my hair and tell me "it felt like steel wool." It was a racially degrading experience when I would return from my grandmother's with my hair braided in corn-row and all would gather around me and make fun of me. Because, of course, this was before white women declared that wearing your hair in corn-rows was fashionable. What you did not know was that I got double punishment in regards to my hair; teasing on the playground and the whopping I would get at home for taking my hair out without consent. I welcomed the whopping for having wasted all the hours of work that had been put into my hair. It was less painful than enduring the humiliating insults from my playmates.

Did you "understand" how insulting it was every September when we returned to school and people would rush to me with the sleeve of their shirts rolled up exclaiming "Look Lorraine, I'm almost as dark as you!" I can remember telling my Granddad about this and he said "Not to worry chile, because if that tan they got don't wash off by December, they be messin' in they pants." I did not feel reassured when he told me that Black is beautiful. His work did not enable me to better deal with my white environment. I ask you, a white person, did you understand the depth of our playmates' jeering at me? And, if so, why did you say nothing? Why did you not — ever — defend me? Just once?

Mary, you say that your first experience of prejudice (and I use your term prejudice as you find it softer than using my term racism) was with your mom in regards to me. Silly me, I had a crush on your brother and with me being in the fifth grade and him in the seventh I hardly think it would have led to marriage. However, your mother may have feared it would and made it quite clear that she would have "none of that." To date Mary, you have not approached your mom on that very issue, and I ask you, is that another form of understanding? When I have asked you, face to face, about this issue you try to pacify me by saying your mom is "just old-fashioned when it comes to things like that." When I further question you on "things like that," you become uncomfortable, you say I am angry and you cannot handle it when I am angry.

I would like to confess and address my anger. You are right when you say that I am angry, as I have grown up in a world that feeds on teaching me that my existence is an abomination. I have sat in classrooms waving my hand to the point of exhaustion in hopes of being called upon with the stark realization that my calling is to remain in silence. I am angry that my women still have to clean your women's toilets in order to "get by." I am angry that my people are still in a position of getting by to survive, and so many of us lack the energies to thrive. Indeed I am still angry at your unwillingness to unpack your mother's philosophy on "it is alright for Lorraine to play with my daughter but it is not alright for Lorraine to date (?) my son." The issue, the denial of the issue, and the uneasiness of it all fits quite comfortably in your safe white world. Think about it.

It is not that I want to pick on your mom, Mary, as I can sympathize with your fear on having to confront her. However, that does not mean I must tolerate your fear, as you have to confront it. Before I move on I would like to talk about one other issue concerning your mother. This issue being your second experience with racism. Mr. Baker. Remember good old Mr. Baker, the grade seven teacher? Remember, he hated me, hated me passionately; he hated me passionately because I was Black. I know you remember him because you were a victim of his mistreatment. He mistreated you because you were my friend. As a matter of fact he mistreated anyone that was a friend of mine. Much to my surprise it was your mom that confronted him on his racist behaviour. Your mom was the fourth mother called to be informed by Mr. Baker that I was not a "good child" and that it would be in her best interest if she did not allow her daughter to play with me anymore. It was your mother who sided with me and informed Mr. Baker that if he did not take back his words she would report his behaviour to the board. His attitude towards me changed (not completely, but he did stop harassing me) and for that I have your mother to thank.

For brevity's sake I am going to list in point form some "other" realities that I would like for you to ponder: grade eight graduation night, when you had the perfect hairdo I had experienced the perfect hair disaster due to the scissors of an inexperienced white woman who did not have the honesty to tell me she did not know how to cut my hair. Our first day in grade nine English class, Mr. West demanded that I sit near the front of the class by the door "so he didn't have far to throw me when he wanted me out of his class." I did not tell you that the real reason I left Westminster S.S. to go to Beal was I could no longer handle being the only Black student in a school. I have never, to date, had a Black instructor, teacher, or professor. Your childhood television watching provided positive role models, mine did not, as the only role models I saw were from shows like *Sanford and Son* (poor Black father and his son always fighting), and *Good Times* (which was really the epitome of bad times; a poor Black family struggling in the ghetto projects). And I could go on and on and on and on... So by now, Mary, have I increased your understanding "to a certain degree" of my experience of oppression?

In closing I will set out to discuss some of our adult differences. It bothers you a great deal when I express to you that I have absolutely no interest in white men. You tell me that dating "should depend on the person and not on the colour of the person's skin." And yet you have not dated outside of your race (not that it bothers me, as you know I don't play that inter-racial thing). In my opinion, inter-racial dating is a powerplay and not a political statement. More often than not the Blacks are denying the reflection in the mirror. More often than not the whites are seeking out defiance of their upbringing, and/or latching on to weird sexual fantasies. Or the white involved often feels he/she has to make up for hundreds of years of oppression towards Black people. And, like Tina Turner says, "What's love got to do with it?"

Lastly, as promised in the opening of this l-o-n-g letter, (smile), I will now attempt some dialogue on my experience in the feminist movement. Initially, one needs to get through the silly, superficial rules; the rules on being a "real feminist" dictate a certain dress code; certain acceptable hairstyles; and rules dictating the way one may groom oneself; ranging from make-up to what parts of the body are permissible to be shaved. After deciding if one could indeed be a real feminist, one would need to know if one qualifies to be a real woman. As I mentioned earlier, some white women have problems seeing Black women as women, since they have claimed that title for themselves.

So Mary, you ask where I am as a feminist, and I am not so sure if I have a solid answer. This last year has left me utterly drained. I am not so sure I have the energy to return to your movement. My dreams of crossing barriers to true understanding were shattered by nightmare realities. I have bitter memories of women who disrespected me and others. The lies, pretensions, the snobbery, the cliquishness and the racism which bled through at every moment at every level has served only to revive my fears. The awful gossip, bitchiness, backbiting, jealousy and the gross lack of love has taught me darkness follows light in the passing of the days. I dark, they light.

The question "Where do Black women go from here?" leaves me in a state of speculation. I speculate that until all women are included in the feminist movement, the theory-making process will render all theory invalid. Black women are still struggling to be liberated as a class. How can we negotiate when we do not exist? There are no easy answers, and there are no quick-fix solutions. What we do know is that the band-aid solution is not working.

So, Mary I have given you much information to chew on, swallow and digest. This is probably the longest letter you have ever received in your life (smile). It is my hope that these words will serve as a bridge and not a roadblock. If you are angry with me you need to unpack it.

I look forward to hearing from you.

Take care of yourself.

Much love,

Lorraine

Nadra Qadeer

To a Traveller

Talking with you is like
wearing high heels.
I can slip into conversation
but I'm uncomfortable.

You talk of travels
Your favourite being South Asia.
You tell me how beautiful it is
You tell me how beautiful "Indians" are.
You tell me, but you never ask me.

Every morning we pass each other
I run to my room
Dripping.
The towel wrapped around me
exposes my skin.
The food I cook you
My name, my eyes.
They are all saying the same thing
but you never ask.
What about my culture, my family, my countries, my
life?

Why is it easier for you to talk and dream
of lands far away
than to learn and ask about them
in your own home?

Nila Gupta

Falling from the sky

I

what could i have remembered?
me, just a child
my sister and brothers
uprooted
hurling across
the yawning seas
we flew BOAC

my only remembering
is our falling from the sky
still
i dream
of falling from the sky

oh yes
i remember
my brother said
"the plane will crash"
and my mother shivered
in 90 degree Delhi weather

II

no one caught us
as we fell out of the sky
no open arm welcome
in kin-kissing Quebec

where you called us heathen
but we would not exchange
our lives for your hell
over the collection plate
my mother is one of you
but you smacked her too hard
you drowned her
in your baptismal
in your abysmal
cup

you tried to pin her
to your cross, woman
martyr
saint

but she reared up
and she jumped down
and she flew off

she just pulled up
her roots
and stalked off

III

french is as english is
as colonialism is
oh canada
i am not proud of your bloody history
i am not grateful
for your two official languages
your new multicultural lie

despite the lessons
you never taught me
history is punching me
in the belly
history is being borne in me

now i remember
now i remember
how we are here because you were there
how you raped and pillaged and stole
the roof from our heads
and then let us in at your convenience
into a land that was never yours
how money is your only god

IV

escaping in
victoria holts and harlequins
oh, the fruits, the sweets, the heat
a tall dark handsome man
hot and tropical distant land
beggars and poor and servants
at your command
you would be a generous queen
in your foreign land

V

my father warned you
it would not be quite like that
not quite like that

VI

desperation
before the quiet revolution
who are you
before the FLQ
the daughter of a man
hosing down ESSO tanks

what would your life be like
with church and sins
and hail marys handed out like aspirins
and more sins and lies
the fantasy does not die

oh holy Quebec
my mother must have said
your priests are strangling me
with their rosary beads
and i cannot breathe
i cannot breathe

VII

though my mother's mother hit her
with vicious sticks
for playing with foreign children
she held her tongue
when she saw the foreign man
you brought home
at least she would have a chance
at a future
father in heaven
and mother mary
a future

VIII

so, my mother you sat
like humpty dumpty
on a wall
you uncrossed your legs
you bore four children
you crossed your legs again
and had a big fall
even coming back to Canada
could not put you together again

the shell of your tolerance cracked
and poison seeps out
you sit in a chair and shout
what you learned
in the turn of a page
in the swing of a stick
in a sermon from the pulpit

you shout out
immigrants steal my jobs, my money
you shout: go back where you come from
go back where you come from
and when i say
mother where did I come from
but from you

you shout that's not true
that's not true
you look at me
you were never borne of me
you were never borne of me

IX

my father says
i am just like a canadian girl
and shakes his hurried head
he drops
in passing
a few words
of advice on my plate
he pleads with me to remember
remember you are an indian girl

i dig and dig
but i am clawing air
father i cannot remember
i cannot remember the feel of my land
i do not remember any roots
that took

my first remembered dream
is
of
falling
from
the
sky

now
there is something
but then
there was nothing
nothing
nothing
nothing
for
me
to
grasp
on
to

Rage is my sister

I

Mother
i see you everywhere
at all our demo's and marches
on the other side of all our pickets

i know it's not you
but that red face
that spit filled mouth
shouting out racist epithets
wanting our deaths
so much like you

when the march passes you by
its collective voice shouting out
shame, shame
for a moment i forgot myself
and hang my head

II

shame
i have known you
your vociferous greed
a present from my white mother
who at two
shackled me to your bed
her raised stick
a flash of colour in my eye
her racist words
an axe
cleaving me from myself
and the love of women
who would have loved me
had i loved myself

III

and oh,
the white sheets
i feared my mother would own
when the KKK moved to town
and took up shop on Dundas Street

IV

shame
my familiar
how you made me carry your cross
i have tried to kill myself for you
but the love of thinking women
saved me from myself

V

shame
rage is my sister
Kali rising
fierce and indestructible
out to cleanse with her sword

Jaimi Carter

"Are You Writing a Book?"

THE MAN WHOSE TURN IN LINE IT WAS ORDERED TWO BIG MACS and fries and cokes for his wife and himself. He looked at me kind of queerly when I reached for his money, almost suspiciously. My hand stopped. "How do you say your name?" Oh, that was it; he was looking at my badge: "Great Service Guaranteed by Jaimi!" I told him. "Jay-mee." He smiled. Then he went on, "Can I ask you a personal question? You can probably guess what it is." Yeah, right. Anything from "Can-I-have-an-apple-pie?" to "Are you married?" But it was "You're not... Mexican are you?" The sidelong glances in case any of the Mexicans beside me heard were a bit much, I thought. But I answered in the negative so he was reassured. "Yeah, I didn't think so. I've got a feeling for that sort of thing." Funny. I always thought it was fairly obvious... "Well, what are you then? You're part black, huh?" Perhaps he was looking for an ally in this veritable sea of Hispanic faces, but "What" am I? *"What?!"* "Yes. My dad is black, and my mom is white." Again he beamed. "What a lovely combination you make." Would I be so lovely to him if I *had* been Mexican? I wonder. I wonder. And now he's thrown me back into the midst of some sort of identity crisis that I didn't know I had until I was nineteen and realised that I didn't know who half of me was.

"My dad is black," I'd said. True enough. Well, true in the sense that he planted the seed in my mother, and there his association as "dad" ended. He chose to leave before that union of father and mother, tadpole and egg, became external and real. So perhaps "father?" But "father" ended with the $50 a month that stopped two months after I turned 18. Then "biological father?" Or perhaps "farmer?"

So when I was six and trying to pinpoint myself, to know me by knowing my parents, and I asked "J.C., how old are you?" was it any wonder that I'd said "J.C.," not "Dad?" His response was in the form of a Catch-22: "Are you writing a book?" I wasn't. I thought that should be clear. "Well, then you don't need to know." Oh. The next time I was more clever. I lied. "Yes." But he was even quicker than me: "Well, then that's one chapter you'll have to leave out."

When I was sixteen, I found I could get no further than the book, and whether it was or was not to be, it could not help me. I found that out when he accused me of lying and tricks and manipulation; said that I could not love and therefore could not be loved. So after sixteen years, I was told by my dad? farmer? that he didn't love me. And to my mother he said "I don't even believe she's really mine. Not the fruit of my loins."

But who else's could I possibly be? Not that I believed it. I look like him. Only lighter. And female. So I concluded he was a sadist and a liar and an asshole. A bastard that had spawned two bastards of his own, because he left before my elder brother and I could be made legitimate, real.

Not that I minded. He had, in effect, given me permission to stop trying to make him into my dad, and I stepped away. But I never got from him that side of me that I had been trying to find when I asked him his age, though at the time, I had forgotten that I had ever wanted to know.

Perhaps I didn't mind because I had always, since I could remember, had a "dad." To whom my mother teased us into saying "Thank you, Daddy Dwight!" after he had taken us all to dinner. (And whose name, by some ironic twist of baby-pronounciation was transformed into De-White.) I wonder if he noticed and felt something?

In his house I grew up, with his sons, my half-brothers, who are just my brothers. So why does he encounter difficulty in describing me, in introductions? Again, the "who" is not the problem. "This is Jaimi." It is the "what." "Jaimi, my..." daughter? step-daughter? wife's daughter? How any of these, when he did not (would not? could not?) adopt, yet has lived with me for twenty-one years. "My daughter." Sometimes. Like in the "Father-Daughter Cake Bake" in second grade; or if I were to be married, and he had to give me away. "Step-daughter." Other times. Like when discussions about financial aid began... But always with the introduction, whichever he chose (chooses), the slight pause, the blush. So, like the man in McDonald's said: *"What"* am I?

I always solved that question by saying, "I'm me." True enough. Why should I be classified by father, absent or otherwise, or by colour? My mother solved it by saying, "You are a citizen of the world!" True enough. But isn't everyone?

So came nineteen, when I said "I'm me." And a voice inside me said, "but you know yourself only by half." And so came the crisis that the man in McDonald's had inadvertently stumbled upon. What is Jaimi? She is half of something, and that she knows. The mother, the grandparents the relatives in England, the house in which she lives; the life she has lived. She is half something else, from a someone who would never tell.

So I wrote to his (the father's? the farmer's) grandmother in Mississippi, to ask. "He won't tell. Will you? I never thought I'd need to know, but I do. I do. Can you help me?" But the reply never came. That is, it never came to me. The father? the un-dad (I shall name him) mentioned not to me, but to my mother, a letter, "sent by my brother" to the great-grandmother in Mississippi. My brother knew nothing of any letter. Of course not. It was mine. How could such a mistake in the identity of the sender occur? Perhaps we are simply one, two half people that complete each other, and so the sender didn't matter. It didn't matter really, because no matter who was the sender, the eventual receiver was the un-dad, who would never tell.

So at nineteen, I discovered that I was bound not to know the un-dad side of me. And at twenty-two, I conclude that I will, I must, define myself out of a half-past, and a present. I am not a *"what,"* I am a *"who."* I am Jaimi, who has a mother who happens to be white; who has a farmer, an un-dad, who happens to be black, or at least part black... I am a body of experiences and thoughts not restricted to (yet not excluding) the *"what"* that people seem to have such difficulty in defining... such a need to define.

I wonder if the man whose turn in line it was would have understood if I had said, "I am a citizen of the world." I wonder.

Nona Saunders

mother milk

muggy july air
mingles with hospital scents

i swallow hard

amid the clatter
of carts in the corridor
i stand outside her room
unseen

watch her nurse
this newest child
a boy

sweet life flows
from pink nipple
his fat brown hand
clutches
her white breast   its blue veined
invincibility
she cannot feed
this brown baby

swallow hard
baby brother
learn early
to keep it down
deep inside

children's games

(i)

one potato, two potato, three potato, four...

april sun toasts children's cheeks
snowbanks shrink along sagging
red staves winter fences

small rubber boots brown and black
crunch cinder-sand on asphalt
recess games

a gaggle of children mostly girls
play dodgeball
winnipeg
its rite of spring

white light smooth
on mittenless fingers
the ball flies through chill blue air
bounces drunkenly out of bounds
that light that leather
thuds softly against a parka

'you're out   you're out'

liar, liar, pants on fire...

two remain in the centre

(ii)

i am breathless
agile nearly the winner nearly
the last one the only one
inside the ring of schoolmates

i dart dodge scramble
escape the soft thud kiss
the ball on my body.
not out still in still in

"blackie"

the ball misses my head

"half-breed"

i stumble
look around the rope of circle
tightening on me

"nigger baby blackie"

i taste copper
my blood thunders
over the school bell

the circle breaks away

(iii)

i walk home slow
alone
poke grey holes in ice puddles

i wait
comb
my favourite doll's
long blond hair

i hear my mother back from work
come up the stairs
the lock's snap
grocery bags' rustle

hiee, how was school

why did you have to
why do i have to

eeny, meeny, miny mo...
catch a nigger by the toe...

why

(iv)

her hand lashes out
strikes my cheek instant hot
she grabs my skinny arms
pushes me seated onto the couch

her face is so close to mine
i can only see parts of it
at once

skin smooth   white
golden hairs above her lip
her green-grey flecked eyes
look at me hard
her mouth set   lipstick worn off
isn't pretty any more

you are what you are

ten

i don't want to be me

(v)

tears sit on the rims of her eyes
they do not fall

they do not fall

pussy willows and pink

beyond tidy rows
of pre-fab homes
with pastel icing paint
sprawls the field
where pussy willows grow

after school
i tramp alone
through brambles and reeds
past wild purple crocus

drink in chill sweet breaths
of snow white lace
seeping in damp soil

fingers stiff
a knife from my pocket
i cut cut cut
brown woody stems
of pussy willows

i bring a stalk
to my lips
close my eyes
turn my head
from side to side

the velvet
is like mine
downy soft new

diane says
i can't play with
her any more
because i'm
a negro

didn't she know
i was
when she showed me
her growing breasts

let me touch them
turn my head
from side to side
feel her pink buds
warm to my tongue

S.R.W.

IN VANCOUVER AT CLUBS, PARTIES AND CULTURAL EVENTS, WHITE women in particular are ever-present. White women also often run "African" cultural events, particularly because of the lucrative, politically correct nature of these events. They can assure themselves that they are good "feminists" helping out in the cause against colonialism.

At Africa Day this summer, my girlfriends, who are also black, and I waited in a line up for an evening event. Several of the African musicians attempted to get us in for free. We walked into the event only to be told by a red-haired white woman, with her hand held out: "Ten dollars please." This was said with a fake African accent to boot. She was offended that black men would be willing to let us in for free to experience our own culture. Three white women had just been let in for free ahead of us but they were friends of hers.

I thought of a story that a mixed girlfriend, whose mother is white, told me. Her mother had been in New York last summer and many of her white girlfriends there were dating black men. These white women said that they *would not* pursue a black man who was married to or dating a black woman. I saw that what I was experiencing was merely one of the many actions that white women take to try to undermine black women, our relationships with black men, our culture and by extension, African people as a whole.

I completely disregarded the redhead and moved past her and the cash box, to speak with any black person I could find. I refused to pay to enter the event. Fortunately, we were let in for free. When we entered the place most of the women present were white.

Later this year, I discovered that the redhead who held us at the door is pregnant with a mixed child. I thought about her disregard and disrespect toward black women and wondered how she would eventually treat her child if she were female. I recalled a white woman friend of my mother's with mixed children. She used to compete with her daughters for attention from their boyfriends. One of her daughters hasn't spoken to her for ten years. She lives in the States now, where her father came from.

I thought about a friend of mine who made a deal to let a white woman bring him over here from the West Indies. After living here a while, he left her to be with a "Mixed race" woman. The white woman is threatening to never let him see their daughter of mixed race. I reflected on the stories two separate friends of mine, who had grown up as "mixed" children of single white mothers, had told me. Their mothers had called them "monkey" or "my little niggers" as children. Despite their protests, their mothers call them the same thing today.

S.R.W.

That Just Isn't Right

A white girl looked at me with envy:
"Though you're black,
you're beautiful because your features are white.
Your eyes are green and your skin is so light."
I said, what you've told me just isn't right.
The grandmother I come from is as black as a cobalt
night.

A black girl looked at me with envy:
"You think you're better than me.
Your skin is light,
Your eyes are green."
So I reminded her that I'd seen my features in those of
an Ashanti Queen.

I said the Queen's lips were slightly heavier,
But her profile like mine was supreme
I've seen my features on Sheba, the African queen.

She was darker than you,
And She was Beautiful
Black as Cobalt night
She looked just like me.
Sister what you said
Just wasn't right.

Michi Chase

One

Look into my eyes,
and you will see a shadow of Hiroshima.
You will see a dark room, illuminated by its single stream of
     WHITE light — flowing from the humming projector as it reels
GREY, WHITE, BLACK image onto a screen.
You will see ten silent rows of seated people,
     formless figures in the darkness.
And you will hear the rusty recording,
     as it comments on BLACK, GREY, WHITE images thrown
     onto the cold square screen:
Atomic bomb "Little Boy" explodes at 8:15 am August 6, 1945...
Epicentre reaches several million degrees centigrade... ground
temperature reaches 3,000 — 4,000... Thirteen square kilometres
completely destroyed... Three hour firestorm with velocity of
15m/sec... Over 140,000 deaths caused by "Little Boy"...
(etc, etc, etc)
BUT — the ears of a small girl have forgotten sound,
     listening only to the naked terror run over the screen...
HELL
Her Eyes stare wide open, in innocence tainted with blood
     As the screen throws daggers into her eyes.
Daggers of Broken, Burnt and Twisted Bodies lay strewn across an old
wooden floor.

LOOK! (in silence)
Pale white light reflects from the screen softly illuminates
        her tired eyes, her confusion, and her small clenched fists.
She tries with one fist, to grasp that "Little Boy"
                that Daddy's country dropped —
and she tries with the other fist, to grasp the firestorm
                that burned in Mommy's country —
But a life of six short years knew only how
        to reach One hand to hold her mother's, and
        One hand to hold her Father's.

Karen Stanley

Warnings (Suspense Version)

"I'M JUST TRYING TO WARN YOU", THE MAN'S VOICE TWISTED through anxious lips drawn into a tight line. He accelerated under flashing amber lights, speeding down the viaduct off-ramp. "Open the glove compartment", he commanded, his hands firmly clenched the steering wheel of the VW bug. He liked his nice clean German car. The young passenger lifted a hand directly in front of her and turned the knob of the compartment. Noticing her silver rings glint in the dim light, she was frightened by the ominous warning he gave. The driver was a volatile man accustomed to using intimidation tactics to get what he wanted. She wondered what he would have her search for in the tiny glove box.

The little door sprung reliably forward and the driver reached brusquely past her with his large right hand. His square finger nails were immaculate as usual. Arm hair poked out thickly from under the pristine cuff of his freshly pressed plaid flannel work shirt.

Extracting a photograph from the dark hollow he barked, "Here look at this, that's her!" A small glossy photo dropped into the timid passenger's open hands. She brought the image right up to her face and strained her eyes in the darkness. She tried to absorb all the details. Each streetlight they whizzed by illuminated a flash more. A bit here, a bit there. Never the whole picture at once.

The driver signalled, checked the rearview mirror and changed lanes very precisely. The girl continued to study the photo up close. She felt connected to the old woman pictured in bright clothing and tried to memorize her face. A proud expression beamed out of the picture.

The old woman stood firmly, like a proprietor, before huge stone gates. Her colourful, patterned pantsuit shone in contrast to the dingy stone; she looked like she owned the place.

The girl silently sorted through flickering memories for clues. The driver offered no further information. Scowling, without a sideward glance, he pushed on the gas. The car jumped forward as tension revved high. It was no use, thought the girl, her brow furrowed in frustration and confusion. She absolutely could not guess what he was warning her of simply by looking at the photo. Divination did not work. The car sped through the night. There wasn't enough time to look at the picture, to imagine all the possibilities. What warning did the driver dare not speak? Why was he so nervous and angry about the photograph? he shifted gears going uphill on Prior Street, the engine became louder, higher pitched. Menacingly, he spoke. "Be careful, I've tried to keep you from it. Be careful," he urged. "I'm warning you."

Ominous warnings fill the small car, raising the temperature. The air is close, the windows fog over. Shrinking away in her seat, the passenger opened the window a crack and wiped the sweat off her face with her coat sleeve. The photo lay in her lap staring up, reproaching her for being too scared to anger him with questions. She leaned her head against the cool car window and tried to breathe deeply. Questions burned in her mind, fuelled by the overheated tension prickling through the vehicle. "Why does he want me to be afraid?" she wondered. "Why is he afraid? What happened to cause this anxiety? Why can't he speak about it?" The old woman in the photograph exerted some force over the man. As they passed the darkness of the unlit park, he snatched the photo from his passenger's lap and snapped it back into the glove compartment. Click, the little door closed and hid the photo in darkness again. The girl rolled down the window a little further, pulled her scarf off her to open her neck to cool air and pressed her right temple against the glass. The car seemed awfully loud, her heart beat faster, she could hear the pounding. She spotted the familiar brick walls of the projects as he turned left on Campbell Avenue. She was almost home and decided to risk his wrath by asking the question. "What is it Dad? She's my grandmother!" All the muscles in her body tensed as he fired back angrily. "She's from Saint Christopher, they call it Saint Kitts. It's an island in the Caribbean!" he snarled.

This is how my father told me where his mother was from. I grew up in Vancouver, far from the Caribbean community in Toronto. Even after this revelation I did not know why my father was so uptight about the fact his mother came from St. Kitts. It took me years to find out. The night he told me this secret was the eve of my trip to Toronto. I longed to meet my grandmother, to get to know her, to spend time with her and my father tried to inspire fear of her in me.

It took me years to understand the implications of his secret. After travelling, reading, spending time with people in the Caribbean, I realized that my father had been passing for white all his adult life. He had tried to withhold from me a rich part of my heritage. He had denied part of himself, part of me. He had tried to devalue part of my identity with his deeply internalized racism/self-hate/sickness. I think Granny accepted his sickness; she told me several times of how he had fallen and hit his head when he was a boy. He had fallen unconscious for a day. He remains unconscious to this day, in many ways. I think Granny forgave him, she'd seen worse. She came from a place where tough silence denied psychological scarring.

Joanne Arnott

Little on The Brown Side

I am a beautiful girl
A beautiful baby
Such pretty brown eyes
Lovely brown skin
*left in the oven too long, little
on the brown side*

I have beautiful
Curly brown hair
I look like an elf
With a heart-shape face
*left in the sun too long, little
on the brown side*

I am a beautiful baby
A beautiful girl
I have a fine disposition and
When I want something
You really hear about it
*some kind of throw-back, eh?
Nigger-in-the-wood-pile?*

little, little, little

Little
on the brown side

Joanne Arnott
Speak Out, For Example

ONE DAY, I STOPPED BY UNEXPECTED AT A FRIEND'S PLACE, knock knock. As she opened the door, she said with pretend irritation, "What do you want *now?*" When she saw it was me, she laughed. "Sorry. I thought it was my mutt...".

No, dear woman, it is not your mutt. It is someone else's mutt at the front door.

At the time I was too surprised, and too unsafe, to do more than focus my attention carefully on whatever had brought me to her door in the first place. But the incident has stayed with me, the sort of sting that crystallizes much into its simplicity.

In 1989, I attended an Unlearning Racism workshop presented by Rikki Sherover-Marcuse, and subsequently have attended and led many such workshops. I have met a diversity of women and men with mixed/ multiple heritages. I will take a few minutes, now, to talk about racism, specifically from a mixed or multiple heritage person's point of view, but there is no way that I can speak for everyone. The format I will use is that of a Speak Out exercise, as taught by Rikki Sherover-Marcuse. It is used as a tool for educating people, and as a platform for people targeted for oppression to speak *and be heard.* I will address these three points:

1. What I want you to know about me and my people.
2. What I never want to hear again.
3. What I expect of you as my allies.

Your job is just to listen. If you are also a mixed-race person, take some time to answer the questions for yourself. Remember to leave space for your feelings, because feelings and experience are essential and need to be channelled, embraced, and cherished. If you are not a mixed-race person, please repeat whatever you remember of what I said in response to points 1 and 3, and bear 2 in mind but remember, I really don't want to hear it again.

1. What I want you to know about me and my people:

ABOUT ME: I am a person of mixed Native and European ancestry, and I know lots about my European ancestry and almost nothing about my Native heritage: this is one impact of racism. I was raised in a white community as a white working class person. When, as a child, I or my sisters or brothers attempted to talk about our relationship to or similarities with Native people, we were punished. Our parents seemed to believe in lies about our ancestry, and we were forced to believe, or to pretend to believe, the same: this is one aspect of internalized racism. At the same time that this white-out policy was in effect, we were constantly being recognized by friends and by strangers, by people not under the sway of the family's survivalist lies.

This combination of input created in me an attempt to sort a world of responses to a Métis person through an insecure identity of whiteness. Confusion, dissonance, incongruity, self-doubt, endless inadequacy, deep shame were the results. The process of healing has been a tearing down and tearing up of almost every constituent belief that I held about myself and my world, and a recentering in the truth of body, mind, of spirit, a reawakening of my deep self and a reconstruction of my social self, my being in the world, on this new/ old/original foundation.

ABOUT MY PEOPLE: People with multiple ethnic heritages are an extremely diverse bunch of people. Our looks are diverse, our habits and heritages diverse, our knowledge of ourselves, our ancestries, our traditions, our families, are diverse. To use the example of mixed Native and European heritage people, some of us are raised on reserve, in the bush, in small towns, on farms, in cities, and/or any combination of these places; as Indians, as Métis, as "breeds," as whites, Blacks, Asians; with great pride, with great shame, with full knowledge, in complete ignorance, with double and triple messages about who we are and about our place in the world. For many of us, the greatest source of racism, hurt and shame is our own families. For many of us, our families are the cradles of safety against racist abuse and rejection from the outside world.

Big Issues: passing, and the not-Black-enough, not-Indian enough hassles we put on ourselves, collect from other people. "Where are you from?" "Are you two related?" In terms of multi-generational denial, complicities, it is important for us to acknowledge the privileges of European people, the very real dangers to our physical survival as Indians, Blacks, Asians in the context of the Americas. The decisions of family members to deny who we are do not come easy, they are meant to save lives. It is one strategy. Many of us choose other strategies, or override the decisions of our predecessors to reclaim the fullness and complexity of who we are and the histories of our families and communities. To attempt to enforce silence is soul murder. To attempt to induce identifications that are, because of racism, too threatening, is to rip a seed from its pod and is pointless: the seed will either ripen in its own time, or it will moulder and die within its protective casing.

Further layers of complexity get laid in when we are raised by people not targeted for oppression in the same way we are, the situation of the black child of the white woman who affectionately called him "mutt" to her Métis girlfriend. Our worlds differ fundamentally, in how we are received and who we are received by, and there are basic truths and survival skills a person of colour must learn that white parents don't know about.

Possibly the most difficult issue for people of mixed heritage is that of belonging, and a part of that is safety: constantly testing the waters to see how I am seen, and what the perceiver's response to their perceptions might be. The wide world that is laid open for people with multiple heritages is a well of potential, centered in a sometimes perilous terrain. The sliding identity that can be so difficult at first can become a very powerful tool for peacemakers.

2. What I never want to hear again:

"Mutt"   "Half-breed"   "Heinz 57"   "Wannabe"

I never want to face another door opened by a mother who calls the child of her own body racist names.

3. What I expect of you as my allies:

Question: What is an ally?
An ally can be a friend, family member, co-worker, complete stranger; but none of these is automatically an ally. Ideally, an ally is someone who is aware of their own issues of hurt and oppression, accumulated over the years, and is healing, and who is aware of the differences between us and who cherishes me, intervenes when they can to interrupt attacks against me, and supports me in my struggles against oppression and internalized oppression.

The possibility for every one of us to be allies against oppression is always present. Mistakes are made, and as allies, we commit ourselves to confronting rather than ignoring them, and doing the emotional and other kinds of work needed to correct and clean up mistakes and misunderstandings.

Notice the great pain carried by many, many, many mixed heritage people. Notice our strength, our great pride. Notice us, everywhere in the world.

Stop making assumptions about the heritage of other people, thinking that if someone looks white, looks European, that they want to hear your racist jokes in a buddy-buddy fashion. Or conversely, if someone looks Indian, that they are an automatic font of deep wisdom via continuous ancient tradition.

As an ally you must never expect me to choose sides, because I am all sides. You must never silence the parts of me that need to be given voice, especially when the parts of me do not agree. I need the fullnes of that space to sort out the contradictions of my life experience, and to solidify a grounded and well-rounded sense of who I am, my place, and what my work in the world might be, based on that reality.

What I expect of my allies is not to divide up the world by race and caste without acknowledging that every single boundary is blurred, and that these blurrings occur not only out of a conquerer mentality, but also out of love and need, and further that these blurrings have a name: we are called human beings. What I expect of my allies is to expect full pride from me, and to foster it.

We all learn the same racist crap, and we all need to stop perpetrating it on ourselves, on one another, and on the young people. Participating in the diminishing of ourselves and of others is how we have learned to survive, and it takes a conscious effort, storming and weeping, and a courageous collaboration to turn things around. There are many things that each one of us can do. Actions large and small can be taken. Alone, together. Heal old wounds, demand the fullness of life. Listen carefully. Speak out.

Anonymous

White Mother, Black Daughter

I AM A TWENTY-FOUR-YEAR-OLD AFRICAN WOMAN WITH THE BLOOD of both the colonizers and the colonized running through my veins. I have a young son who has just recently begun to call me MaMa. A touching experience. I look at him and wonder whom he will turn into. I know he will grow to be a man and strange as it seems, now, when he is so dependent on me I will never fully understand his experience. As a male, his stories will be different from mine.

This all leads me to reflect on my own mother. My European mother through whose sacred place I passed into this world. My European mother who nurtured me into what I am today. My European mother who also will never, can never understand me and my life as an African woman. These differences, male and female, black and white. These differences complicated and beautiful yearn to be recognized in a world that sets a mono-standard against which all is measured.

My personal and political journey to a place of consciousness of what it means to be Afrocentric and black in this profoundly racist country, has been one of the most intense experiences in my life. Being culturally rooted is struggle and joy! But this place I've reached leaves me stranded from my mother to whom I've suddenly become a stranger in a strange land. My mother acts in very racist ways at times. I still can't bring myself to say my mother is racist because like all of us, I've been brought up to believe racists are violent/evil people and not the next-door neighbours they really are.

What shall I tell my mother who is white? What will she hear? My mother like so many other "white liberals" considers herself enlightened on racial matters. But she/they constantly invade my space, presume to speak on my behalf, assume what I need and organize on my behalf, refuse to acknowledge the podium of privilege from where they speak and act.

The Women's Studies department in my home town recently created a course to study women in a cross-cultural perspective i.e. let's study the Others, the ones who fall outside the sphere of feminist normality, the "non-white." My mother was personally invited to teach this course. For me, how embarassing and infuriating... The one limited space made for our stories to be told and once again our voices are silenced. When I voice my concerns/my rage to my mother I am told "You have a chip on your shoulder," "Your father (African) doesn't see it that way," "You're the only one who feels like that, most Black women I know (i.e. those with a professional/colonized mentality) aren't angry like you" and "there are a few other women like you but you're all just bitter and obnoxious and I refuse to feel guilty like you want me to" and on and on until I want to scream but I feel like I've shrunk.

To be told your experience is untrue, worth nothing, by white society hurts. To hear it from your mother's mouth cuts even deeper.

This is all a mess. I don't even know where to begin untangling it. I'm in pain from it. My mother and I used to be very close. We're still friends but there is this heavy space between us I can't make peace with. It will only fall away when we can look gently and honestly at this race thing.

I've had problems in the past embracing my European side, I need to connect with it. Making peace with my mother could help facilitate this process. In no way does this mean I don't identify as an African woman because in this time/space it's the only thing I can and want to be. But to not feel like I'm at war with one half of myself, that's what I need to achieve.

I love my mother. I hate her racism. I can't separate the two, the mother, the racism, the love, the hate. Where to go from here?

I find it extremely difficult to continue challenging my mother on race issues but if I want growth I have to do it. I think of some good friends of mine who are an inter-racial couple and about to marry. I find it difficult to bless their union as I dream about their child/ren. I think of the tears they may shed in coming to terms with themselves, their mother (European), the world.

I find myself alone on this path, my siblings and father choose not to participate for their own personal reasons. But I am an African-identified woman and I am not alone. I stand in a community of other radical African women and men, ancestors and living who refuse to be broken down and silenced. We are the dissenters, the creators, the ones they call crazy and fringe. I call on Oya,[1] Whirlwind of change to be with us. We are the brave carriers of Africa's seeds in this new land. And I refuse to have that Black power/Black spirit stolen from me. Not even by my mother.

---

[1] *Oya* is a Yoruba Goddess.

Nila Gupta, Lezlie Lee Kam, Claire Huang Kinsley, Stefanie Samuels, Lisa Valencia-Svensson, and Anne Vespry

Mixed Race Women's Group — Dialogue Two

LISA: ... when I see an Asian woman with a white man (which is my family) I get a knee-jerk reaction. Right away, I want to protect them, I want to tell all the Asian women "Beware — stay away from him!" Even though I know that's where I'm from, and ultimately, if I were to tell them all "Don't do it" then I wouldn't exist. But it's so strong in me. I just feel I can tell what's really going on, and they can't tell what's going on between them.

STEFANIE: I think there's truth to that, again, it's also different because my mother is a white *woman* and my father is a black *man* and my mother's family had nothing to do with their marriage for the first five years, and every bit of her culture got left at the doorstep, including down to the kind of church she could worship in. It is different, like you said, I do react differently when I see a black woman and a white man. I certainly do acknowledge that some upwardly-mobile women of colour think a white man is a key that will give them some kind of satisfaction or material wealth. Yet, at the same time, all I know is my family, and these kind of reactions to black and white simply did not exist — your parents are your parents and having white in my immediate family obviously allowed me to see the similarities, not the differences.

LISA: ... It took me the longest time to even realize — Oh, there's two races in my family.
(laughter)

STEFANIE: I didn't until somebody else pointed it out.
(laughter)

LISA: I suddenly was hit by all these stereotypes of Asian women, and at the same time I was reeling because my mother and I had dealt with the same stereotypes. So I extended my own anger at those stereotypes to her, realizing that she has also had to deal with the same shit. All the white men that I get pissed at for looking at me as some exotic, innocent, submissive Asian doll; is my dad like that as well? I had to sit and go through my memories to figure out whether that was a factor in all our family history. I came to a conclusion, it was more an intellectual one than an emotional one, for sure, there were a lot of stereotypes both ways. For my mother, my father was the American man all Filipinas dream of marrying. My father, being born and raised in the States in the forties and fifties, there's no way he could not have had those stereotypical views of Asian women.

NILA: In my experience, it's more in terms of parents not talking about the colour issue in the family. I recall an incident where my dad was upset with my mother about some embarrassment she put him through. My mother was really racist when I was growing up, and somehow my father and I got into a conversation about what I had gone through in terms of growing up with my mother. I said, "You know, Dad, Mum is really racist. She is a racist." He looked at me with these innocent eyes, really perplexed, and he looked at me and said, "Well Nila, how can she be racist, she married me." And I realized that that was the extent to which he had analyzed the situation. And this woman had made such derogatory, racist comments during the course of my history growing up, and he was there, you know, and he *heard*. So I don't understand how he could... They didn't talk about it. I mean, they *did not* talk about it.

LISA: I know, I remember my father making the classic "Asian driver" comments, even when my mother and I were in the car with him. And it was like "Hello? Something is getting missed here."

LEZLIE: Listening to all of you talking, I realize I'm on my own again in this because both of my parents were brown. The difference that came out to me when I was growing up was that my mother came from money, and she was more East Indian than anything else, and my father was working class, and he was what they call in Trinidad "Heinz 57" so he really did not have any status of any kind. My grandfather was very Indian and he decided my mother was to marry one of two men he had chosen, one was white, and one was Indian. My mother rebelled by going after my father who was more Chinese than anything, and I remember being told that my grandfather pulled a shotgun on my father when he found out that they were seeing each other. But it was not until I came here, and like I said I find myself in a very isolated position when you're talking about the mixture of races and how sometimes we feel we have to identify. I find that sometimes what happens is people trade on making me exotic. If you're not one or the other but you happen to be a lot of different races, which I am, my experience is not given any value because they make me into this "whatever they want me to be." When I say I'm mixed race, or I feel this way because I'm mixed race, they say "Look at all the places you can get into, what's the big deal, you don't have to worry." But you know, in my work place I'm the diversity of one. Somebody calls up, they want somebody to do a workshop for the Vietnamese community, they want a woman of colour, they get me. I feel I am used. People exoticize you and use you to their benefit. It just makes me feel sometimes I would like to be able to choose my place, and not have someone trying to put me in it. I remember when I first came out in Toronto, going to the bars, I would go with my black Canadian friends, and they'd be treated so differently. Again, talking about the shadism and the colour. They would experience direct racism, and I would be treated like "Oh! What part of the world are you from?" And white women still do it. When you talk about backlash, and there is a backlash. I've been to the bars recently, and see that when you're a mixed race woman you're treated differently than when you're perceived as a black woman. So they would treat you differently than they would treat me, sometimes. And you wonder, where is the analysis in how they treat someone?

STEFANIE: And also in what they perceive as mixed race. I mean most of the white women I deal with, they're next to shocked if I happen to mention that I have a white mother. They expect mixed race to be this beautiful, grey-eyed mulatto.

LEZLIE: To look like them.

STEFANIE: They always expect you to look like the woman, Vanessa something, who won the Miss America contest. When I was born in Toronto, the nurse thought there was something wrong because the child was the wrong colour. She was freaking out, and my mother is saying "No, she's just the right colour." It's strange, in a lot of ways I didn't have that ticket, and I know what you mean by that ticket, but by having kinkier hair, that's how a lot of white people determine, if your hair is long and straight then you're a viable bi-racial person. This is not something that happens as much in the black community as in any other communities because I think that we're better able to know these things, and to see that spectrum. That's really hard in a lot of ways, I'll be walking down the street in arm with my mother who is now looking like this big Ukrainian baba, and no one gets it. We've had conversations and she's said she wonders what she has not been able to give me as a white woman. It's interesting, at the same time that I am bi-racial, I don't feel that I have the same access, as other bi-racial women, because I have darker skin.

ANNE: Well, the other thing is, that because there is the perception in the black community of not wanting to admit to white heritage, there are a lot of people who may be lighter than you who are saying "No. I'm black." So that it ends up being a bit of a mindfuck for people who are left saying "The last time I saw someone your colour they said they were `black, and that's it.' So, now what are you saying you want to be called? I have to learn a new word for this?!" *(laughter)*

CLAIRE: Do you think that's just a matter of not wanting to "admit" to white heritage, though? I mean, I'd understand that the rape of black slave women by white men was so prevalent, like Stefanie was saying earlier, that most North American black people who are descendants from slaves have at least a bit of white ancestry, and some have quite a lot, even without any recent intermarriage. So that someone might be lighter-skinned than Stefanie but have four out of four grandparents who consider themselves black, and have been treated by society as black. Isn't it logical enough for someone in that situation to identify herself as black, period, even if she does have some white ancestry from way back?

ANNE: Sure, for people — like my father, for instance — who doesn't know who their white ancestor (or ancestors) are, and whose immediate family (parents and grandparents) identify as black, for them to identify as mixed-race makes as much sense as white people identifying as Native because they think they were Native in a previous life. What I'm talking about, though, is women who have a white parent but find it more convenient in the feminist communities' atmosphere of white guilt to deny their mixed-race and go about vilifying all that is white to try to gain power. I don't particularly care how people identify themselves. What pisses me off are those who try to put me down for how I identify, or who insult half of who I am by insulting all that is white. When those people have white in their immediate family I begin to think they should be "outed" as mixed-race.

NILA: I just wanted to say something, jumping off from what Stefanie said about walking down the street with her mother and people are shocked to see them together. I'm sometimes shocked to see my mother at the door. I've been in the women of colour community for over a decade, and so I've only been with women of colour. When I see my mother, and I don't see her very often, it's a shock to me that she's my mother. That a white woman is my mother. So there's that kind of internal shock as well.

CLAIRE: That's interesting because, my parents, I'm definitely aware of what race they are, but at the same time, this sounds kind of corny, but first and foremost they are my parents. I love them so much and they are so dear to me that they have to be my parents first, and whatever race they are is second. Which is not to say that their race is irrelevant to me or that I can't analyze issues that have arisen within the family with a racial analysis, but I guess I have to think of them as "Mommy and Daddy" first and other stuff after that.

NILA: I think that depends on people's personal family history...

CLAIRE: Definitely, definitely...

NILA: And their relationship to their family, and if there's a history of racial violence that highlights the issues more. In my family, my mother was racially violent in the family, so for me there was the experience of not wanting to own my mother because she did not want to own me as well. She would say that we weren't really her children. That's confusing for a child. My mother was also mentally ill, so for me the confusion was "Is this racism?" which I also experienced outside of my home in the era of "Paki-bashing," and then, I walk into my home and there is no safe place. Here is my mother being racist, and the confusion is, "Is she racist or is she mentally ill? And, does it make a difference?" In my family, my mother did not want to own her children, and I know this is not an uncommon thing with women who have ambivalent relationships with their spouses or boyfriends or whatever and they take it out on the children. I've seen that happen. I've seen bi-racial children running around, and their mother yelling out and using a racial slur to call the children. I've seen that happen and it pains me a great deal. My mother would also say things, now when she's a lot more functional, and I'd tell her that I'm involved in the South Asian community and starting a theatre company and whatever, and she'd purse her lips and say "What are you involved with South Asians for? You're not South Asian." without defining exactly what I *am*, only what, in her eyes, she wants me *not* to be.

STEFANIE: It's interesting, we did not have any close family living in Ontario, just one aunt in Manitoba and another one that I've never seen, but the family really did have to create it's own armour against all that shrapnel. Even in the church, we were this juicy exotic foursome, and everybody wanted to know what the goods were and what was going on. It was also wierd. My mother is a very big woman, five foot eight and a "strapping lass," and my father is five six, dark, quiet, middle-class Jamaican type, and we really did have to, I feel, have a certain kind of privacy that we tried to keep up. My mother was always really bad at this because she is very gregarious. My father was always very private and protective about family matters, and all of this really showed up to be true when my mother and I went on "Just Like Mom," a game show that they used to have out of CFTO. It was like the "Newlywed Game," except for mothers and daughters. They ask all the daughters a question while the mothers are away and the mothers come back and have to try to guess what their daughter said, and all the daughters have to make something and the mothers have to guess which one their daughter made. So we go on this show *(laughter)* and they ask us questions like "What family secret would you least like to talk about on TV?" then they ask us "What does your mom do in the bathroom that you don't do?" Throughout my whole school career, whenever there was a problem and my mother had to come to school the first thing people would say is "How are things at home?" So often people want to slot people of mixed race heritage into this tragic, confused, messed up whatever. It's awful. This is the real work people have to know going into mixed race marriages.

NILA: I have a story to tell about children of inter-racial marriages being seen as "confused." I was in a women's studies course a couple of years ago, the year that *This Bridge Called My Back: Writings by Radical Women of Colour* came out. It came out at the end of the term. Part of the curriculum in this class was to do journal writing to document how you progress and what you learn in the class. So, my professor was really taken up — this woman professor, feminist professor, who is still teaching at University of Toronto — she was really taken up with me and wanted to meet with me at the end of the term. She'd invited me over, and we sat on the grass outside New College, and we talked. She gave me the book, *This Bridge Called My Back,* and I asked her for a reference for medical school because at the time I wanted to get into medicine. In the class, part of the curriculum was to talk about male bias and how it works even in the university system, and how women often experience having male professors write them references and say "She is married to ..." and reference her to a spouse and make derogatory and sexist remarks in the reference which are totally irrelevant in the matter at hand, which is a person's qualifications or capability or whatever. So, she gave me a reference letter and I was able to read it, and in it she said, and this is a direct quote, "Nila has had identity problems common to the offspring of interracial marriages." Now in my journal I had written lots about racism, but I hadn't written about being bi-racial or about my family history. So I'm sure the medical school committee must have read this and said "She's not stable mentally, we don't want her!"

LISA: When you were talking about privacy earlier, and when I was talking about being really furious when I see Asian women with white men, at the same time that I have those feelings I know I also have this feeling that no one else better comment on this situation to me. Don't ask me if I think it was race problems that caused my family to divorce. I don't want to hear it. I just don't want to hear it. Unless you're mixed race, I feel that you have absolutely no right to comment on this. Also, the confusion thing; when I first started exploring race issues, I had one white friend (I still have one white friend). Her long term partner is black, and she started thinking "Oh my god! Lisa! Am I going to be making a big mistake if we have children?" I was sharing my pain with her, and I just did not know how to respond. I can't say "no, don't" because then I'm saying my life is worthless, but how can you dare ask me that? It's like "Oh, is your life really so worthless that I should not have kids because they would be as fucked up as you?"
(laughter)

NILA: I think I can envision that what would make interracial marriages healthy, would be if people were racially conscious: if they understood the history, if they did their research, if they did their learning, their growing. That would take a lot of the pain away. It could not shelter you from the larger societal context, but in terms of the family, it could give you a place of strength and empower you to go on with your life. I can envision that. It's not the fact that we're bi-racial that is problematic, it's that there is so much silence, and ignorance, and racism.

STEFANIE: ... I mean, my family was warned by my mother's family, by her sister, who had been her best friend until then — in fact, my father dated her first — and they said, "Don't have kids, they won't know what they are." ... One of the things that's very frustrating for me is that my white aunt (on my mother's side), who has been a teacher for the last 35 years, is completely clued out... I'm disgusted at her ignorance... She's a loyal friend to my mother, but has never made an attempt to educate herself or understand anything about my father's life, family, or her niece's and nephew's blackness... I've never sensed a genuine intent to understand my father's experience or way of life. That's what's upsetting to me, that's where I have to admit, though I don't like to admit, that most people believe integration is an assimilation into their world, and that we can all just pretend that we're white, rather than learn and understand...

CLAIRE: I think that the point about all the people involved being aware is very important. I have friends, a black woman and a white Jewish man who are planning on getting married. And they were talking around me one time about all the discussions they've had on how they can raise their children to have both a black identity and a Jewish identity. They were saying they had even talked about what they could name their children so that it will fit into both heritages. I said "If you have a girl, you could name her Rosa. That would be both for Rosa Luxemburg and Rosa Parks." *(laughter)* To me it was a really good sign that they were talking about that sort of stuff. You can't just go into these kinds of things with the attitude that you love each other so much everything will be just fine. Once in a blue moon that might work, but you can't assume it's going to.

STEFANIE: It also gives more to their kids. Just that this is something that they've thought about, that they've worked through. For the first seventeen years of my life I never had a serious conversation with my parents about my bi-racialness or their racial intermarriage. I think giving children that right to speak is important.

LISA: Another thing that pisses me off: less than a week ago, yet another bunch of people who are not mixed race had the discussion in my presence of how they think that people of mixed race are a racial salvation because...

LEZLIE: Yeah, the wave of the future...

LISA: Yes, we really hold the key to the understanding and the resolution of racial issues. And I was just thinking "Oh, we're the only ones that are going to do any of the work?" We are the ones, probably with less problems than most of the rest of you around this issue. Give it a break.

ANNE: The thing is that there was a big part of my life where I had internalized that belief. I figured that the world would cease being fucked up at the point where everyone was of mixed race, or everyone admitted that they were mixed race. I think that a large percentage of the people who don't admit it, are anyway.

NILA: There's no such thing as "pure race."

ANNE: Now that's going to get backlash.

NILA: I'm really debating whether or not to be anonymous in these tapes, whether to have a pseudonym... Partly because I'm dealing with personal family history. So part of it has to do with that, and part of it has to do with this community, and I'm talking specifically about the Toronto lesbian of colour community. And I'm feeling that it can be both a very supportive but occasionally a very hostile place depending on who you have the fortune or misfortune of meeting or running into. And it can be hostile on numerous issues, not just this issue, I have to say. So part of it is that I'd like people to talk about it, so we can unpack it.

STEFANIE: I feel the same way... When you talk about that kind of hostility... Though I don't feel I want to be anonymous, but it's something, and I know I probably would not have had this freedom to speak in some circles.

ANNE: For me it's really easy, as easy as anything, because I feel I've already burned all my bridges.

LEZLIE: Yes, exactly.
(laughter)

CLAIRE: The only friends you have left are your true friends...
(laughter)

ANNE: Also, because when I first came out I was involved in the women of colour community or the lesbian of colour community very very briefly because I kept on hearing things about white women and inter-racial couples that made me not want to have anything to do with those communities. I've created my own little bubble where I interact with lots of individual people from varied parts of the lesbian communities. So I think I don't have as much invested in the lesbian of colour communities as some of you do.

STEFANIE: It's a great way to know who your friends are.
(laughter)

ANNE: Yes, but it's very depressing when you find out there's only one or two of them.

STEFANIE: It's very sad. I did a piece at a theatre cabaret that was supposed to be empowering black women artists, and my piece had to do with a white mother, and I could hear the snickers and the back stabbing. And then there were these women who came up to me and said "white mama blues," and really identified. And other women who just said thank you for being so honest. But when I turned around and saw people laughing and pointing and then heard something that I hope you'll never hear from the community from which you seek validation, the same sort of recorded messages of "confused, mixed up." Talking about mixed race means you're mixed up. You're right, this is a great way to know who your friends are.

CLAIRE: Maybe I've been lucky — I don't feel I've had those kinds of experiences. I mean, I haven't been around what's known as the "lesbian of colour community" in Toronto for very long, and maybe I've just been lucky in the individuals I've happened to meet, but in any case, I haven't personally experienced that kind of hostility.

LISA: I have told this story before, but it's important here. In the precious first days of my coming out — utter confusion, complete depression, and continual race confusion as well. I went to a lesbian for advice, and the conversation went this way and that way, and it eventually moved to an argument about bi-sexuality. And she said "Bisexual women pose the same problems..." and she looked at me, like she had me pinned. "Bisexual women pose problems for lesbians the same way as women of mixed race do for women of colour." She was a woman of colour. Four months after, I finally started getting angry about it, at the time I was just so devastated. It felt like she was saying that, because of my racial background, I am fundamentally a problem.

STEFANIE: I can identify with that totally.

LISA: Now I would say, "And I enjoy being a problem!" but at the time... you don't say something like that to someone who is feeling so tenuous, who is struggling in so many different ways.

STEFANIE: ... I'm not trying to slash away at something, or throw darts at these communities. I think what we're trying to do is point out where they don't include, and why they feel the strength of their politics may be threatened by someone talking from their own experience. I think it's more exclusionary than it is oppressive. I don't know how deliberate that is. It is interesting when we talk about colour, because colour is non-white but then within colour there are all of these other classifications. Within colour, it is important for women who are dark, just like Lezlie said, when you walk into a club and people can treat you one way and someone who is darker than you a different way. There are politics that go between those sides all the time. And people that are bi-racial and one looks more "ethnic" and one looks more white. I think these are the things that aren't spoken of, and we're touching on some of those chords that are extremely sensitive.

CLAIRE: But as you say, the fact that it's sensitive is no reason to tiptoe around it. I think my uneasiness — my impulse to tiptoe, as it were, is partly just connected to knowing that there are a lot of people out there who are very quick to label criticisms of racism or homophobia or sexism or whatever, as attempts to be "politically correct" and "silence free speech" and so on. So it's easy to imagine these PC-baiting types reading this and saying "Yes! We always knew *those kinds of people* were just trying to impose a rigid political correctness, and look, we were right!" These women are concerned about the pressures within their own community, and if they feel these pressures are rigid and unproductive and unfairly hostile, then it follows that all the people who've been hassling me about racism and homophobia and whatnot are *also* being rigid and unproductive and unfairly hostile, and I shouldn't have to listen to them. But again, that's no reason not to talk about this stuff. I just wanted to bring out into the open my own edginess about the possibility of that kind of reaction.

LEZLIE: ... I would like for us to challenge each other, to hold each other accountable on how we treat each other... how do we celebrate our differences and use that to strengthen and support each other? That's how I see this.

LISA: Yes, If I had been able to read this in those desperate first days when that woman told me that bunch of bullshit, it would have been amazing, then I'd have been going *"Right On!"*
(laughter)

LISA: So I do this for someone else, so that for all the ten people that say "oh, yeah," there'll be one person saying, "Thank God!"

CLAIRE: It's interesting that you talk about having been able to read this when you were younger. Because when I was thinking about who I imagined reading this anthology in the first place, the archetypal image in my mind was someone kind of like me, but younger. Someone in the position of wondering about stuff and trying to figure stuff out, who would come across the book on the library shelf and read it and say, "Hey, I'm not the only one!"

NILA: In some sense a lot of women who say these (hostile) things may be hypocrites, because they may be involved with white women or with men. I had this experience when I was invited with my lover, who is Sri Lankan, to this Indian woman's house to watch Hindi videos. So there I was, and there was another South Asian woman present who was living with a white man. The Indian woman, whose house it was, was in a relationship with a white woman. The details of the movie are that this raj who is married to a beautiful woman, played by Shabana Azmi, becomes obsessed with an Anglo-Indian girl and kidnaps her in his sexual obsession. The Indian woman watching the video, whose house it was, started talking about how ugly the mixed race woman in the movie was, and how stupid she was. Not critiquing the script or the reason behind the man's fanatical obsession with the Anglo-Indian girl, or the analysis that's being presented in the movie, but attacking the physical looks of this mixed race child in the movie. I'm sitting there and I'm thinking, "OK, she made this comment, maybe she thinks this woman is ugly, and I'm looking and looking, and I don't think she's ugly at all, I think she's beautiful. I think a lot of the characters in the movie are beautiful." She went on and on about how ugly this mixed race woman was, and I started to feel extremely uncomfortable, what was I doing there? Up to that point, my experience was to identify as South Asian, that's been my experience and my history, and how I'd been treated in society. This was the first time that I started to experience this kind of hatred towards people of mixed race (apart from my experiences with my mother). This was the first time, in this political setting. So I'm sitting there, wondering why is she attacking the looks of this woman, this woman is clearly not ugly, so what's going on here? I felt this to be a personal attack on me. Because I am of mixed race, and she knows that, she's been over to my house, she's seen my family photos, we've shared dinner.... Then, the other woman joins in, and there's this chorus of voices in this room attacking the mixed race woman and her beauty or her lack of beauty. I'm thinking this is very, very strange, and I wanted to leave. My respect for these two women plummeted to the point where you can't touch this point, it's way down in a bottomless pit, that is where the respect is. I've never confronted them.

STEFANIE: They had to have known about you...

NILA: Yeah, I think for the Indian woman it was a lot of jealousy that I was in this relationship. We were the only two South Asian lesbians at that time in a coupled relationship, we'd been together for a couple of years. I think partly it's also her own internalized shit, I remember her making a comment before this incident that she got so angry with white women who would ask her "Are you Anglo-Indian?" By attacking Anglo-Indians she distanced herself from any identification with them. It's like a closeted lesbian staging a homophobic attack. Except in her case it's about not wanting to own any privilege white society may give her because of their perception of her as being perhaps more like them.

STEFANIE: I feel like I was in a very similar circumstance, and I get the feeling so many times when I meet people who have swung so much to hostility towards people of mixed race, that they had been a very different person until a political awakening that hit them like a ton bricks and they constructed something that was entirely different, which is why there are holes. I was at one woman's house and I had to leave. I was with three black lesbians and they were talking about white families raising adopted black children, and they were talking about how the parents won't be able to give them Afrocentricity or whatever, and nobody seemed to be raising questions that I wanted to see raised and eventually I asked, "Did your parents give you Afrocentricity?" *(laughter)* That was mistake number one, and mistake number two was to ask what would be better for a child, to be in an orphanage or to be with one family? And one woman turned on me saying, "We know that you have a white mother, and you're not a part of this discussion." I just got up and walked out the door. I just left. This was something that had been going around in circles, up until then I had had this feeling that these people from three years old onwards were educated in Yoruba,... *(laughter)* I did not know any of these women very well, so when I, in my naivete said "did your parents..." It touched a nerve that was *very* sensitive.

NILA: On a similar plane is when women of colour say when you identify as a mixed race woman you want to be white. Internalized racism is not unique to women of mixed race. All of us (women of "pure" race, and women of mixed race) who grow up in a white society internalize racism. What the women you're talking about are doing is obliterating their own history, obliterating the pain and projecting that all onto us.

LISA: We embody the struggles that are going on in their minds (and ours).

STEFANIE: It's interesting what you say, with regards to jealousy, when you meet light light skinned black women that are on the verge of passing and they need to tell people. Their blackness must be so important in their lives. And yet, there's always this strange dynamic, with black women especially, (where) skin colour and hair and body shape are the determining factors for beauty. And it is something that is hard to deal with on a personal level. I think that those women may have had to, may have needed to tell that woman on the television that she was ugly. They have to say that to themselves and in turn attack you for being something that for their first twenty years they wished they could be. And one against three just ain't a good ratio to...
(laughter)

LEZLIE: That's a good point, because sometimes I get the feeling from "pure race" women that it's easier for me because I'm a mixture of so many, and it's not easier for me because I'm so many. But you get that animosity sometimes.

LISA: Yes I get the feeling they think I'm about halfway there...

STEFANIE: What kills me is that it's black people who can best see those differences. I don't think the average person who's looking at your job application can even see those things. I think there is something to be said (about) privilege, when you look at old photographs of the first blacks to be admitted to schools, they are light skinned. Even today, I think that when people are hiring out their racial quotas they won't hire someone that is very dark...

CLAIRE: Or has a quote, unquote "accent"...

STEFANIE: or has an accent, or even a mode of behaviour that isn't white.

LEZLIE: A non-North American accent, I have to take exception to that.

CLAIRE: I said quote, unquote "accent".

Heather Green

This Piece Done, I Shall Be Renamed

AS A PERSON OF MIXED RACE, I EMBODY SOME OF THE MOST unresolved contradictions in current human relations. Beyond just the mixing of physical traits, there's the fact that my blood has ancestry from two different continents. This means that, even before the experience of being born and raised in a land which is not my own, I have two or more vastly different histories, heritages, belief systems and ways of life which exist in my soul, in my spirit, in my DNA, in my heart of hearts — whichever you prefer.

This very pure and simple reality (about the only "purity" to speak of) which follows from the mixing of human races, has become less the exception and more the rule considering the long history of human contact. These days just about everyone who is born in the diaspora has been mixed with something over the generations. And for anyone of mixed race, the number of resulting experiences is endless. These depend on which races are being considered, how many in one person, the generation(s) of mixing, which gender of which race for which parent (and child), the circumstances under which the egg actually accepted the sperm, and so on.

The questions that I ask (and the answers that I get) in considering my mixed race condition depend not only on the support I have in my life, and on a certain freedom of thought, but also on how fundamentally curious I am — and what my gut political angle is in this world built on geo-political-socio-economic-sexual-racialized ways of seeing people. As a woman of mixed race, how eager am I to decipher my past experiences and present life? Do I even care that it matters? Do I know that this information may save my life, the lives of those I love or of people I may never know?

People are funny. In our minds, hearts and spirits we are granted the capacity for so much comprehension. Yet we tend to simplify things that go on around us to either/or; good and evil. This male European view has infiltrated and dominated almost everybody on the planet, and many of us have absorbed a similarly two-sided approach to life.

With this approach, the history of racial mixing has been obscured. Gender, class, culture, ability, sexual orientation and race have been compartmentalized into narrow definitions. Women are considered women only by qualities of "feminine" weakness and passivity to male control. People are defined as "members of society" only by degrees of productivity, type of work and the usefulness of our labour to capital. Otherwise we are considered the dregs of society — the unemployed. A person with a disability is looked upon as "unable" or "non-able" and not for consideration as a human being. Lesbians are not seen as women since our purpose in male-controlled reproduction is lost and we are therefore non-existent in society. These power-based values of purity become major tools in oppression, keeping us from being all the things that we are.

Then there's racism — the creation of European/Christian/ capitalist/imperialist self-proclaimed super-human superiority. Within this thrives the dualistic, puritan reasoning of white/Europeans who often believe that any person of European descent mixed with Black (African), brown or yellow (Asian) or red (Native American) is "tainted." By virtue of this "impurity," I am *not* European = not good enough = "theirs, not ours" = "other, not this"... "This," of course, being their (euro)centralized, most legitimized form of life.

Still there are times when the opposite is true, and racism is camouflaged through the erasure of colour difference, and through the assumption that no matter what our race and heritage, ultimately we all "want to be white." Racism is made real for me by the Europeans in my family and in my life when they *choose to adopt* me into their world, either literally or figuratively. I have been officially "adopted" as the daughter of a European patriarch, and made "legitimate" under his name. I have been just one among a few of my kind, "adopted" by European schoolmates and co-workers... under their European gaze I became their "exotic" change from the ordinary, their "curious mascot" who it's cool to hang with, the "child" for their patronage of pretended self-importance — to fulfil their desire for power over others, for lack of knowing and loving themselves. In all situations, "underprivileged," "deprived," "undeveloped," "disadvantaged," and/or "minority" is the status which Europeans prescribe for me. Their adoption of me then becomes a symbolic gesture which they use to absolve themselves of any real attempt to challenge the power privilege that the European race continues to gain through racism.

And when an economic squeeze is on, when there's a tough personal choice to make or a crisis with white family or friends, I have learned well that as a Black woman, I am more likely to be pathologized, ignored, abused, disowned, disrespected, disregarded, misunderstood, sent on my way, or simply "put in my place" within this adoptive status. When I proudly assert the true "colour" that is in me, when I begin to make white people aware of their power and responsible for their history, when I start to identify just a bit more with others of colour and their control is called into question — they fear me — fear my Blackness. Fear who they do not understand. Fear who they've never truly known. Fear to admit that there are places where they don't belong. Fear that there are times when their presence is not wanted — and not needed.

Such adoption can only be described as ownership, occurs everywhere in human relations: parent-child, husband-wife, employer-worker, partners, siblings and friends. The problem in these relations of ownership is the power which is misused and abused. It is this power which would encourage me — and anybody — to say or believe that someone belongs to me, and that she must not question or challenge my values and practices or else she is not of me, not with me, not good enough = exploitable = disposable. It is this power which falsely seeks to find and define "humanity" in the domination one can exert over another or group of others.

The European adoption, literal or figurative of anyone of non-European descent is this type of ownership. It is *inherently* a power imbalance, a master-slave dynamic. It is played out as ownership because of historic and current European attitudes of supremacy, which have become insidious and blatant practices of racism, all entrenched in structures and institutions of global power. It is compounded when I am a child, when I am a girl, when I am a woman, when I am lesbian, and when I do not conform to the misogynist familial and societal dynamics which are the dominant culture.

For women of mixed descent, of colour and white, much of our experience parallels the violence of the externalized and internalized racism, classism and sexism of the larger society, but with an added element. For us, these realities are immeasurably more twisted, upfront, intense, painful and traumatizing because we witness their destruction first-hand in our families, in our homes, and in our very own flesh and blood. We are the embodiment of an ownership/power imbalance which started at least one generation before us. But our parents and their generation may or may not have acknowledged, confronted and begun dealing with the issue of power. They may have, as is the most common scenario, *chosen* to consider race, class, gender and power external and unimportant to who they are as individuals and unimportant in their lives, therefore shirking this responsibility to themselves, to each other, to society, and more importantly — to us as their children.

The effects of this mixed existence, in my case, have ranged from the superficialization, effacement, subordination, exoticization and erasure of my African descent and heritage — which means me — to all the simultaneous power abuses through violence against girls and women such as the pummelling of our self-esteem, rape, battering, neglect and the branding of subservient roles and duties — which still means me. The most twisted, painful and contradictory part is that these messages come so acutely from all sides of the family. They are acts committed by the European relatives and friends who predominated in my world. And they also come from people of colour who have come into my life; who have taken the violence and hatred that has been part of our condition for centuries, internalized it and then used it against each other.

But I am one woman of African and European descent whose existence is here and now. I state the obvious. I declare it — in order to unearth from its meaning that part which has rarely been understood at all: the factors which have shaped who I am, but are never discussed, deconstructed, admitted or even revealed.

I exist. Yet I was not conceived by accident, in some harmless isolation. Nor have I lived comfortably, finding ignorant bliss in segregation. There's a context and history to how an African sperm entered a European egg one cold winter day at the end of the 1960s. Just as there is a context and history to the anger and pain which comes as I learn to identify myself in 1990s Canada. I know that I have already lost what could have been two decades to grow-up knowing my *whole* self — lost to the mind-and-spirit-numbing complacency of growing up very literally whitewashed by white Anglo-Saxon small town life.

In this European-American, male-power driven world, I have learned that I can no longer *choose* to ignore my reality — to not know my *whole* self. My brown skin, locks of nappy hair, African woman's body and, not least of all, my African ancestral convictions do not permit it. My reality as a human being has to relate to other people of all ancestries, in my direct life and on this earth. And this reality is no ideal world of "everyone is equal" or "people are people and it doesn't or shouldn't matter what the colour of my skin is."

Such a world will never arrive. Not as long as the European race maintains the power that allows individual white men and women to *choose* to ignore and inadequately respond to the reality that people suffer and are killed because of their global ideology. Such power will never be shared. Not as long as individual men and women of colour, and indigenous women and men (mixed or not) *choose* to accept the ideology of class privilege and European supremacy, which often transforms us into self-serving, self-hating individuals and uses us to oppress ourselves and our own peoples.

For the past five-hundred years, Europeans have, above and beyond any other race, been the most abusive, violent and destructive people, especially to those who do not resemble them and to this planet which was granted to us for the prosperity of all races.

Both directly and through the colonized minds of our sisters and brothers of colour, Europeans continue to commit genocide against Africans, Asians and indigenous peoples everywhere. From the burning of witches to the Christian imperialist wars and inquisition; to the colonization of Africa and Asia; to the rape of the Americas; to the corralling and killing of Native Americans; to the enslavement and displacement of Africans; to Asian indentureship and forced migration; to the imposition of a capitalist world economic market; to the current non-European global migrant labour force; to the international prostitution and domestication of girls and women of colour; to imperialist debt sanctions and structural adjustment policies; systemic sterilization of African; Aboriginal and Asian women; strategic selling of weapons; artificial free trade zones and treaties; nuclear experimentation of the Pacific islands and islanders; theft and sale of the rainforests; hoarding and controlling the planet's resources; selective and biased documentation of history; manipulative and culturally-effacing education; police brutality and systems of justice so separated from the reality of all human experience — European's have a lot to account for in thinking that their presence among people of colour can continue to be so painlessly accepted.

And knowing just these few facts about my European ancestors and their descendants, including my family members, means the possibility of me finding some "internal peace," balance, compromise or reciprocity between my African blood and my European blood is nonexistent. Especially given my upbringing.

Imagine... growing up as the only child of colour adopted into a British family in small-town Ontario. It taught me much about England and the needs of white men everywhere. It painted a very *"pretty and pure"* picture of white girls and women for me, and *generously* hinted that as a Black girl (seen as crudely masculine and erotic) I should aspire to be like both white men and white women in very specific ways, though — clearly — I could never succeed. It's no wonder that I resisted that straight European lifestyle so stubbornly, retreating at every chance into the private freedom of sports, the acceptance of good grades and the safety of my own thoughts.

Looking back I now see that I must have seemed *so preoccupied* being taught these things and living by them, that there simply wasn't the time during my first eighteen years for my parents to tell me that my adoptive mother is really my biological mother, that my biological father is Jamaican and living in nearby Hamilton, nor for them to ensure a space for him in my life, or a connection with other Black people and Black heritage. They tell me there just weren't the means for this upwardly-mobile working-class European family to teach me about Jamaica or Africa or to even point them out as places of significance on the map. Clearly, there was really no need for this European family of five plus one, to mention to this youngest, Blackest one (or even to themselves) how Africans had had no choice in becoming Jamaicans, or how it happens that Jamaicans would have to leave such a beautiful island for such a cold cold place as Canada. It would have actually required a real amount of honesty for everyone to contemplate how a married English woman became pregnant by a Jamaican man, with me, the unexpected little Black girl, and how I grew to be so quiet and self-effacing and frighteningly mature years before my time, or how I came to be exploited as a sexual plaything by my white-man elder brother, an alien(ated) opposite by my snow-white perfect elder sister, and a stereotypic athletic novelty by my entire high school.

No. It obviously hasn't been at all desirable, let alone pressing for these white middle-class people to trouble themselves about this in their very stable, comfortable and unadventurous lives. Naw. I'm just the baby of their family. I'm only adopted. And after all, there's only one of me so why should I be accommodated?

Why would my "adoptive" mother have wanted to ruin the logic and safety of her and her husband's European lie — telling me when I was three that she had had a stillbirth and in its place adopted me... erasing through her entrusted words any connection for me to my actual blood heritage? Why would my white adoptive father have made it a priority to tell me that I'm mixed and *not* the daughter of a Black mother and Black father, as I had so naturally concluded for myself? Why would they have seen it as their duty to teach me about my racial origins, and their painful and exceptionally significant implications?

Why would my mother tell me the truth that *she bore* me, became pregnant with me through the male violence of *RAPE*, and that *THIS* is the nature of the world in which she lives and which I am entering... Instead of risking that in this truth I might *have the power to assert my own choice* to connect with my Jamaican and Black heritage, while at the same time taking on (from the age of three) a very healthy distrust of all men, including her white husband.... Instead of catering, like her, to this "well-intentioned" patriarch whom I learned to so *gratefully* refer to as "my dad"?

Why would my white mother have just told this truth in honesty, and not out of fear of losing me when at eighteen years old I found the courage to ask "Who are my biological parents?" Why, when she could more easily escape her own painful reality — *leave unchallenged* the power she holds within her patriarchal, racist and sexist reality — via a bottle of brandy and a solid dose of privileged conformity?

I have come to understand that *being* of mixed race is a genetic fact and a socio-historic reality. However *politically identifying* as mixed race, and nothing more, is telling. It can reveal a desire to be or to function as a balance between all the races I am, giving equal importance to each. But I know that if I were to aspire to strike some balance between Black and white, between African and European, trying to be the wizard mediator between oppressed and oppressor, I would be sacrificing my entire being. It is not possible. It is not wise. And it makes no sense for any one woman to take on what humanity as a whole is so far from taking seriously — the power and destruction of white supremacy in the family, in friendships, at work, at school, in systems locally and internationally — in all its infinite manifestations.

On the other hand, revealing that I am of mixed race — mixed with European — to African peers and other people of colour can be most painful, another side of the double-edged sword. Acknowledging my mixed heritage speaks to my wish that they accept *all* of me, including the European side of my experience which has been imposed on me externally and also insidiously mixed into my flesh and blood. Naming this experience is coupled with my intense vulnerability to being rejected by African people — the very race of people to which I turn (however unrealistically) for unconditional acceptance and understanding. The pain is felt when the sheer existence and/or acknowledgement of my upbringing in a European family — and whatever access to economic privilege, wealth or power I may have by virtue of my blood = whiter appearance, European upbringing — becomes grounds for distrust or rejection in the African community.

For centuries, African people have been strewn across the globe as cheap labour for the privilege of many. Along the way we have mixed with other races with resulting ranges in appearance and skin colour. The particular mixing of Africans with Europeans everywhere has contributed to conflict among ourselves — in our own communities, by fuelling that competition of self-hatred and self-effacement because some of us continue to measure ourselves and seek acceptance by the white man's standard.

Here, issues of race and class go hand-in-hand. On the range from "white" skin through light skin through brown skin and dark skin to Black, each has its particular equation with passing; being privileged (racially, economically, socially); holding power; buying in; selling out; moving up; forgetting my roots; acting superior; walking and succeeding on the backs of... and I know the list goes on.

History shows how Africans and other people of colour mixed with Europeans, have used whatever privilege this mixing has brought to step on their sisters and brothers of colour, in the pursuit of personal gain. (As have people of colour who are not of any European descent, also contributed to the domination of their own peoples in this way.) Knowing this I understand that being "of colour" does not guarantee me the trust of others of colour automatically.

Though Europeans have virtually everything to answer for in recent history, in order to even begin to *earn* the trust of non-Europeans, people of colour ourselves, including those of us with European descent, must continue to analyze our history and *ourselves*. It is time we women of colour take conscious and active measures to gain the life-sustaining trust and solidarity of our communities — of other women of colour. As part of my contribution to undoing the destructive whitewashing to which we are all exposed, I know that I must begin with myself. I know that I have to demonstrate, sometimes differently than non-European-mixed people of colour, an awareness of class and race and power privilege.

As a woman of mixed African and European descent, I am confronted in adulthood with the opposing behaviours of actively *or* passively siding with the power of European supremacy, ownership and cultural domination — and *actively* siding with the promotion, nurturing and survival of African peoples, and other people of colour. But in this land, in these times, I do not have a choice in this. It's not just Black and white. If I do anything short of vigilantly embracing my African identity — consciously, wholeheartedly and without illusions about African realities — then I may be swept away, co-opted, consumed and sucked into the European power structure, culture and mindset which preaches that because of my African blood, I am inferior = sub-human = exploitable = disposable = ...

Identifying as an African woman, as a daughter of African people and African ancestors, I vow that I am not and will not become part of any value system or mindset which seeks to crush other races through its way of life, by imposing its beliefs and its needs not on its own people, but on all the other peoples of this earth.

In claiming my African identity, and as I participate in struggles for justice and liberation from various oppressions, I will need to communicate the detangling I have done: that out of sheer necessity to remain sane and alive, I have had to and will continue to embrace — with courage — the challenge to understand the race, class, power and gender dynamics which gave birth to me and which are my mixed experience. And in return I will expect no less than an equal amount of recognition and understanding from other Africans and people of colour — of the seemingly impossible, the sometimes confusing, and the always painful contradictions of being African mixed with European. For those of us who embody Black and white, holding the privilege of access (in varying degrees) to European status in one hand can never balance the cultural and racial annihilation which is held in the other.

Africans of European descent, need to stop obscuring our experiences into that one, monolithic, fictional and stereotypic "Black experience." We must no longer be self-censoring or partially absent.

As people of colour now write our own history books, it is time to acknowledge the revolutionary work of Africans, Asians, and indigenous peoples who have been mixed genetically and culturally with Europeans, and how this has affected their individual and the collective consciousness of race and class. Recognizing the struggles of those of us who are mixed, including those who resist buying into the European power structure, becomes essential to dismantling some of the betrayals of power which divide people of colour and our struggles. Both despite and because of the contradictions of our ancestry, people of mixed race have become some of the most vigilant and revolutionary leaders working for social change in local and international communities.

Of Africans, Bob Marley is a most outstanding example. Before he began his musical life in the tenements of urban Kingston, he grew up with his African mother in rural Jamaica, who had become pregnant by a European sailor. But it is likely that few non-Jamaicans know this fact about Marley, and how this circumstance, among others in his life, contributed to the development of his conscious and revolutionary creativity. Which person today who knows Bob Marley's music, can deny what the wisdom and prophesy of his lyrics have meant to African people and people of colour working for change everywhere?

The day I read that Bob Marley was of *African and European* parentage, was the day I began to lay down my burden of being mixed with European blood and feeling "unauthentically" Black — "unauthentically" African. I decided that I would burn the whip with which I beat myself for not being pure enough. I stopped biting my tongue every time I wanted and *needed* to say, "As a Black woman... As an African woman..."

From this one "small" piece of information about Bob Marley, and about many other people of colour since then, I have learned that if a mixed African names her European ancestry, it doesn't have to automatically imply division, but can in fact help empower those of us, like myself, who have been cut off from our heritage, from our communities and from ourselves. Whether it happens through the destructive pursuit and use of white power privilege, through the violence and brainwashing of isolation, or through daily feelings of self-loathing, being "closet-case half-breeds" will forever do a disservice to us and to all people of colour and the changes we are trying to bring about.

Holding this perspective, I find that I'm able to gain more confidence and more respect about being whole in who I am and in how I live. This means revealing, discussing and having a strong presence behind the intricacies of my African lesbian identity. By writing about my experiences and the huge implications of being of mixed race within these, I know I am going beyond the Black and white reductions of mainstream life.

Hopefully, I am challenging and surpassing the limitations of the closed-minded, short-sighted thinking that thrives on keeping people, especially African, Asian and Indigenous peoples, separated from the truths — the real, profound truths — about our contexts, our backgrounds and our histories. By undertaking an unlimited and unending analysis of my world, I am seeking to expose for myself and others, that only when we are willing to see how many pieces there are to the puzzle of our lives, will we see the patterns of power behind the destruction and exploitation of human history. And seeing these, being real in these, will free us up to contribute in solidarity to that which keeps us going strong — the colours of our humanity.

Myriam Chancy

Je suis un Nègre

I.

"He literally jumped
right out of his skin"
I think as the Catholic schoolgirls
sitting on the bus
behind me giggle at the sight
of a man, yellow with age,
passing over the seat next
to mine to stand in the aisle
propping himself up on a cane
"right out of his skin"
I will say later talking about
racism in this country
to an Uncle visiting
But I forget to say
that when this happens
I look out the window
pretend not to notice
as if I am watching
the moving road
and that all I see
is my own reflection
my black hair, brown eyes,
a tear refusing

to roll down a chestnut
cheek made transparent
by the sunlight

II.

"Je suis un nègre"
my Uncle jokes
knowing this is not all he is
negre, nigger
language blurs
We are branded by words
not of our making
I remember, at age four,
the neighbour woman who said to me
one day: "Je veux devenir nègre
come toi" bronzing
in the sun
who refused to let me in
her house to play with her daughter
Now in my twenties I try
to laugh with my Uncle
who is also old enough
to begin to take such things
lightly, and as we chuckle
I only remember myself, then,
a foreigner
wanting to shed that skin
to be no colour at all
like rain

Yolanda Retter

Quincentennial Blues
(An observer writes in the first person)

It's five hundred years since the invasion.
Colonizer minds siguen buscando fresh sacrifices.
Aqui estoy,
no longer the maiden on the high altar of the Aztecas,
but the brown lesbian on the low water bed of
a white colonizer butch.

cortez
alvarado
pizarro
coronado
they now have names like
linda
judy
kathy
susan

They are not looking for gold,
but they are prospecting
at the periphery of our colour circles,
where the more susceptible ones li(e)ve.

Malcriada shouted at the white girls:
"If you're gonna lie down with us,
you'd better learn to stand up for us!"

So later, when they said,
you must report Malcriada's latest outrage to the
authorities,
(they had their own agendas),
I meekly tucked a white butch under each arm,
like crutches they carried me to the authorities,
and I reported Malcriada, my misbehaving
compañera of colour.

In flashback, I fall into the sexual abuse abyss (again).
I lie, cheat and do not heal.
"The history of colonization is a record
of betrayal, of lies, and deceits."[1]
I come from a long tradition/tra(d)ición.[2]
Sigo corriendo.
No soy mi brown father.
I'm not my white mother.
I take on the colour of whomever I'm with.

I talk brown,
I sleep white.
(More of us do, than don't).

Malcriada said: "una palabra lo describe: `Blancarota'."[3]

---

1. bell hooks, *Talking Back*, South End Press, 1989
2. *tradición* = tradition, *tración* = treason
3. *bancarota* = bankrupt, *blanca* = white, *rota* = broken

Are we home yet?

return to self and cultures

Diana Abu-Jaber

The Honeymooners

I SPENT A CHILDHOOD SWEPT IN DREAMS, SURROUNDED BY THE long skirt of nuns, the eleagic sound of *The Honeymooners* drifting from the windows, and Jackie Gleason was the man in the moon. Jackie Gleason reminded me of my father who was always gone, endlessly working as a janitor, a security guard, a dock loader. He would come home so late, when all the world had gone away, and sometimes I would wake, the thin dime of light from my bedroom door swinging over my face as he looked at me, their voices murmuring, the sound of the TV, rooms away in the night, the sound of safety.

Or he was away for weeks, months, long nights of watching movies in bed with my mother, through a film of sleep. He was away in the Old Country, Jordan, getting a job, getting a place for us to stay. At school one day, everyone said the Martians were coming, *for real,* and my mother let me sleep with her that night. I still remember my dreams filled with pale, descending saucers, dropping from a sky like a bowl of milk.

Madame Boop, my grammar school French teacher, brought my father in for Show and Tell. "Diana's father is a *Moslim*," she said. "That means he does not believe in God. He believes in Mohammed."

My father had no specific response to this statement. He entertained questions from the class on everything from machetes to family curses. "We Moslims call everybody else infidels," he told my second grade class. "You have so many gods, the father, the son, the aunt, the uncle..."

The class was a terrific success, without hitches, until his leavetaking. Dad made a sign against the evil eye over the class, blessed our teacher's hand, then said, "So long kids, farewell Madame Boob."

Arabs don't have the letter "p" in their alphabet. My father immediately read his phonetic error in all of our faces, then tried, "Madame Poop." Finally, as he backed toward the door, we settled for Madame Poob.

We moved from New York to New Jersey to the West Bank to Jordan, all by the time I was seven. In Amman, we lived on the first floor of a stone building surrounded by a garden of figs and sunflowers and great mint plants. My younger sister Suzy and I would pick the glossy mint leaves and my parents steeped them in tea and sugar. We bought hot rings of bread from boys who carried wide trays of it on their heads, walking up the streets. We got fresh berries from women who carried them bound up in their skirts. And we stopped vendors whose donkeys carried vats of hot butter and corn on the cob on their backs.

At the mosque in the Arab quarter of Jerusalem, 1967, an old man performing ritual oblutions before prayer, stopped us. "If you take them in there, you'll never see your wife and daughters again."

I sat down in the white dust and cried. I'd heard him clearly. Suzy, who at four, spoke no Arabic, stared at me quizzically. Monica was still just a baby curled along our mother's shoulder. Then the imam came out of the mosque and took us in. We carried our shoes, tiptoed across the great praying room and looked out of the minaret at the city, its light-pricked edges glowing in the dusk. Everything inside the mosque, walls and ceilings and columns, were engraved, blasted with words, scrawled with the great Arabic calligraphy in banners of gold and ivory, turquoise and obsidian: "*Il hum du'illah,* All praise to God, there is no God but God; *Allahuaqbar,* God is great," painted, chiseled words, so stretched and dizzying and slashing, swirling bold, dashing the length of entire rooms, I felt them pressing on me, weighing my chest, I couldn't breathe.

Every night of the year, I heard the muezzin climb to his window in the minaret and cry out his loud, melancholy song to the faithful, his voice like the very curtain of evening, calling sunset down over the world; his voice the matrix of loneliness, of amber stillness.

In Jordan, I first understood that I and all living things must die.

Toward the end of our stay there in 1968, the sky began flickering with strange lights at night. All the neighbourhood stood out on the street, staring, pointing. A man in a car would drive through, shouting, "Get back in your houses, lock the doors."

No one would move.

My mother and I listened to daily radio reports, broadcast by Palestinians: "I, Ibrahim Al Mansour, testify that I am alive and well in the city of Ramallah... the city of Nazareth... the village of Salt. I send greetings to my family across the bridge and pray to Allah to hear your voices again soon."

There were soldiers in the streets who spoke a language I was just beginning to understand. I knew when they were talking about food or their families. Once, one of them stopped me because my shoe laces were loose and he tied them for me so tightly, I thought they would never come loose again.

Then I was eleven and we returned to America. I never knew why we moved from one place to another, only that we did. Movement was a fact of existence, restless flight from home to home. My father worked as a reform school guard, a rug salesman, and in a glue factory. I myself have not made a home in one place for more than two-and-a-half years.

Some of the greatest struggles of my childhood were over my gender: whether I should be married, at age fourteen, to my fifteen-year- old cousin Hassan, whether I should be allowed to go to dances, to sleep-over parties, to movies with my girlfriends — I wasn't. My father told me when I was fifteen (and still single), "Never trust men, you don't know how their minds work. The *horrible* things they are thinking about."

I just assumed boys thought about sex.

I dreamed about being a crew member on *Star Trek*. I never loved the macho heroes, I always fell for the robot, the logic-driven alien, the mild, cold-blooded android.

Sometimes I had dreams about bombs; bombs lighting the horizon, bombs opening a whorl in the sky that sucked everyone in, and I would be thinking: now I'll know what it is. What death is. Now it's going to happen. Now.

Now, the first question I hear at almost every reading I give is, how autobiographical is your work? I especially get this question if there's a lot of blood, mayhem, and havoc in the story.

I say a lot of things in response. But honestly, the answer is that I don't know. As a graduate student, I had dreams where I saw in absolute detail the faces of corpses — faces that I'd swear I have never seen before. They are vaguely green, dissolved, they lay in what I recognize as the white dust of the Middle East.

My mother has green eyes; she is American. I have her eyes.

So what happens to the past, the invisible dreams, when people can't see it in the grain of your skin or the deeps of your eyes? In my family, the first generation boys receive Arabic names: Tarik, Nezar, Nasser, Ahem, Zaid, Tile, Adel, Maged, Munir, Salih. The girls are named: Linda, Pamela, Judy, Loretta, Rose, Monica, Suzanne, Diana. We are claimed and not claimed by the Old Country.

My middle name is Ghassan. So are my two younger sisters'. Ghassan is my father's first name — we are branded like property. Ghassan means "Jumping up and down."

Now that my father is retired from hospital administration — a job that would never promote him beyond the fact of his Arabness — he talks incessantly about moving back to Jordan. My mother tells me that he plans to put the house on the market and then fly back this August. I say, don't let him! Tell *him* to go, but you keep the house. I say, trying to be psychologist rational, how do you feel about this? Where do you want to live?

She shrugs, Catholic-stoic, I see her mother in her face. She says, maybe I'll go live in a convent.

It seems that there must be a certain age for everyone when parents turn inevitably heartbreaking, when the time isn't enough, when the things you would like to say, to ask, remain there, behind your eyes, and you can't quite get them out. I have a friend, a fine writer, who told me she didn't begin to write until her parents died when she was in her forties. A Norwegian friend of mine and I have theorized that first generation women may sometimes have more ease in writing than others because our parents aren't fluent in the language that we're writing in.

And now I dream in Arabic, long conversations between myself and others in my first language. The words that I learned to refuse when I was eleven, and again at fifteen, come back to me now. And there are other scenes, my relatives calling me during the Persian Gulf War: come back home! Americans hate you, don't you understand? My father saying, we will all move back home where my grandchildren will dance around my knees. The swastika someone slid under my office door that year. The call from the FBI, for the *protection* of Arab-Americans, our house broken into, someone scrawling "fucking A-rab" on the kitchen floor, the bed slept in and every door and window open to the sky.

If that's the way it's to be, then I'll keep the doors and windows open. I'm tired of translation, family secrets and public, pleasant deception. One of my closest friends Deborah and I are forced to dissemble, we tell my father her *grandmother* is Jewish, nothing more. I won't mention the marriages, lovers, and other alliances destroyed by politics. I plan to let my various countries in; I will go visit my father if he moves back. But I will live in the places I have learned, New York, Nebraska, Oregon, and I will try to speak again in the original languages.

Nona Saunders

tapestry I

daddy said
grandma
collected rags
cut strips of bright colour
from worn out things

he drew pictures
for her
on flour bags   potato sacks:
of a woman
        a child asleep in her arms
        bent over green garden rows
        reining in a billow of white sheets

grandpa
made a hook
that didn't blister
her hands so much

with a hook and rags and bags
she made rugs
two dollars for a small one
maybe five for a large

daddy said
almost every house
in town
had one of Lena's beautiful rugs

rich people
hung her life
on their living room walls

tapestry II

mama reads
the clothes
my brown heart wears
and weeps
her white tears.

forty years'
accumulation
of rags.

my fingers
knit weave
dream shreds
hope tatters
yard upon yard
of shame
of fear tangled tears
love threads
anger knots
knit weave knit weave.

it must be
finished
put together
or i

will shiver
from the cold
a lone wind
dread
alone wind.

i bind
the threads
create
a coat
of colours
know
at last
who i am.

mama, don't cry.
don't be ashamed.
grandma
too
made tapestries.

Carole Gray

Heritage

THE ISSUE OF HERITAGE HAS ALWAYS BEEN A TOUCHY ONE IN my family. Both of my parents were born on the Prairies, as were all eight of the children. We were a large, Catholic, working-class family. I am the fourth eldest, fifth youngest child. I am probably the whitest of all the children, though my hair and eyes have always been dark. As I get older my eyes are losing their chocolate shade, and my hair is rapidly turning white.

As a child, I would sometimes ask why two of my sisters were so brown. Were they adopted? No, they weren't. The family resemblance was/is too strong to deny. And what about the "patches" so many of us have? The darker children have light patches, and for myself, I have at least one dark patch that I have spent hours, as a child, trying to scrub off. The reason was something vague about "skin pigment", "dark Celts" and the "nigger-in-the-wood-pile" smile, nudge, nudge.

The only person who ever spoke of us being of Native American descent was my father's only sister; mainly when she was drunk, and when there were no other adults present. My father, with his raven-black hair and red-brown skin, denied it flat out. My mother had no idea at all. I remember running barefoot through the trees and fields on my aunt's farm. Searching out the fresh, steaming cow pies to sink my feet into and feel the manure ooze between my toes. Lying in the long grass, carefully pulling out the centre stalk, chewing and eating the pale end of the grass. The part that had been safely wrapped in the outer blades of grass. Sometimes I would be lucky and find that special type that was so sweet to chew and suck on. I would continue on my way, sometimes

318

with my younger sisters, sometimes alone. Running as fast as I could across the barnyard, arriving breathless and laughing at the back door of my aunt's house. She'd come out and stand with her hands on her hips laughing at us all grubby, beaming and breathless. She'd shake her head, her wild black hair resisting all her attempts to tame it. "You little buggers!" she'd say with affection, "It's the Indian in you that makes you act that way. Now go get washed up and come in for supper." The smell of cooking food wafted out after her. We'd sit on the step, drop our shoes on the ground beside us, and find sticks to scrape the shit off our feet with.

Some years later, I am visiting my aunt again. Most of my family has moved back to her little prairie town after our mother left. I had followed a few months later than the rest. One of my sisters and I were sitting in the kitchen with our Aunt, drinking coffee and listening to her stories. She was making white sauce to put the peas in for supper. She told us about how once, before they got the new store, she'd stashed some money in the fire box on the old stove. They hadn't used it for ages, and she didn't want our uncle to know she had this cash. Out she went to do the chores, and to her shock when she returned there was our uncle, warming himself by the fire box. She said she ran over to the stove and opened the door, hoping to save some of her stash. I can't remember if she was able to save any of it — seems to me she said she was too late. And very disappointed! We all laughed. Our uncle had thought she'd gone mad! She told a good story. I'm not sure if it was me or my sister that asked her if we were Indian. She paused, drew a long deep breath, and said yes. She got a wistful look on her face, and she said, "Momma... she was so beautiful. She was a halfbreed, and her Momma was a beautiful Indian princess." I found the princess bit hard to swallow, but by the look on my aunt's face I could see that her Grandma really was a beautiful Indian princess to her. I'll probably never know what status she had really held, or what Nation she was from. Finally I had been told. In those softly spoken words of my aunt, yes.

319

Bernardine Evaristo

Letters from London

To my Father Who Is Nigerian and a Fighter

I DO NOT KNOW WHAT DREAMS CARRIED YOU BY BOAT FROM LAGOS to Liverpool over forty years ago. I do know if you have ever returned. When you first arrived here you were not welcomed. Doors were repeatedly slammed in your face. I wonder how this affected your lively, hopeful, young Self?

You met my mother and courted her. The first (and last) time you walked her home, her mother came rushing to the garden gate in a panic, waving at you to go away in case the neighbours saw you. In spite of fierce opposition, you married and in your wedding photo your face is plump and happy. You fathered eight of us children and worked like blazes to support your family. Your wife and children always came first. You were so tired when you came home from work that you had dinner, switched on the news and promptly fell asleep. You didn't talk of responsibility, you lived it.

Back home you had been an amateur boxer. Here you did not turn the other cheek. When people made your colour a problem, you dealt with them. You sometimes lost work because you stood your ground, but you kept your integrity. You took the shots for us. You opened doors for us. I am so proud of you.

The Lagos you left behind is now a fast and furious city. You would not recognize it as your childhood garden. You have sunk roots deep into the British earth. Daddy, as you age the flesh moulds onto the bones of your face, sculptured. The story it tells is that for you home and homeland are not one and the same.

Love XXXX

To my Mother Who Is White and Made Black Babies

In a photograph of you as a child in 1930s London, you are playing with a little Black doll. As a teenager in a convent school run by the Daughters of Jesus, you wanted to be a missionary in Africa. You didn't go there but you met Daddy and gave birth to mixed-race children. Personally, I think it had been on the cards since you were three.

Your family were against your marriage. They said you would ruin your life, become a social outcast, your children would be born inferior. But your religion supported you, for what they told you contradicted God's teachings. You stood your ground. You were a devout Roman Catholic girl and you decided to have a large family because it meant that you would enable lots of souls to be saved in heaven.

It wasn't easy raising eight children on little money, but you budgeted and managed. It was hard work — all those mouths to feed, nappies to wash, infants to rock to sleep, stockings to fill at Christmas and sixpences under pillows when baby teeth fell out.

Today when you say you did not give us a Black identity I say to you: "Give yourself a break, don't you think you had enough to do!" You gave me a mother's love and I grew up strong, secure and proud to be me. I learned Black pride later, so did you. You have grown with your children. You have been a dutiful daughter, dutiful wife, dutiful mother — now you are discovering Self — enjoy!

Love XXXX

To my Grandmother Who Never Left Suburbia

When your only daughter fell in love with my father you went up the wall. For you it was the most inconceivable nightmare; with one fell swoop all your dreams were crushed. You made it your mission to stop the marriage. In post-war Britain it simply wasn't the thing to do, and after all, what on *earth* would your neighbours say!

The first child born to my parents was the light brown of girls in adverts today. Not caucasian but definitely not *too* negroid looking. You were shocked, relented, and held the child. How could you not love this beige delight? The colour of the grandchild had won the day. Battle over. No dead. No victories.

You loved us all and we took turns visiting you on Sundays. You always wanted the best for us. I loved you because you were sweet, kind and had always been there. But nana, you were born in 1904 and your view of the world was Victorian. The perimeters of your life were set before your birth, for you lived a prim morality which consumed you. Your Self was probably ironed and starched out of you in childhood. The words rebellion, non-conformity, passion, were as alien to you as the word penis which you only discovered in your eightieth year. It had always been called 'down below.'

A year after your death, your first great-grandchild is born. Blonde hair, blue eyes, ivory skin. Your identical image. You would have *adored* her. The line continuing as you in your heart of hearts wanted it to be — white. My father names her Iyabo which, in the tradition of Yoruba, means Mother Returns.

Love XXXX

To my Niece Iyabo Who Is Four-and-a-Quarter

I hope that you will grow up proud to have African blood in you, that you will embrace all parts of yourself and love them equally. You can pass, easily; let's hope you never want to because your ancestral past will catch up with you in the end and you'll wonder where you lost your Self.

You see, when I was growing up, the images of our people in books and films were untrue and derogatory. I was taught that our people were semi-human savages who were lucky that Europeans brought us civilization. Nothing could be further from the truth.

There are things they did not teach me in school — about the great achievements of Africans who developed science, medicine, numbers, writing, astrology. There were advanced civilizations, huge empires, thriving cities, the first libraries, brilliant scholars, ingenious doctors. The history is rich and fascinating. It is also empowering knowledge, which is why it has been suppressed. You will learn all this because I will teach you.

Little Iyabo, you are already saying that your dolly Pandy is a bit too dark and that you only like straight hair. When you are older we'll talk some more and I'll get out my history books and we can go on voyages of discovery. The world you are growing up into is a vast planet. Explore it. It is yours.

From Auntie who loves you. XXXX
P.S. I think Pandy's a *lovely colour*.

To my Cousin Olufemi Who Sent her Boys Back Home

When you flew into London from Lagos over sixteen years ago you were a young bride in love. You worked to support your husband through college, he got his PhD and buggered off. You were shattered but pulled yourself together to look after your three children.

But a mother's love was not enough. Your two boys, only ten and twelve years old, were falling by the wayside. They were getting into serious trouble in school (expulsion), with the police (arrests), and on the street (mischief-making). You tried to control them but the odds were stacked against you. You could not bring them 'round. You gave your Self to God. All your free time, and your children's, was spent within the walls of your gospel church. Still they went astray. They were breaking your heart.

Eventually you made the hard decision to send them home to your parents. The choice was that or to see them destroyed in a society that does not care for them. Now they are at school in Lagos where discipline is tough. They are in the care of the community and hopefully will grow to be responsible, thoughtful, self-motivated and educated young men.

Femi, you were never taught to raise children on your own. You were brought up as part of a huge extended family where a child's upbringing is a shared responsibility. You were then forced into a situation where you not only had to do the job alone, but you are in a culture you feel alienated from. You miss your boys badly, but what choice did you have?

Love XXXX
P.S. Please stop trying to find a husband for me!!

Letter to Myself. I Have the Wanderlust

You are a Londoner. You like fish and chips and *Eastenders*. You speak English fluently, of course. You are also learning Yoruba. You like England, warts-and-all. You were born here, went to school here, live and love here. You know this place. Your father's nationality is also your identity. To you Africa is a spiritual homeland and you spend time there. Your African Self is intact and always growing.

You are European. Indeed you have often travelled across Europe by car. It is old ground. Africa's ancestors laid claim to Europe for thousands of years. Europe has been home to a host of Black people from the Grimaldis to the Twa in Scandinavia, Moors in Southern Europe, Huns in Germany, Libyans on Crete, Black clans in Scotland, King Goremund of Ireland, Septimus Severus, Coleridge-Taylor, Lucy Negro, Hannibal, Pushkin, Seacole, Charlotte Sophia, Dumas, three African popes... oh yes, this is well-travelled land.

Today's frontiers are man-made, marking out territories, proof of ownership, with a limited life-span. Migration is and always will be. The land owns itself in the end.

You are always seeking, searching, exploring. It is the wanderlust which drives you to travel beyond false boundaries. You will not be kept out or restricted to ghettos. You say that borders are doors to be opened. Barriers are gates to pass through. Today people are given passports as proof of identity. It is the entrance fee. Your passport is European, and you use it.

Signing off
Bernardine Evaristo

Ngaire Blankenburg

Halifax[1]

I love it here
black limbs
shaking with laughter
or sorrow
or righteous indignation
breasts and bums as full as lips
and the smells —
Oh the smells
pervasive acrid sweat
meaty body smells
bursting out of masking
floral deodorants or
elegant proper musks

no more questions
this time, the right assumptions
I am one of you
understanding many things
which I thought
were mine alone to bear
a glimpse of real, sensual, casual acceptance
erasing ever so slightly
the invisible lines of uneasy belonging.

---

[1] Halifax/Dartmouth has the largest black population in Canada.

Kukumo Rocks

Route to my Roots

MY NAME IS KUKUMO ROCKS. I AM AN AFRICAN ASIAN SCOTS woman. My father is from West Africa; Nigeria. He was born in Lagos and is from the Yoruba tribe. My mother is from Bombay, India where she was born. I chose my name because I wanted an identity I could own. In Yoruba, Kukumo means "This one will not die." I wanted to belong, to come out as black, as African, so people would immediately know, when I spoke my name, that I belonged somewhere, had roots, a connection. The decision to change my name felt scary, dangerous, but it also felt strong, political, powerful, peaceful, at home, 'me,' being forged every time I wrote the words Kukumo. This journey to be able to write this was not an easy one and it is not finished yet.

It began at the age of fourteen. I began to question myself, who am I, black or white? Although I was black, I lived with all white people till the age of ten. Therefore, I was confused and nobody acknowledged my colour. I came to the conclusion that if both my parents are black then I must be also. I felt a great sense of relief. I experienced much racism as a child but I didn't consciously think about my identity. My only wishes were to survive — to survive the hurts, that I wasn't different, and that the images of me were not only of slaves.

As I grew older, I began to think again about my identity. The decision I reached was to call myself a Scot who happened to be black. As I knew the Scots' culture, it eased the confusion within me and the isolation I experienced daily. I found myself clowning around to be accepted, to stop the names. I felt forced to act in this way as often as

327

my experience was to be treated like a second class citizen. I thought there must be something wrong with me but my body worked perfectly well, it must then be my colour that is wrong. This nagging feeling of being wrong, unacceptable, stayed with me. I became shy but played the fool afraid to be me, the black person, the different person. As I began to listen to music and the radio in my twenties I was aware of the impact of civil rights had gone right past me. In this all white working-class town, it never touched my life. Only when I heard the Motown sound filter into my life i.e. Black is Beautiful. I thought (*yes!*) at last, a positive image of me — Diana Ross, Angela Davis. I then conceived of myself as a black woman who just happened to be Scots. It was a very freeing experience and I sang the song *Young Gifted and Black* many times over. It strengthened me and made me happy.

But still something was missing. I had no black friends, saw few black people, knew nothing of my cultural roots, therefore had no positive reinforcement of my identity. Isolation was my friend.

In my late twenties I began to study, read books that explained how I felt. They called it prejudice, discrimination, racism, alienation. I voraciously read Angela Davis and George Jackson. I began to understand, to intellectualize my thoughts, but the hunger to be recognized, to be accepted, led me to consider how to achieve this. Meaning I would have to meet more black people and learn about and visit Africa and India. The difficulty would be the lack of black people around and my internalized racism, as I still saw my white friends as better.

After university, I got a job in Community Education as a development worker in a Black Women's Centre. The women who used this service were from Africa, India, Pakistan, China and South America. Fantastic, I thought.

Now I began to make black friends. I began to feel more complete. The journey was not easy and being accepted was difficult. Some of the African women said "You're not really African, you're Scottish."

The Indian women said "You're British." I felt rejected. Often in Asian-owned shops the owners thinking I was Indian would speak to me, ask about my parents. When they knew I was mixed, the conversation would stop, they would lose interest.

I felt hurt, rejected, lonely. I felt like a "nowhere" person. Where do I belong? The British say "Nigger go home to your own country" and people from my parents' homelands say "You don't belong." Result — confusion, anger, frustration. I wanted to hit back, but at whom.

I still tried to connect to Africa as I was brought up by my father and I looked more African. It was then that I decided to make the political statement changing my name to Kukumo. People refused to call me this, but I insisted. It made me African, so I thought. Other Nigerians recognized it and they began to accept me much more. The African and Asian women wanted me to belong to each group. I was very torn. I went with the African women and felt guilty of denying my Indian side, but it was less confusing to me. Then, when I got to know the women from India, I began to feel I belonged. This frightened me. I couldn't cope then with being both in my heart. The women began to see the benefit of me being both, I helped them break down the barriers between them. They said I was the future. This made me so proud of being both and less isolated. I realized that my mixed heritage was of benefit.

I began to be asked to perform at African benefits for the ANC and for Africa Day celebrations. This meant so much to me! Africans saying to me, your words and your poetry speak to us of our struggle. I nearly cried to hear this. Acceptance — *yes!*

Invited to many parties, I still felt the outsider, knowing nothing of the African culture. I knew I needed to meet African Asian Black British like me. Can I *ever* find *anybody like me?*

The future is moving to London where lots of black people live, to steep myself in the black experiences. This is my next move to feel complete. My journey must also take me to India and Africa. I long and am desperate for this experience. To laugh, to talk with my African aunts would be bliss (I will go soon). I need to learn where some of my personality traits come from. Already I have noticed that my poetry is in the oral African Tradition.

I also need to go to India to find my complete heritage. I know my mother was an Indian classical dancer and that I *love* to dance. Therefore, in my journey I have discovered I am *not* odd or different.

I am a Black African Asian Scot woman. Still searching and seeking to be complete, to put the pieces together. It has been a painful journey. It still is a route that hurts. I hope when it is completed the pain will lessen. That I will have accepted and understood myself culturally, emotionally and intellectually. Less importantly, I will be accepted by others for being me Kukumo Rocks Black African Asian Scots Woman Poet.

Pam Bailey

Naming and Claiming Multicultural Identity

> Where are we moored?
> What are the bindings?
> What behooves us? *(Rich, p. 12)*

WHAT ARE MY MOORINGS? BEING BROUGHT UP IN AN upwardly-mobile (working- to middle-class) "traditional" family with whiteskin privilege and no knowledge of my past. A family of Chef Boy-ar-dee "italian" and canned "chop suey." A family that ignored and denied the richness of its diverse cultural heritage. A rather oppressive family with only the barest semblance of tolerance for differences. Most of this occurring in the very segregated south, u.s.a...

...remembering ...*in sixth grade, my mother refusing to drive me to a school play that i was in because it was in the "bad" (read:black/ african american) part of town... she said she didn't want anything to happen to her new car, but i went to school there every day.*

But is my past really where i am moored? Perhaps it is more what binds me — that persistent, nagging, racist, heterosexist bigot that hides in the back of my mind, keeping me from finding the "i" who i want to be, who i want to become. My past is the bindings that hold me down and prevent me from flying to a place where i want to dwell. A past that restricts my movements, calling me back into the oppressive patterns it would be oh so easy to fall into.

Yet, do I know what and who I want to be? Isn't that the whole question?

So i am casting about for new moorings. Some of my moorings i have found — my lesbianism, my struggle against and unlearning of the bigotry that i have inherited and been taught, my life as an activist academic, my radical dyke separatism — other moorings i am not so sure of. Specifically, how do i moor myself, if at all, on my multicultural heritage?

At this point, i do not know what it means for me to claim my identity as a womon of irish, german, french, hungarian and native american/cherokee heritage. On which of these identities, if any, should i moor myself? Is the claiming of some of these identities more "acceptable" (and according to whom?) than claiming others? Is saying that i am irish, for example, less problematic than saying that i am cherokee? To what extent should my whiteskin privilege be factored into the problem? I have grown up with this privilege, but at the expense of not knowing the full richness of my family history.

...remembering ...as a girl, bragging to my friends that i was descended from royalty because my great-grandmother was a "cherokee princess". Now i know that this was a false claim, a claim that could only be made from the ignorance and prejudice of the eurocentric view. But i still wonder... what truth is there to be found in this statement? Was my great-grandmother part of the governing group of the time? My ignorance about cherokee history and culture, as well as a lack of information about my great-grandmother, leaves me without an answer.

What behooves me? I often wonder if my desire to claim my multicultural identity (specifically my cherokee heritage) stems from disaffection with white society and the "great white way." Am i asserting my cherokee past to distance myself from the crimes whites have committed against those they (we?) consider to be "different" or "inferior"? But i have/had whiteskin privilege and all the benefits that arise from the dubious honour of being considered white. Benefits gained through the oppression and exploitation of others. As such, i am (at least in part) responsible for the oppression that happens in american society. Consequently, to distance myself from the actions of the rulers of america is, on the one hand, extremely irresponsible. However, it might also be the best thing that i could do, to not buy into the power structure and perhaps weaken it a little with my refusal.

One possible solution would be for me to renounce my whiteskin privilege. In fact, this has — in a sense — already happened. In coming out as a lesbian, i have lost most of the claims to privilege and power that i might have had in this society. This loss, however, is contingent upon my being visible as a lesbian, a difficult task in a society that often refuses to admit that lesbians even exist. In addition, none of this addresses the problem of inter-racial dynamics and racism within lesbian communities. Furthermore, i can reclaim my whiteskin privilege any time i want by simply hiding my lesbianism.

Another way that i could attempt to distance myself from my whiteskin privilege would be for me to accentuate my native american ancestry. But how would i accomplish this? Grow my hair long and wear braids? (But that goes against my lesbian-feminist principles.) Start wearing turquoise jewellery and moccasins? (But jewellery is too expensive for a student's budget.) Get a deeper tan? (But i don't want to risk skin cancer.) All of these possibilities are unsatisfactory at best, for they all, in one way or another, buy into the racist, homogeneous stereotypes that europeans have imposed on diverse group of peoples. In addition, they also ignore the fact that i am more than cherokee, and that i have little knowledge of what it means to be cherokee.

Perhaps the best way for me to renounce my whiteskin privilege would be for me to refuse to perpetuate it. I can, and have, resolved to stop myself and others when we are being racist and oppressive. I have also begun the process of unlearning my racism. In recognizing that i have this power that american society has given me by virtue of my apparently white skin, i must also be able to displace and undermine it.[1] I must continue to find ways in which i can confront and destroy racism. While these actions do not stop others from treating me as "white," there is little i can do about how others treat me, except to continuously work on racism in all of its manifestations. If the concept of whiteskin privilege or, better yet, the entire concept of privilege is eliminated, having skin that is considered "white" will not be a power issue. (Although i feel that i must emphasize that i am *not* talking about the "melting pot.") Thus, while i don't have any say in the colour of my skin and very little say in how i was raised, i do have a say in how i conduct my life.

Another way that i could solve my dilemma over my identity would be for me to just give up this searching. However, if i were to deny my heritage, wouldn't i be falling in to the trap of the "american dream" — the dream (and it is only that) of assimilation and homogenization? To give up my quest would be to fall back into the pre-processed, pre-packaged whitebread (and white bred) world of homogeneity. If i abandon the questings and questionings about my identity, maybe i would be contributing to the destruction of those who may be my own people by eliminating one less instance of diversity.

Why is it that I have been concentrating on my native american identity? It is, after all, only one-eighth of my cultural identity (going on strict mathematical/genetic formulas). Why, for example, don't I find the claiming of my german heritage to be as problematic? The answer, I believe, is twofold. To begin with, I do find the claiming of all my identities problematic, it is just that I am more familiar with the other parts of my identity (due to the eurocentric nature of this society) than my cherokee heritage. Second, and connected to the first, all the other parts of my identity are part of the realm of whiteskin privilege. As such, the claiming of my irish, french, german and hungarian heritage does not involve the same problem and consequences as claiming my cherokee heritage.

But does a bunch of genetic material give me any right to claim a cultural identity? Or is it that i am perpetuating the role of the colonizer, claiming that which i really have no right to claim? (And who is it that decides on rights, anyhow?) Have i become yet another incarnation of the anthropologist that steals the coroma $q'epis$?[2] Is there a way for me to claim my heritage in a responsible manner? Maybe i can just say that there is a connection, a claim, because i feel that there is a connection.

...remembering ...*visit from my grandmother; she has unearthed some old photographs of my family, one of which is of my great-grandmother (cherokee) and great-grandfather (irish). As i look at the photo i am struck by the difference in size, he is about twice as large as she is (in height and weight). I look into the eyes of my great-grandmother and i can only wonder. Did you marry for love? Did you marry for survival? Were you forced into marriage? Were you raped? These questions, like many others, i have no answer to, for my family does not like to talk about our "jaded" past. I don't even know her name.*

However, for me to simply say that there is a connection because i feel one is to be much too solipsistic, not to mention irresponsible. For to leave identity completely in the hands of the individual opens one up too many problems. Under this solution, it is conceivable that a person could just walk into a given group and claim that she belonged there simply because she felt like it. (An event which is becoming all too common.) There has to be room for recognition and responsibility, a way for the group to say that an individual does not belong.

"Europeans did not listen to the souls of their dead... ancestor spirits (have) the answers."[3] So i am trying to listen to my ancestor spirits, *all* of my ancestors. In listening to them, i hear the call of my diverse cultural heritage. While i know that i am a far way from hearing all that they have to say, i do know that i am being drawn to explore and examine my multicultural identity in all of its richness.

There is yet another problem that needs to be considered in my questing towards my identities. As a radical separatist dyke, i have — at least in theory — separated from the values and the world of the patriarchy. Consequently, should i even concern myself with claiming cultures that are part of the male-dominated world? But to simply abandon my quest on the grounds that all cultures are part of the heteropatriarchy; to erase the existence of a matriarchal (perhaps even lesbian) irish/celtic past; to deny the fact that many native american tribes were based on equality for all, including homosexuals (although, as far as i can tell, this was not the case with the cherokees); to abandon all questings into the past of all my identities, (a quest which might uncover a few surprises) to simply reject all cultures without examination would be to erase the significant contribution that women have made in the formation and perpetuation of a given culture. Unlike Tashi (in Alice Walker's *Possessing the Secret of Joy*), i don't need to mutilate my body, accepting patriarchal, heterosexist definitions and strictures, in order to claim my identity and become part of my cultures. Instead, i can reject those parts which are unacceptable (homophobic, racist, sexist, etc.) and claim the parts that i find to be womon/lesbian-positive in a responsible, thinking manner. I will, like Tashi, avenge the deaths of my sisters at the hands of womon-hating societies and kill the *tsunga*, the circumciser. We have recognized that we can claim our heritages in a life-affirming, womon-positive manner.

> *my feet*
> *recognize*
> *no border*
>
> *no rule*
> *no code*
> *no lord* [4]

"We don't believe in boundaries. Borders... we pay no attention to what isn't real."[5]

The elimination of boundaries, divisions... recognition of the messyness and multiplicity of life. Perhaps in this recognition i can finally solve my questions of multicultural heritage. If i can see that there really is no division, i can begin to integrate all the parts of my selves. To travel the many paths that my life encompasses. *"Invent yourself a name."[6]* I will create my own reality, not in isolation, but in careful relation to all of my facets and concerns. What can i take that will help me to learn and grow? What can i bring and return to my cultures? Whatever i take (or maybe borrow?) it must be more than meaningless river stones bought at a spiritualists conference[7]. Like Trinh T. Minh-ha, i will conduct a careful "grafting of several cultures onto a single body — an acknowledgement of the heterogeneity of my own cultural background.[8]"

"Yaquis also understood that a person might need a number of names in order o conduct all of his or her earthly business."[9]

"I can't settle down with any single name, any single work."[10]

"[A]s soon as you move from the position of a named subject into the position of a naming subject, you also have to remain alive to the renewed dangers of arrested meanings and fixed categories — in other words, of occupying the position of a sovereign subject. "Non-categorical" thinking sees to it that the power to name be constantly exposed to its limits." (ibid. p. 173)

...remembering ...*as a child in elementary school, other children asking me "what are you?" "I'm american" was my simple (naive?) reply. "No, really," they said "what are you really?" I didn't have a reply*

337

for them. But should i have? How was i to name myself? How am i now to name myself?

My moorings, then, will include a recognition of my multicultural identity, but i must moor myself in a way that allows for change, for growth. Perhaps i can accomplish this growth by not having any bindings, anything that will hold me down and prevent me from moving. I also expect that in the future i will find other, different moorings, ones that will fit my newer self (whatever that may be). Even so, the moorings that i have, had, and will have will remain a part of who i am, dwelling in my memories and hopes. In the recognition of the potential fluidity of names/naming, as well as the power of names to constrict, i can begin to see that my past upbringing, while important in how it has shaped my life, is not the ruler of my destiny. I need to see that i can cast off the bindings of my past to find and create new moorings for myself.

So i will invent myself a name (or perhaps many names), a name that claims all of my identities in a conscientious, responsible manner, a name that includes my separation from the values of patriarchy, a name that acknowledges my past complicity in the oppression of others, but a name that also recognizes the wonderful possibilities that come from the being who i was/am/will be. This new name will not be an easy one, i do not expect it to be. It will also continue to change and grow. I will build my own stone hut[11], a many-roomed one centred around all of my moorings, working my way into villages, looking at my own oracles to see where i should be headed.

1. Trinh, p. 170
2. The *q'epis* are bundles of sacred textiles which symbolize and embody the coroma communities, called *ayllus*. Through the *q'epis*, the coromenos maintain their sacred relationship with their ancestors and are the focus of much of the ceremonial life in the *ayllus*. Many of these sacred garments were either stolen or illegally purchased from the coromenos by western collectors and merchants. The loss of the garment(s) is equated by the people with the kidnapping of the spirit of the ancestor(s) and has resulted in the disintegration of their community identity. On a positive note, the past few years have seen the gradual return of many of the sacred textiles. Taken from Susan Lobo, "The Fabric of Life," *Cultural Survival* (Summer, 1991), pp. 40—46.
3. Silko, p. 604
4. Alarcon, p. 15
5. Silko, p. 216
6. Silko, p. 216
7. Silko, p. 217
8. Trinh, p. 141
9. Silko, p. 227
10. Trinh, p. 146
11. Silko, p. 228

BIBLIOGRAPHY

Alarcon, Francisco. *Snake Poems.* San Francisco: Chronicle Books, 1992

Rich, Adrienne. *An Atlas of a Difficult World.*

Silko, Leslie Marmon. *Almanac of the Dead.* New York: Simon and Schuster, 1992.

Trinh T. Minh-ha. *Framer Framed.* New York: Routledge, 1992.

Walker, Alice. *Possessing the Secret of Joy.* New York: Harcourt Brace Jovanovich, 1992.

Maxine Hayman

Shortbread and Oolichan Grease

I GREW UP IN VANCOUVER — THAT IS TO SAY, I SPENT MOST OF MY physical life in Vancouver — where my father's family is from, but my heart and spirit were often two hundred miles up the coast in the little Indian village where my mother is from. My mother, a Kwakiutl Indian, married a third generation Scottish Canadian. Hence, I am a half breed and have been exposed to two cultures. I learned a lot about white cultures during visits with my paternal grandparents and plenty about native cultures during visits with my maternal grandparents. During these visits in my grandparents' homes I also experienced very different feelings.

The lessons with my white grandparents generally took place on Sunday afternoons when my sisters and I were dressed nicely, having just returned from Sunday school. The short drive across the Second Narrow's Bridge was full of warnings from our mother: act lady-like; children should be seen, not heard; speak only when spoken to; sit properly, no fighting; and above all, *act* lady-like. Consequently, by the time we arrived at Grandma and Grandpa's house on Cambridge Street, my sisters and I were not exactly ourselves and we were certainly not free to be children. Instead, we played the part of little ladies (like our mother) and sat with our knees together, said please and thank you, and answered politely *when* we were spoken to. In short, it was stifling and intimidating.

Sometimes it was frightening to be in the presence of Grandpa Hayman. He showed very little emotion and there were definitely no displays of affection. We, in turn, kept a respectful distance from him. Now and then he complained about the economic ruin that Canada was in because of the immigration of too many "Japs and Hindus." Because his racism was directed at immigrants, I remember hoping that he thought Indians like us were okay. Even so, I sensed my mother's discomfort when he spoke in this harsh and racist manner.

Visits with Grandpa were lessons to be endured in order to see Grandma Hayman, whom we truly enjoyed. We took delight in her offerings of oatmeal cookies, fruit cake, and melt-in-your-mouth shortbread accompanied by ice-cold milk. The house itself was lovely too, and my sisters and I were fascinated with Grandma's pretty things and well-kept garden.

Those Sunday afternoon visits were a significant part of my childhood in Vancouver; however, I longed for my other set of grandparents. We used to go to their home in Fort Rupert for school holidays and I often wished I could stay with them permanently. Granny and Papa's house was full of love and action. There was a constant flow of cousins and villagers moving through their house. During those visits we learned about respecting elders; however, we also learned that this respect was mutual because we saw how children — grandchildren, village children, white children — were all respected and welcomed into that house. I felt so much love and acceptance there and, of course, my sisters and I were free to be children. We never had to hide who we were and, similarly, our mother seemed equally free to be her true self. In fact, there she spoke the language of her childhood, Kwakwala. Even though I didn't understand Kwakwala, I did nevertheless, understand the feeling of being happy, relaxed, and surrounded with love.

Unlike Grandpa Hayman, my Indian grandfather was openly demonstrative in showing his love for my sisters and I. I can remember sitting on his knee learning Kwakwala children's songs, complete with hand gestures. As a child, I also enjoyed running behind him on the beach or through the village. And just as there were food treats in the home of my white grandparents, there were also food treats for my sisters and I in Fort Rupert. However, up there we were treated to smoked or barbequed salmon, crab, seaweed, and oolichan grease. Because we also ate "Indian food" in Vancouver, my sisters and I were no strangers to these delicacies. Once, to the delight of Granny and Papa, my sister Marsha drank a whole bowlful of oolichan grease proving that she was a real Indian.

The hard part about visiting Granny and Papa in Fort Rupert was saying goodbye. When holiday time was over and my sisters and I were loaded into the station wagon for the long trip home, we'd wave from the car window and pretend not to see our grandfather crying because he was so sad to see us go.

Back in Vancouver, there was our other set of grandparents and our other life. I feel fortunate to have been exposed so deeply to these two cultures. The polite visits to the house on Cambridge Street taught me about propriety in our white culture and staying with Granny and Papa in Fort Rupert broadened my horizons, reminding me that white culture is only one in a sea of many cultures.

Seni Seneviratne

Cinnamon Roots

Cinnamon sweet wood spice
Once more precious than gold
When I look for my roots
I find you yellowish brown
Like my winter skin
Native of Sri Lanka
Growing wild in the jungles
Of the Kandy Highlands

1492 Columbus never finds you
Sailing westwards to the lands
Of the Arawak Indians
He promises spices and gold
Trophies for a Spanish Queen
Brings her Taino slaves as 'gifts'

But Portugal travels East
To an island that falls like
A teardrop from the tip of India
Finds your soft sweetness
Wraps it in hard cash
Grows rich on your rarity
Founding a spice trade
That deals in blood

The Dutch make plantations
Tame your wild fragrance
That can never sweeten their breath
Demand quotas of your bark
Enforced by death and torture
Burn down your August harvest
Fabled fuel of the phoenix fire
To keep up the prices

Dutch East India
Becomes British East India
Your acres grow in the rain
And heat of Sri Lanka
Filling the coffers
Of the British Empire

1992 I buy your ground aroma
In pre-packed jars fry you
With aubergines and coriander
Look for my roots
Find you yellowish brown
Like my winter skin
Native of Sri Lanka
Growing wild in the jungles
Of the Kandy highlands

Shanti Thakur

Domino:
Filming Stories of Interracial People

You have no choice but to identify with the oppressed group, the colonized group. They're the marginals — they need the voice of representation, not the mainstream. *(Matou, 38, Congolese/French)*

My interracial heritage has given me the best of both worlds. The Japanese and British cultures are so opposite but so similar — you learn to bridge the similarities, while never forgetting the differences. *(Elizabeth, 23, Japanese/English)*

Learning about my interracial heritage at 18, distanced me from my brothers because it was understood that we were in fact half-brothers, and then they knew why I was a light-skinned Black: my father was Chinese. *(Leith, 43, Black/ Chinese/European)*

I want to have a child with another mixed person, because that child would represent the global growth which is happening today. *(Rebekah, 27, South Asian/British)*

THREE YEARS AGO, I WANTED TO BREAK THE ISOLATION I FELT as an interracial woman and plunged into researching "who" my community was. This exploration pulled me towards producing and directing the one hour documentary *Domino*, which portrays the personal histories of interracial adults.

345

I was curious to know how other people of mixed race experienced the role of being a cultural broker within their families since we're the ones who are usually overlooked.

The six subjects portrayed will share the insights they have experienced during their "rites of passage." The "rites" in a mixed child's life are often the turning points where cultural contrasts emerge. The stages range from birth, adolescence and dating, to career choice/education, to partner selection, to starting one's family and finally the death of our parents. These are the turning points in our lives, where we refer to our most profound beliefs. When we have two or more "races" or systems of cultural beliefs, we turn to the values which we believe in. Our identity oscillates throughout our lifetimes, and I think that our rites of passage are fertile ground for people to relate their stories.

As in every family, kids represent a sort of mirror of the parents' subconscious reality which they haven't faced yet. As the product of a racial mixture, we have to find answers to questions our parents haven't come to terms with.

Interracial people know that race is a social construct. Yet, whether we want to or not, we internalize the racism which seeps into our consciousness: through the media, school, the extended family, our peers, etc. But race is not the only issue. It's a lot more complex. Interracial families' dynamics are dependent upon many factors: demographics, political climate, language, religion, not to mention individual temperaments!

I was born in Vancouver and I'm the only child of an East-Indian father and a Danish mother. My experience crossed the borders of culture, language, religion and colour. My dad emigrated from India and my mother emigrated from Denmark. On my father's side, choosing a European wife was a reflection of other personal choices. Hindu at birth, he decided very early that religion wasn't for him. Later, while preparing to leave for the States (in order to do his M.B.A), his parents did everything they could to dissuade him from going to the "corrupt

West." Coming from the Brahmin caste (which is the highest on the caste scale, composed of priests and intellectuals) his career choice was seen as stepping down the caste hierarchy. My parents married in Vancouver.

When his parents got the news, they were furious because they had planned an arranged marriage for him. They also thought he would return to India. (The choice of a European wife symbolized embracing the "West" and rejecting his own country). On the other hand, in a small farming town, my mother's family accepted my father with open arms.

Today, my parents are still married. But 30 years ago, they thought that their love would conquer all forms of racism.

Once in Canada and in the corporate world, my father opted for total assimilation. He wanted to be Canadian to the bone — at the expense of forgetting his Hindi and Bengali languages. Assimilation to the dominant culture in Canada was a question of survival. It was also a strategy used in India when the British were in power. Assimilating to the culture in power at the time facilitated entry to the institutions. Unfortunately, he still believed in the myth of assimilation — that to take on the dominant culture would immunize him (and me) from racism and discrimination.

I was raised as the "Canadian" kid: my parents felt their languages and cultures weren't "useful." Being ignorant of my background did not immunize me from being the scapegoat, of being a "Paki." Growing up in Vancouver in the 70s, there was an influx of South Asian immigrants which created a "threat" to the dominant society. Violence and racist media coverage against South Asians were everywhere. Being the only brown kid in school, I was the one who "smelled" and was "stupid." The teachers were totally unaware of what was going on: my grades took a nose-dive. I couldn't understand how I was being associated with the immigrants, as I hadn't been educated in any way about South Asians. At ten years old, I wasn't capable of understanding the roots of racism, I only knew that I was being identified with people I didn't know anything about.

My parents were as distressed as I was. They wanted to protect me from racism, but at the same time, I wanted to protect *them* from what was happening. My European mother didn't have the reference points for telling me how to deal with racism... but she tried her best to get me to talk about it. On the other hand, my father didn't want to talk about it. (He was experiencing it himself and didn't have the answers either, having come from India as a privileged Brahmin). So I was told to ignore the comments, and that the kids were "jealous" and "ignorant." Our family unit was everything — it was the one safe place to be. And we guarded it by remaining silent.

Survival strategy #1: Keep busy reading, swimming or playing the piano. Strategy #2: Do not read the newspapers because the racist coverage of immigrants only underlined that it wasn't only kids who were "ignorant," but society at large.

At fourteen, we moved to Montreal and my life changed radically. We weren't isolated anymore. The school I went to had 80 percent immigrant kids. There was a mixture of class, language, religions and visible and invisible minorities. My differences, which were so repugnant in Vancouver were considered natural, even interesting in Montreal. For the first time in my life, my peers accepted me and I could start to accept myself.

By the time I was nineteen, there was a great distance between my father and me. My father realized that when he spoke to me, there was no reflection of himself. I was as "westernized" as he had raised me to be... independent, living on my own, supporting myself and choosing a financially insecure field: filmmaking. With that realization, his reaction was typical of assimilated immigrants: we needed to return to the "old country," India. The place he rejected, the "unimportant" culture, was suddenly very relevant.

I was thrilled — finally a chance to discover "my" culture. I didn't realize that a lot of frustration was ahead of me. I imagined being embraced like a lost child by my relatives in India and long, intimate talks with my grandparents. Once there, I was seen as the "other," the Canadian, who could never appreciate the wealth of Indian culture. The voyage allowed me to measure the distance which separated me from the Indian culture and also my Indian parent. Once I was able to see where my father was from, I could appreciate and respect him in a very different way. It motivated me to understand the culture more in order to understand my father (and myself).

On the other hand, when I visited my grandparents in Denmark, an immediate distance was wedged between us because I did not speak the language. It was heart-breaking. Today, my parents realize they should have taught me their languages. Back in the 50s, 60s and 70s, assimilation was a symbol of the cultural amnesia needed in order to survive. But in rejecting their differences, they denied their children the self-esteem, pride and tools for managing racism.

Through the experiences of speaking to a wide range of other interracial people, I'm not ready to group such a wide range of experiences under a banner of "mixed race culture." The experiences I heard were very different from each other: some identify as one culture, both or neither culture. Mixed race people can experience racism from either one of their parents' backgrounds. Some mixed race people experience racism at its worst: within the family network and by society's imposed reactions to them. Others may experience only isolated incidents in comparison.

My contact with so many interracial people not only inspired me to make a film — it also empowered me to understand who I am — a woman of colour and a woman of two cultures. Now I can understand that I'm not alone in this experience.

Mixed race children are the minority within the minority. To combat being slotted into a category we have to form our own identity. The importance of transcending our cultural boundaries is essential for knowing who we are — as members of a community which shares similar ideas and values.

Nila Gupta

The Garden of My (Be) Longing

That day
before the flight
i twirled
delighted
in your garden
dust devils
dancing at my side

before my mothers hands
stilled my dance
aghast at your question
you wanted me

but she would not let me go to you
that day before the flight

when i fell out of the sky
my mother
was a cloud
i passed through as i hurtled
down

and crashed
this land
my mother's hatred
a vast desert
where i lay, unable to take root
parched and bleeding
i learned i do not belong here
or in her heart

i do not belong anywhere

i heard you calling me
that day i meant to kill myself
when my bare feet danced on the ice
and i twirled and twirled
icicles shattering in my hair

and you come back to me
in dreams
dancing in your garden
calling me there
you, the woman
no man touched
touched me
your lap as soft as petals
and your garden
my only home

i do not belong anywhere
but my longing returns me to you
when i wake
the scent of your garden
is in my hair

Gitanjali Saxena

Gitanjali's Bio

ANJALI WAS BORN IN THE TWILIGHT OF AN AFTERNOON MIST IN a small town in Germany, to parents who did not have the ability to see one another. She seems to have been looking for them ever since. It made for a fairly difficult situation because they could, as a result not see her very well either. Now and then they would catch breathtaking glimpses of one another and it would remind them that they must somehow be mysteriously connected.

Whenever her mother would put puffy little girl dresses on her Anjali would crinkle up her little light brown face and cry. She felt like she had somehow "Wallflower" disappear-per. She was only truly the scarlet *lederhosen* blue as the sky. It made invisible hands up in *von deiner Sorte!!*[1] Lit-what her mother meant pondered that if there

grown petals like a ing into the wallpa-happy when she wore with a heart as clear her mother throw her the air to declare "*Funf* tle Anjali wondered by the remark, and were others like her, then she would certainly like to meet them.

One day, her parents grew tired of looking for one another and they had a divorce. Her father went to marry a wife who was more visible and her mother went to look for herself.

Anjali followed her mother out to the Prairies, a city named Edmonton. The people wore intriguing cowboy hats and she fell in love with their music. She learned to ride horses, drive cabooses and tractors. The hat people grew suspicious of Anjali when they saw that her mother looked much paler than her. They would ask, "What are you?" She wasn't really sure, and said, "Second Generation, Once Removed." They said, "What?" So she said "German" to make it easier on them. It turned out they were rural Albertan Nazis with Imaginary Deficiency. "No such thing as Brown Germans. No Brown Cowboys either." And they sent a couple of Motorcycle Mamas to teach her some Manners.

At that time Anjali decided some self-protection was needed. She split herself from her body and created an amnesiac called Gita. She learned how to deal with multiple identities, holding down jobs such as truckstop waitress, drug dealer, credit card thief and furniture refinisher.

Through this time, Anjali was never far away, but remained invisible. She would whisper wise things in Gita's ear. "The possibilities of colour are wonderful. A study entrancing and unlimiting."

Gita decided to clean up her act and go to Toronto to attend art school. She spent five years there. Making art was the only time Anjali and Gita could directly communicate. During this time they both remained invisible to everyone at the school except for the paintings, drawings, sculptures, videos and films that were made on a regular basis. Anjali would whisper, "A filmmaker just keeps making the same movie over and over all of her life, just in different ways. Life is actually a big long movie." "When a movie becomes tiresome, it may be because the motive is not worth the effort." Gita learned to trust the voice that spoke inside of her. It was extremely perceptive and *never* wrong. Sometimes the artmaking brought up painful things. The whisper said "Art must also be useful to the community, it must contribute to healing. The more doubtful and painful the process, the more power it contains. It is only a gift if it is given. Reach deep inside of your experience and be willing to look honestly." the voice also warned her; "The more power you have, the more vulnerable and valuable you will be to people's political agendas."

Gita started going to queer bhangra dances, she met a beautiful woman there, very seductive, dancing on the dance floor. The woman made graceful come hither motions with her hands. She had the most beautiful hands. Gita's stomach nearly went through the floor. Their eyes met. It reminded her of someone she knew but could not quite remember. Gita was in love instantly. She went shyly forward, swaying awkwardly to the music. But alas! The woman seemed to have changed her mind and her exquisite hands were making gestures that were pushing her away. Gita was crushed. Then the come hither gesture started again and the whole thing went back and forth for a while. Finally Gita became frustrated and asked, "What on earth are you trying to do?" She said,"this is bhangra, these moves come from punjabi folk dancing." So Gita joined in and learned some of the same moves as they circled around the dance floor... The dance became a lot of fun once you didn't take it too seriously. She looked around and noticed all the women doing the same moves to each other. The women became curious and asked her, "So what are you?" She looked down into her cowboy hat because she wasn't sure so she said "Avocado Vegetarian Turtle." They said "What?" So she decided to make it a little easier on them and said "South Asian." They smiled politely because they were from nice brown homes in the suburbs, and they shrugged their shoulders rhythmically, as they whirled away, hands clapping across the dance floor. Anjali looked on, quite pleased, and started to pack her bags to meet the family in India.

When they arrived the strangest thing happened. Gita was hardly seen at all and Anjali appeared, smartly garbed in Salwar Kameez. She embarked on an epic journey through a land she could not see. Pretty soon Great Big Galleries and Great Big Funding Bodies took interest in Gita's videos. She walked through these Big Galleries and felt a chill. This was not the home she had imagined for her work. She became very sad and almost decided she would return to the street and be a pedestrian again. She began to see her name written in unexpected places. She remembered what the voice had said about political agendas. She said, "I think I need a `New View, New Eyes.'"

She found a door marked ENGINEERS OF CHANGE with a HELP WANTED sign taped to it. She remembered her times driving the caboose. She brought her resumé and met with the hiring committee, and they immediately wanted to hire her based on her Previous Life experience. "Hmmm, ENGINEERS... *Engineers of Change?*" she glanced at them. "It looks and sounds like some kind of middle-class occupation, I seem to be moving something in the world." She joined many many anti-racism committees and boards of Arts & AIDS organizations.

The voice whispered in her ear. "The Emperor has no clothes."

One day, Gita was invited to an anti-racist lesbian conference in Berlin. She went to a bhangra dance there, and she met a group of five other funny/funky looking women. They were exactly like her, wearing sexy *lederhosen*, jaunty cowboy hats and elegant Kulu shawls, shuffling joyfully to the rhythms. Gita could not believe her eyes and immediately rushed over to see if they wanted to start up a support group.

"*Bolo! Bolo!*" she said, *"Kuch To Bolo!"*[2] They all began to spout anti-sexist, anti-racist, anti-homophobic, anti-classist, pro-addict, pro-artist rhetoric. All at once. She could not keep up! She just could not keep it up! She began to scream and scream and scream.

When she was through screaming, she opened her eyes, all the women in bhangra dance had cleared out of the room. Even the DJ had left. There was a sinister looking row of teeth hovering and gleaming in the smoky multicoloured air in front of her. She was about to begin screaming again, when she was caught by surprise. The teeth broke into a huge grin and a laugh, a huge laugh which echoed every which way. Gita also got the joke; she finally realized what her mother had been trying to tell her so long ago. Their laughter mixed in together until they were indistinguishable. Slowly around the grin Anjali appeared wearing a magnificent wedding dress. The heart on Gita's *lederhosen* turned orange like the big autumn sun.

They got married on the spot. The truth *is* indeed stranger than fiction.

355

1. Tamhari tara panch! (Five of your kind!)
2. Sprich! Sprich! Sag mir etwas! Sag mir dass du liebst mich (Speak, Speak, say something!)

GITANJALI'S VIDEOGRAPHY AND FILMS INCLUDE:

The Avocado Vegetarian Turtle © 1988. 16 mm colour, claymation, oils on glass
dist. Women in Focus (Vancouver) Canadian Filmmaker's Distribution Centre (Toronto)

The Wallflower © 1989. 16mm. 5:05 min. claymation
dist. Women in Focus (Vancouver) Canadian Filmmaker's Distribution Centre (Toronto), London Filmmaker's Co-op (England)

Second Generation, Once Removed, © 1990. 19 min, colour. video
dist. V-tape (Toronto), Video Out (Vancouver)

Bolo! Bolo! (with Ian Rashid) © 1991. 31 min. colour, video
dist. V-tape (Toronto), Video Out (Vancouver)

New View, New Eyes © 1993 50 min. colour, video
dist. V-tape (Toronto), Video Out (Vancouver)

Lesbian Flirtation Techniques (work in progress)

Ausgangspunkt (work in progress)

Do Me Justice (work in progress with Melina Young)

Kathy Ann March

Like Koya

THEY TOLD HER WHEN SHE MARRIED: DON'T MARRY WHITE. And she says she didn't — look at his kinky head. He's not white.

Look at his father's kinky head — the lightest of his bunch.

He told her that he had a recurring dream. The blacks and the whites were fighting and he didn't know which side to take.

"On occasion a customer will approach the receptionist at work and ask for the black chap they had been dealing with... and the gal up front will ring for me. I know it's not me they want, — I don't do customer relations, there are only two of us, but I always answer the query. "No, the fellah I'm dealing with is black. Sweetheart, it's something you'll have to deal with for the rest of your life."

She laughs at him strong in her identity, strong in where she came from and yet, her light skin-ned-ness took her into and through the maze of Jamaica's class/colours where brown brothers and sisters could not/ would not go.

A privilege, a passport without geography, an abbreviated history. No legacy of land that gives us a body the security to know, and be satisfied with, what is. An identity from which to clearly speak; not the emulation of a promise that can not be accessed. We are not white, we are not black. We are more often than not, what others perceive us to be. Positioned in the collectivity of the moment as best suits the communal purpose.

And she came to Canada and they asked her if she was nanny to her own children.

Pursuing a posture that looks like but never quite is... you. Drawing upon the authenticity of another as a space from which to speak. I have lived through white academic women who have introduced me to myself through women of colour texts they have explored. Privy to their realms of endeavour as the "polite" other. Offering the ever so interesting voice of the ethnic without being up in anyone's face. Credibility constrained to speaking only of issues about this body. My thoughts, my knowledge of other topics is somehow incredible. Without brownness I don't make them uncomfortable. It is never spoken — I know this.

Looking to my blackness for comfort I can enter so far.

Black History Month, I volunteer, do the work.

My whiteness means I enter only so far, no matter how much work I do.

I cannot be a "daughter" of the Black Women's Congress.

I cannot represent issues of blackness — white folks will get the wrong idea, black folks get annoyed.

What issues of blackness do I have?

What beauty of blackness do I have?

And if I answer you with; body, rhythm, and song, I am giving you stereotypes, embarrassing essentials.

I was born and they asked her if there hadn't been some kind of mix-up at the hospital. Is she really yours, they would tease.

Blonde ringlets, pudgy and pink that would change in adolescence to wiry, kinky bush and lean defined muscle. The panic and anxiety of a head to be tamed. A father's desire... the hair should not be cut short.

And she struggled with wide-toothed comb, grease, plaits, conditioners, ribbons, and relaxers over this head in the laundry sink. This head, its skinny frame firmly clasped between her thighs and muttered "yuh head is like koya, I don't know why he doesn't just let me cut it all off."

Between the two of us, she could spend the better part of a week's wages at the hairdresser. "Beauty feels no pain."

I am the ugly white girl.

Dad, no Farah Fawcett hairdo, no demure smile.

I am the only black girl my Scottish friends know. They are quite clear that I am black. I have always been aware that this was not a supportive affirmation on their part but rather a clear message that my blackness was not to be confused, genetically or otherwise, with the heroic genealogy of the Scot. For the longest time they were my only friends.

In the row house where I grew in Canada, there were two prints of black market women. Every other picture in the house was a landscape devoid of people. Landscapes are not satisfying, and I continue to search for images that represent me and places I am comfortable with.

The walls of my apartment are bare.

I have not been back to Jamaica in twelve years. During a family conversation it is said that back home white people are being shot... my brown-skinned sister throws a quick and nervous glance my way. She and our cousin are making plans to hang out in Jamaica for a while; to see if they can make their way, to see and feel family. The last time I was there I went to visit my grandmother, my mother's mother, on her plantation. The local boys threw rocks at my car and yelled white girl!

And I duck my head,

As my girlfriend shouts and crouches down in the booth. The glass ashtray sails overhead and smashes against the wall. I turn to look and through the din of the bar's heavy metal squall the biker and I lock gaze. He stares, turns on his heel and lumbers, all belly and leather, into the crowd.

I'm drunk and confrontational — what the hell is going on? His sidekick intercepts me and explains: "To my buddy a mix like you is worse than a nigger." He hands me a KKK calling card. In disbelief I show the card to the people I'm with — they're shooting a chummy game of pool — the chums they are playing against produce their KKK cards.

I leave.

"What the hell were you doing in a place like that in the first place?!" I am in there because I passed through the door that day and many times before.

And slowly I come to know that it is the task of carving out a space for myself outside the tyranny of belonging in one or the other. I have been a traitor to no one but myself.

Slowly, dear cousins, I begin, with an effort as this.

("Koya" (coir) is the beaten husk of the coconut used as stuffing for sofas. Refers to something that is hard to manage.)

Faith Adiele

Learning to Eat

White-people emotions happen in the head
Reasonable-like
A tense, short journey to the mouth.
Sadness. Satisfaction.
The mind at rest.

Yellow language circulates the chest:
Entering the heart is understanding,
Exchanging it, trading truth.
Unhappiness, the wasted heart.

Black thoughts need slow chew.
Swallowed
Palm wine added
The slippery descent that is consideration.
They go home to the stomach to rest there,
Searing as curry, as solid as yams.

i don't want to waste my heart
i don't want to waste my shape
i am looking for my tongue

Faith Adiele

The Multicultural Self:
USA to Finland to Nigeria Journals, 1987— 1989

1.FINLAND
24 June 1987.

HERE'S SOMETHING I WOULD HAVE NEVER EXPECTED: MIDSUM-mer in Finland! Grandma's longed-for homeland is unlike any place I've ever been. The countryside is exquisite, the cities (if you can call them that) are Soviet-ugly, and the sun shines twenty hours a day! I feel like I'm in a "Twilight Zone" episode where nothing changes. The birds go on singing all night, and my body doesn't know when to slow down. The quality and intensity of the sunlight doesn't vary a bit, from five at night to two in the morning!

I ran into Damon and Jeff in London and we travelled to Turku together, where we made quite a hit — they with their Jewish Mediterranean looks — and I, the lone black person — looking completely unlike anyone in all of Finland! Wherever we went, crowds of people stopped and stared open-mouthed. I was equally stunned at the thought that I could have come from a country filled with so many towering blondes.

The wedding ceremony was beautiful, moving, a mixture of Christian, Hindu and Apache ritual, spoken in Finnish and English, followed by Israeli folk dancing and a feast of moose and reindeer. Friends and family were there from the U.S.A., India, England, Sweden, and northern Finland. I cried like I was mother of the bride.

The groom laughed happily upon seeing me. He said he had

known all along that I would come. He had seen a vivid image of me in a dream of the wedding long before I got the money together.

As people in the wedding party heard from the bride and her mother that I was Finnish, they approached with fascination and delight. I was surprised. I certainly hadn't expected a homecoming. Marjatta's brother-in-law urged me to stay in Finland. He offered to be my agent, claiming I could be a superstar — sort of the Finnish Grace Jones! The return of the prodigal daughter and all that. "We are a small country, eager for the outside world," he enthused. "We would love you — anything you do or write would be of great interest to us!"

He asked what region our family was from, and I realized I had no idea. Mom or Grandma had paid attention to those things. Several people looked surprised, and one said, "It seems that you are not too interested in your Finnish heritage." That shocked me. My entire childhood was spent feeling like a strangely-dark Scandinavian, hearing Finnish spoken, with a wreath of candles in my hair. But have I indeed stopped feeling Scandinavian since leaving the farm, since Grandma's death? I guess I've been thinking of myself more as black lately, though I certainly don't know what it means to be a black American — anymore than I do to be Nigerian. So what does that leave me?

The next day all the international guests went to the country to join Paul and Marjatta at their wedding cabin, where we spent the week fishing, swimming, wandering the woods and taking saunas. I took to sauna like a fish to water — it was like discovering a hidden talent that has been waiting and waiting for years to be used! We spent hours until we were nearly faint with heat, nearly raw with beating our bodies with aromatic birch branches. Then we would run jumping screaming into the icy lake, or tear naked through the woods, the rain hissing as it hit our bodies, rising off as steam. One time, as I staggered back to the cabin, my heart stopped, and I could have sworn I saw God!

To get to the cabin, we had taken a series of long bus rides from Turku. The last bus let us off at a lonely spot on the road. Flat, dewy meadows stretched for miles around. There were no farm houses, no people, just the occasional cow. We seemed to be at the ends of the earth, untouched by time or human hand. Suddenly, miraculously, a large, old-fashioned taxicab appeared out of nowhere. Speechless, we got in. The driver, a young Finn with spiked hair, had on a pair of stiff, new, stone-washed jeans and flashy sunglasses, though the sun was cool and hazy. As the car careened over cow paths extending towards the North Pole, he turned on the radio, and the car was flooded with — of all things — deafening rap music. I chose to take this as a sign.

2. USA

March 1988. Two nights ago I dreamed I was related to one of the security guards at work. Even in the midst of dreaming I was surprised: I barely knew the guy. My single interaction with him occurred a few weeks ago. I was wearing my one Nigerian outfit — the lavish *akwete* tunic my father had sent when I was twelve, the last time I heard from him — and as I ran to the elevator, Peter followed me. "Oh," he had cried, clapping his hands, "that dress is very beautiful! It makes me very happy to see you wearing it today."

At the time, I was half-proud, half-relieved. I never before dared wear the dress in public. African clothing isn't popular, and I had never seen anyone — African or otherwise — wearing a similar outfit. Every time I go to put it on I find myself wondering, is the style outdated? Tacky? Will Africans laugh at me, or worse, become indignant? What if it's a ceremonial robe? I wasn't even sure if the dress was actually as beautiful as I thought, or if my attachment was merely the residue of garish childhood taste.

Sometimes when the old feeling of being alone in my skin resurfaces, I put it on. It feels as if somehow my people were with me, as if I've put on an African self, as if the years of cultural ignorance have melted away and I am no longer alone. That morning the dress had looked strong, beautiful, like an old friend. I decided to wear it.

The occupants of the elevator turned and began to murmur

appreciatively about the dramatic cloth with its red, yellow and green silk over-weaving. Someone asked if they could touch the embroidery, and Peter said. "That material is very expensive."

As I looked at Peter's proud face, my own pride turned to shame. At age twenty-five, I have to learn from a stranger in public that a piece of clothing I've owned for over a decade is valuable! Just as I was about to ask Peter where he was from, the elevator door closed.

Then yesterday I arrived at work uncharacteristically early. As I exited the elevator, I ran into Peter on my floor doing his rounds. I had already forgotten the dream, but seeing him brought on a strange, nagging sensation. It was like trying to remember a conversation abandoned in mid-sentence.

He greeted me joyously. "Ah, so your office is on this floor?" he asked. "Which one?" I pointed to my cubicle. He nodded with grace, his smile beatific. He stood beaming at me silently. Suddenly my memory of the dream flooded back, and I wondered what could be the possible reason behind dreaming that he was my brother?

"Are you Nigerian?" I finally blurted out.

"Yes!" His eyes widened as did his grin. "How did you know?"

"So am I... I mean... so is my father. My name is Adiele. My father is Magnus Adiele. Perhaps you've heard of — ?"

Before I could finish, Peter erupted. "You're Nigerian?" he cried, surprised, rocking back on his heels and bringing his hands together with a resounding clap.

I nodded.

A cry of joy burst from him, a long "Ohhhhh!" rising steadily from deep in his throat as if pleasure itself were coursing through his body. The sound travelled up my spine, fingering each vertebrae, and soared to a plateau high above us. It hung there, resonating with emotion.

I was amazed. The word "Oh" appeared frequently in African books, but I read it in an American context, flat, an indication of mild surprise. But in Peter's mouth this simple vowel was more passionate and expressive than speech itself. It seemed as if an entire world of communicating and feeling had suddenly opened to me.

Peter shook his clasped hands over his head with religious fervour, crying, "Praise God for showing my sister to me!"

I was entranced. This was the loving, all-embracing nature of Africans I had read about all those years alone in Washington. I realized that this indeed had been my fantasy all along: that eventually some Nigerian would turn to me and say, "Welcome, sister."

When he finally calmed down, Peter asked to which tribe I belonged. Upon hearing that I was Igbo, he leapt up, shouting praises to God all over again. I gathered that he too was Igbo.

By then we were both giddy from laughing. We determined that our families were from different states — mine from Imo state and his from Anambra — and he finally floated back down to earth. He asked after my parents, and I explained that my mother was white and lived in the U.S.A. too, and my father lived in Nigeria.

He nodded and then frowned. "What was your family name?" he asked.

"Adiele," I said. He cocked his head, looking puzzled. I repeated it, as my mother had taught me — A-dee-el-lay — and his frown grew deeper.

"A-dee — ?" he faltered, shaking his head.

I repeated it a third time, my voice shaking.

He looked confused. "How do you spell?" he asked.

With a shock, I realized the painful, humiliating truth: Peter could not understand my pronunciation. I did not know how to say my own name.

On the verge of tears, I spelled the letters out loud, as he traced them with a finger in his palm. "A-heh!" he exclaimed, his face lighting up once the name registered. "Adiele!"

Silently I mouthed the name as he had pronounced it. Three syllables, not four, with a lilt that rose and fell on the middle syllable: Uh-dyel-lay. It took time to say — or rather, sing — properly.

"Yes, Adiele," he said, as if to console me. "It's not a common name." He murmured it again, punctuating the accented syllable with a nod of his head. Suddenly he frowned. "Adiele?" He tilted his head sideways and knit his brow. "There is a an Adiele who was a Minister or Commissioner..."

"Yes," I said, "that's my father. Commissioner of Education, then Health. You know him?"

Peter's jaw dropped. "You are the daughter of our Commissioner own?" he whispered.

I noticed his use of the possessive. I nodded, grinning.

"Ohhhhh!" he beat his chest as if the shock would kill him. He then clutched his head with both hands and rocked back and forth, glancing about as if unable to believe that such momentous news were not being witnessed by a crowd of joyous onlookers. Grasping my hand in both of his, he pumped my arm. "Would I be here now, if not for your father?" he cried. "Would any of us be? Welcome, sister. Welcome!"

I began to cry.

At lunch time he appeared shyly at my desk. He had salvaged some discarded scraps of yellow cardboard from the trash and traced the letters of the Igbo alphabet on it. I was touched. Written in one corner was the Igbo name he had chosen for me. He was quite shocked to learn that I did not have one. How could my parents not have given me an Igbo name? Therein lies an individual's power, child's potential. He had looked worried.

"It was the first auspicious name that popped into my head," he explained. "It means a gift from God,' which is appropriate in light of our meeting."

I was stunned. I knew the name. Apparently it could be a feminine name in Peter's home state, though it must be masculine in ours. It was *Chinyere*, my father's Igbo name.

3. IN TRANSIT

29 March 1989. Had a long lay-over in London's newly-reno-vated, newly-neon Gatwick Airport. Surrounded by countless, obvi-ously Nigerian travellers (I can tell by their supreme confidence and superb dress), it hits me that this time I'm not on another European vacation but actually, finally going to Nigeria! It also strikes me that I am woefully underdressed for the country. Everyone is the height of fashion in dramatic batiks, billowing lace, shimmering hand-woven fabrics, intricate tie-dye, gold embroidered silk, stiff lines and rich damask brocade. Even at five o'clock on a foggy London morning, the fabled Nigerian charm is evident. They are laughing, shouting, embrac-ing, arguing. I am no match for this. They seem to notice me and bend towards each other to whisper as I pass.

My seat partner is a very sweet white Nigerian. He tells me that there are only a thousand or so actual white citizens among 100 million blacks. It used to be that when he stood in line for Nigerian nationals, people would always try to correct him gently. "Now they are beginning to realize that such a thing is possible — just as the Brits are beginning to conceptualize the black Englishman. "He says with a grin. "Of course, *Nigeria's* only twenty-nine years old."

He says he admires the Igbo for two main reasons. The first is that no matter who or where they end up, they always build a home in their ancestral village. Though they may never live there, they are driven to maintain that sense of history and origin. Perhaps this explains my own quest. He is also impressed by how they strive to educate as many members of their families as possible. He was living in Port Harcourt at the time of the Biafran war and feels great sympathy for the Igbo, whom he feels suffered greatly during as well as after in their loss of life, property and goods. I find myself wanting to identify with what he says. It feels strange and yet not so strange to be learning about my people from a white African.

4. NIGERIA

29 March 1989. The flight is short, just six-and-a-half hours, and suddenly after a flurry of gracious British service (such a relief after six hours of cattle-car American airline surliness), we are THERE.

I step into the airport terminal and can not stop grinning. The plane did not crash, my fellowship was not rescinded, and Nigeria is outside the window. I have spent twenty-six years waiting to get here. In a minute once again I will find myself navigating the new waters of a strange airport. Finally it hits me. I realize I know nothing and will really have to become my best to move with ease through this coming year. I am terrified that no one will meet me, though I float lightly along the corridor, grinning and marvelling: *I am here. I am actually here. This is Nigeria.*

Immigration was a parody of efficiency. An agent impatiently shouted, "next! *next!* as if he actually wanted things to happen quickly. All he did, however, was seize my passport, thumb through it officiously, and then pass it to a second man who repeated the ritual. At the third official, my passport disappeared, so I assumed that something might actually be happening at this point. Fast-talking touts slithered in and out of restricted areas, striking deals within earshot of the fat, sleepy officials who lounged everywhere in brown or blue uniforms. They didn't appear to be armed but omnipresent and rather pompous. Occasionally one roused himself to bully the odd traveller.

In the mêlée no one remembered or noticed us, the confused and easily cowed first-timers. The third and fourth immigration officials cried out garbled names, each of which was invariably claimed by several confused travellers. Finally there were less than ten of us left. I had been paged twice by my ride, which was waiting outside. Finally my name was called and an official motioned for me to come to the back of the booth. Prepared for difficulty, I clutched my letter of admission to the university, my proof of financial responsibility and my return ticket. The man looked me up and down and addressed my breasts, "Where have you been? I've been calling your name for twenty minutes." Since I'd been standing in front of him for forty minutes, a mere sheet of Plexiglass between us, I could think of no reply! He handed me the passport with a leer.

I asked if I was all set. He nodded, staring at my breasts. I asked how long my visa was for and he looked startled, as if this was the first time he'd heard about a visa. "You know," I reminded him. "I intend to stay here for a year but I only have three-month visa..."

"Oh," he replied curtly, unconcerned. "You have three months. You must take it to headquarters in Lagos to have it extended." I flashed a big floozy's smile (though I felt like flipping him off), thanked him and left.

Four yards away, everyone who had gotten through Immigration forty minutes ago was now standing and waiting for their bags at the luggage carousel. My bags went by just as I arrived, and I grabbed them without thinking how I'd get the huge Nigerian-size caches of gifts to the end of the room, through Customs, then out the door. Most people were renting carts but I had no Nigerian money! I looked around the room and saw a flurry of brilliantly-dressed travellers in a wide range of outfits. Finally, a tall, soft-spoken woman with a distracted air pushed her cart up to me and told me that I should get a cart. I explained that I have no Nigerian money and, and she offered to take mine with hers.

We approached Customs and I clutched my currency declaration forms, remembering all the horror stories I've heard about Nigerian Customs. On all sides Nigerian travellers were bellowing curses or paying bribes, or both. The soldiers eyed our bags unenthusiastically. They asked to see my companion's passport, then waved us through a set of doors.

It took a while for my host — the brother of a friend in Boston — to find me, since he was expecting me to be alone. Finally we met up, and he and his neighbour welcomed me and my benefactress heartily. They thanked her for rescuing me, and carried her bags. As we walked out of the airport, something comfortable and wonderful hit me: air thick with humid odours, glowing red earth, tin shacks among lush, brilliant greenery. It was my initial impression of Jakarta, Mexico City, Bangkok, Karachi. The vibrancy was overwhelming yet somehow reassuring. It was real life, filled to bursting with real people.

We left the airport, a huge ugly grey cement monstrosity and began a journey past countless billboards heralding a proudly consumer society. The black statue of a drummer welcomed us. Masses of people lined the highway, men impossibly pristine in spotless white robes and embroidered caps, women with baskets on their heads, ready to cram themselves into rickety buses and rusted taxis. My host roared with laughter when I confessed that I was convinced the plane would crash before I actually got to see home. He began a litany on "this chaos known as Nigeria." I listened eagerly to tales of month-long electrical blackouts, water running in the tap a few hours a week if at all, rampant corruption and crime, stolen mail and poor sanitation, daily six-hour traffic "go-slows," and a ban on western goods. His last sentence thrilled me: "Yes, Nigeria is a crazy place, but it is *yours*."

30 March 1989. Today Juliet, a young cousin of my host's who visited last night, came to take me to lunch. I had slept twelve hours and was so woozy and befuddled from the heat that I almost fell into a ditch by the side of the road several times. The roads are horrifying, and motorists come upon one from all angles without warning or slowing speed. There are many schools in the area (Anthony Village is a relatively new middle-class development near the airport) and some of the children shouted "*oyimbo* (white)" as I passed! Everyone stares. The neighbourhood looks like Thailand, the stucco and glass houses enclosed by walls with crushed glass set atop, petty traders at the side of the road, the little shops. But the people's clothes and the hours they keep, from dawn to dawn, distinguish them. I do not yet have the courage to brave these streets.

Today we had a power failure and already there is no water in the tap, so I'm getting the real, complete Nigerian experience! However, one hears the latest rap and dance music everywhere, and I watched *Moonlighting* on t.v. before going to bed to dream of home.

31 March 1989. Today was a very bad day. I am bored to death at being trapped in this sweltering apartment. I found the *Nigerian Handbook 1982*, which was quite interesting. Then my host's girlfriend Elizabeth came by on her break to bring me fruit and the Nigerian equivalent of the *National Enquirer: 60-year-old prostitute in Benin say "Women no dey old. When I dress finish, rub powder, you no go know me again."*

Soon after Juliet came by and we had a soda down the road, over which we swapped stories of Nigerian men. Horrors! I think she may also be my host's girlfriend.

1 April 1989. Of course, today was much better. Elizabeth came at ten to take me to the market in the Surulere district, where I was quite the bewildered hit. It was just like an Asian market. I almost fainted from the smells and the fact that I am bleeding and hadn't had anything to eat. What overwhelmed me most were the clothes. Western dress is much less common than I had supposed, given the expatriate community in Boston. All the men wear gorgeously subtle robes and caps, while the women vary more — traditional dress or modern suits made from traditional fabrics. They're not as consistently fine as the men's clothes, but the best are truly superb. We passed by a Yoruba wedding party, which was amazing — all creams, ecru, pale blue and icy linens!

It seems so odd that I'm considered white, and yet that I'm accepted as Nigerian because of my father. I suspect if my mother were the Nigerian one, or if I had an English surname, it would be different. From the first night, I was struck with the realization that must hit every member of the African Diaspora when s/he returns home: God we *own* this country! Just the simple act of watching t.v. and seeing all blacks

— in the commercials and reading the news — brought that notion home. And there was the additional thrill of recognizing these people as my compatriots. I might be strange, but I am accepted, damn it, by virtue of birth and the prominence of my father. Now here I find myself in a country that claims me almost overwhelmingly but cannot offer much more than that: identity and the opportunity to fight for some kind of life within these parameters. The same old struggle.

April 2, 1989. Though Nigerians own this country, they are ashamed and defensive about it. It makes me sad. As usual, colonialism has done a number on an entire nation. Nigerians don't see the beauty or interest in traditional things. They feel it is a form of patronization to take photos of age-old rituals in village compounds or of the crazy beauty of sprawling urban settlements. *You're just perpetuating the prejudice that we're not civilized and don't have developed areas too,* they cry when I take out my camera. But I'm Nigerian, I say. I'm not using this camera like a white person. *Maybe not you,* they say. *But an American will see your photos in that way.* Am I so western that my appreciation for my own traditional culture is merely cultural imperialism disguised? Am I feeding off my own people?

This evening I heard a refreshing opinion from one of my host's classmates. He was a big, articulate, intelligent and jovial man who is a public relations officer for some firm. His wife (beautiful, equally intelligent, but a bit more reserved) is an immigration officer. They live in a huge, modern, expensive house in a new suburb with their new son. It was their first child, and they just radiated happiness. They said that the house girl told them that "Hyacinth had come home with a white girl."

"He has never come home with any girl, and now he brings a white one!" the husband had exclaimed. "In that case, let him be shown up immediately!" They gave us fresh iced palm wine, which is quite delicious and yeasty. Like everyone else I've met, they were delighted to find out who I was: "Daughter of our Honourable Commissioner own, you are welcome!" They were also thrilled that I has chosen not only Nigeria but the Igbo homeland for my fellowship location. The wife said I could qualify for a one- or two-year resident visa on the basis of study or reunification with parents, but that I would always require a visa, since I had a U.S. passport. It turns out that Nigeria does not allow dual nationals. The policy surprised me, given all the children in my situation.

When we first came in, the husband was talking to another visitor about a huge fraud scheme recently discovered by the police but not prosecuted. "These people," he said, "they kill you for fraud. They go to a newly-dug grave awaiting burial and they bury you beneath. Then the next day the other burial takes place, and who will know or dare to dig up another in search of you? Only when someone confesses, such as this one, so they get permission to exhume. Ah, this country!" But then he laughed and said the kindest thing about Nigeria I've yet to hear from the oh-so-critical intelligentsia: "I will never leave this country!" he declared. "In time we will surpass America. We have just as many men and women of resolve. We are only twenty-nine years old! What do they want? What do we expect of a twenty-nine year old man? Nothing. You are not yet married and do not even have children! Give us time, I say."

And I had to think. This country, my homeland that offers me so little and promises so much, is only twenty-nine, only three years older than I. What do I expect of it, and of myself? I, who am only twenty-six, and who am seeing home for the very first time.

Faith Adiele

remembering anticipating africa

this is how the journey home began:
at 25 dreaming a stranger to be my brother
discovering my real brother a stranger
with my habits my laugh
a sister wearing my face

> *Sister, welcome home*
> *We've been waiting for you*

on the verge of africa
words half-listened to for a lifetime
return

> *You'll need a briefcase full of money*
> *to move from one side of town to the other*

throwing each other to the tarmac
babies strapped to women's backs
we trample and bloody each other
to board the only plane to the capitol

> *They'll greet you with open arms*
> *You'll make lots of friends*

my brother my sister
calling to me
at dusk
on the village path
beneath black banana palms
teeth gleaming
slowly nodding this evening
Good evening
Auntie
Peace be with your household

  Everything is for sale
  Even human head

smoldering trash in roadside ditches
crowds of children churning up the dust
they chase me shouting
white lady! white lady!

  Sister, welcome
  We always knew you would come

shouting
white lady! white lady!
at me
a nigger for 25 years

Contributors' Notes

DIANA ABU-JABER

I was born in Syracuse, New York. My father is Jordanian/Palestinian and my mother is from New Jersey. My PhD is from SUNY - Binghamton, where I got my first inklings that it might be all right to write about being half and half, about myself. I now teach creative writing and post-colonial literatures at the University of Oregon.

DEANNE ACHONG

Born in Montreal, January 20, 1963 of mixed Irish, African, Spanish, Chinese and other unknown ancestry. Profession: artist. Currently completing my M.F.A. at U.B.C. Vancouver. For the present, my work is photo-based. I am a lapsed painter. I also enjoy making pots, tea-pots in particular. I have moved around a lot, from St. John's, Newfoundland to Halifax, back to Newfoundland and now I'm residing in Vancouver — a very picturesque city. I'm looking for work. Recent exhibitions: September 1993, M.F.A. Graduate Show, U.B.C. Fine Arts Gallery; June 1993, Telling Relations: Sensitivity and the Family, Grant Gallery group show.

FAITH ADIELE

I am a thirty-year-old woman of Nigerian (Igbo) and Finnish/Swedish descent. I was raised by my Scandinavian mother and relatives in a rural, segregated (Anglo, Native and Latino) town in northwestern U.S.A., and spent several years in women's spiritual communities in Southeast Asia. In Nigeria, at the age of twenty-six, I met my father for the first time. My memoir, Black American, White African: Moving from Scandinavian Childhood to Nigerian Adulthood, explores identity issues of gender, geographic estrangement, class, and being North American/African/black/biracial/multicultural.

378

ANNHARTE

Anishinabe Equay/Eagle Clan Poetta[1] (cross with celtic confusion). Chapbook/performance - Coyote Columbus Cafe.

ANONYMOUS

I am a mixed race woman of African (Trinidadian) and European (British) descent. I was born in Canada and currently reside in Toronto where I am studying to be a librarian. I use writing to get in touch and come to terms with my feelings — it is a healing tool. My main areas of personal interest are identity politics and afrocentric spirituality.

JOANNE ARNOTT

Joanne Arnott is of mixed Six Nations and Western European ancestry, originally from Manitoba. Her first book, *Wiles of Girlhood* (Press Gang, 1991), won the Canadian League of Poets' Gerald Lampert Award for best first book of poetry. *My Grass Cradle* (Press Gang, 1992), her second book, focuses on mixed heritage issues. *Ma MacDonald*, a children's book about birth, (Women's Press, 1993) is illustrated by Mary Ann Barkhouse. Joanne facilitates "Unlearning Racism" and "The Political Context of Mothering" workshops. Mother of three, she lives with her family on the west coast. Joanne is very interested in hearing from other writers of mixed Native/non-Native ancestry, with a view to compiling an anthology of our words. Please contact c/o Press Gang Publishers, 603 Powell St., Vancouver, B.C., V6A 1H2.

PAM BAILEY

I am currently dwelling in academia, dreaming of Utopia and pursuing my PhD in philosophy in upstate New York. My hope is to one day live in a multicultural lesbian-feminist society that is fully open and accessible to *all* lesbians.

---

[1]Italian for poet.

379

MERCEDES BAINES
I am of mixed heritage: Afro-Canadian, French, Irish, Danish and Native. I struggle — sometimes with joy, sometimes with tears of rage or confusion — to find my identity in all the bloodlines that have come together to create me. I actively resist being boxed into any one of my cultural/ethnic identities. To allow myself to be labelled as only part of myself limits my creative/spiritual expression. I am a writer, performer, drama teacher, and director based in Vancouver.

A. NICOLE BANDY
She is an undergraduate in History planning to return to her home in sunny California immediately after graduating from college in the frozen hinterlands of St. Paul, Minnesota. While in college, she founded a group for mixed race students and developed a passion for researching the experiences of mixed race people and understanding the nature of race relations in the U.S.

SHEILA BATACHARYA
She is a Bengali/Irish Canadian lesbian born and raised in Southern Ontario.

NGAIRE BLANKENBURG
I'm of mixed race — black, white and unknown, South African, New Zealand, working with words and images and imagination, with video, with poems, with the known and the unconscious, the collective and the immediate...

CAROL CAMPER
Carol is a Toronto-born woman of Black, White and Native North American ancestry. She is a writer, visual artist, women's health worker and mother of two young adults, Michael and Cicely. Adoption by a White family, the extreme cultural isolation she experienced and the conditions of society in general, have made racial/cultural identity a major issue for her — which is why this anthology came into being. Her writing appears in various anthologies and periodicals, including *Fireweed, Piece of My Heart: Lesbian of Colour Anthology* (Sister Vision Press) and *OutRage: Dykes and Bi's Resist Homophobia* (Women's

Press) for which she also did the cover illustration.

Future projects include beginning university, painting more women more often, an anthology on transracial adoption, getting the bikes fixed and trying out for *Jeopardy!*

Carol (a Leo) is in love, keeps her cat as long as she can (lover hates it) and she enjoys gallons of perfectly brewed tea as only she seems to be able to make it.

MARILYN ELAIN CARMEN

She is of Cherokee-Creek-Algonquin, African and English descent, has published poetry widely in the U.S. in such journals as *Heresies; Phoebe,* and *Paterson Literary Journal.* Her fiction has been published by Hurricane Alice and Home Planet News in the U.S. and Grain in Canada and Slow Dancer in England. *Blood at the Root,* her novella was published in the U.S. by Esoterica Press, after winning a Fellowship in 1990 by the Pennsylvania State Council on the Arts.

JAIMI CARTER

A recent graduate of Macalester College in St. Paul, Minnesota, Jaimi was born and raised in Southern California. She inherited her love of words, language and the outdoors from her mother and grandmother. She inherited her looks from her parents, both of whom she somehow manages to closely resemble. Jaimi currently lives in Los Angeles with her mother, stepfather and two of her three brothers.

MICHELLE CHAI

A callaloo dyke of Chinese, African and Portugese heritage — hailing from the land of calypso, steel-pan and limbo. Bad like yaz and living for bacchannal — santimanitay!

MYRIAM J.A. CHANCY

She is a Haitian-born Canadian woman and her writing explores the connection between her identity in Canada and in the U.S. as a Black woman and the reality of her mixed-race — Francophone, Spanish, Afro-Caribbean background. Her writing on this and related subjects of multiple oppression has appeared in *proemCanada, Frontiers* and *At the Crossroads.* She recently completed a PhD. dissertation on Afro-Caribbean women writers in exile from their home islands in Canada, the U.S. and Britain and has begun work on a novel.

MICHI CHASE (Adrienne Michiru Chase Onizuka)
I was born in Fukoka, Japan and at the age of two moved to Indianapolis, Indiana where I lived for eight years. My parents, recognizing the value of my multinational/ethnic heritage, and wanting my sister and I to be familiar with both sides of our heritage, moved our family to Kobe, Japan where I attended an international school for seven years. When moving from America to Japan, my family took an invaluable one year trip across Europe, Africa, India and China. Currently I am a junior at Macalester College, majoring in Studio Art, with interests in writing, dance and feminist spirituality.

ELEHNA DE SOUSA
She is a psychotherapist who practices her healing art from the Shamanic perspective of Huna. She has travelled through many realms in her search for purpose and identity, and looks forward to the day when she will be able to move freely in a world without artificial boundaries imposed by passports, status and citizenship.

LARA DOAN
I was born in Toronto and received my degree from York University. I still live at home with my mom, three cats (Dudley, Puddy and Buggy) and two dogs (Mocha and Alfie).

LOIS ROBERTSON-DOUGLASS
Lois was born in Cross Roads Jamaica. She was educated in Jamaica and the United States, where she has been a resident of Ann Arbor, Michigan on and off for the past 22 years. Her goals include publishing her poetry and short stories as well as the long-term goal of publishing a novel based on Jamaica and her personal experiences with racial intolerance.

MARILYN DUMONT
I am Metis. Dislocated from the Alberta Metis Settlements and my extended family, I grew up first, in logging camps where my parents worked and second, in a small southern Alberta farming community. I have been writing for an audience for twelve years and publishing for eight years in literary journals such as: *blue buffalo, CV II, A Room of One's Own, Other Voices, Newest Review* and in three anthologies: *Writing the Circle, The Road Home,* and *The Colour of Resistance: A*

Contemporary Collection of Writing by Aboriginal Women. A first collection of poetry is soon to be published. At present, I make my living from freelance writing and video and film production in Edmonton, Alberta.

BERNARDINE EVARISTO
I am a Black British woman born in 1959 to a Nigerian father and English mother. I attended drama school and left to co-found Theatre of Black Women, Britain's first Black women's theatre company (1982-89). I wrote several plays for the company, and my poetry, essays and reviews are published in several anthologies and magazines. My first collection of poetry, *Island of Abraham* (Peeple Tree Press, U.K.), is forthcoming. I currently work as a freelance arts co-ordinator and am writing my first novel.

VICTORIA GONZALEZ
I was born in Chile to a Nicaraguan father and a white, American mother. I grew up in northern Nicaragua and lived there until 1983. I went back home to visit in 1986, 1988, 1990-91, and 1992. I am currently living in New York and am completing a master's degree in Latin American history.

CAROLE GRAY
Carole Gray was born in Manitoba in December, 1958. She is from a large, working class family of Native and West European descent. In 1980 Carole moved to Vancouver and began drawing in pen and ink. In 1982 she moved to Melbourne, Australia. There she had some of her drawings published in the book *Monsters Aren't Real* and in June/July 1991 she had the first exhibition of her work, called *Drawing It Out*. Carole returned to Vancouver in January 1993 with her two sons, where she continues to work on her art.

HEATHER GREEN
Writing the piece for this anthology (already a biography within itself) has marked the beginning of an end, and the end of a beginning for me... the new name I want to take will be the final transition in this. Excavating hidden information about my past from my mother, breaking free of the control of my white relatives and then confronting

past abuses, including their racism (which remains current), has brought me to a much more real place of understanding — of myself and the world. These steps have coincided with a ferocious desire to know the history of African peoples, an increased connection with people of African descent, daily interactions with women of colour, and making my way into my new African and lesbian of colour families. Changes continue to be both painful and glorious all at the same time. Working with and for women of colour will, I hope, always be there to reinforce my strength. My new name is *Datejie*.

NILA GUPTA
Nila Gupta was born an Aries in 1961 and immigrated with her family to Canada from Jammu, India in 1967. Her father is Indian and her mother is French Canadian. Her first collection of poems entitled *The Garden of my (Be)Longing*, is forthcoming. She is a founding member of the Saheli Theatre Troupe, a South Asian feminist theatre group.

MAXINE HAYMAN
Maxine Hayman lives with her sweetheart and three children on Denman Island which is equidistant to the birthplaces of her mother and her father. She is currently a student at North Island College and in her spare time does maid work with three wonderful "waspy" women. Her goal is to learn to play the bagpipes (Seriously!) She is half Native.

DORIS HEGGIE
She received her Bachelors in Art Education from Tufts University and The Boston Museum School of Fine Arts. She is a mother, art teacher, herbalist, and canine animal behaviorist. Her works are exhibited nationally and she has conducted African textile workshops for children and adults. She is a teacher of the arts and strives to work from within and to help others use the arts to access their power within.

CAMILLE RAMDWAR-HERNANDEZ
I am a TrinCan of Trinidadian/Ukrainian-Canadian heritage. My soul and spirit belong to Trinidad but at present I am physically planted in Toronto. I divide my time between studying, writing and raising my son and daughter. My work (creative and academic) revolves around the

idea of "race", the notion of "interracial relationships" and a comparison of the construction of "race" in the Caribbean and Canada.

IJOSÉ

I am a poet and visual artist born in Nigeria where I obtained a Bachelor's degree in accounting. I have been living in Toronto for approximately 18 months now. Born to a Nigerian mother and a Chinese father, I started writing from the young age of eight years, probably from the aloneness I felt as a result of my parental and social isolation. My work has appeared in *Fireweed* and *MetroWord*. I read at various poetry reading cafes and pubs where I also display my visual work (which often complements my poetry). I am also a pioneer member of *Matrika*, a women poet's group organizing monthly reading series and art performances by women.

LISA JENSEN

I am a feminist activist, born in Calgary, committed to just being me and doing all I can.

CLAIRE HUANG KINSLEY

She unintentionally subverted the stereotype of the tragic mixed-race heroine by having one of the happiest childhoods of anyone she knows. As an adult, she works at the Parkdale Community Information Centre, teaches women's self-defence, is intrigued by the etymology of obscure words, likes cats, has been known to go starry-eyed over both women and men, isn't crazy about the word "bisexual" but can't think of a better one, drives her friends crazy by pausing in the middle of sentences, agonizes over ethical dilemmas, works herself perilously close to burnout, but is still pretty cheerful most of the time. The same impulse that leads her to scrutinize people in the subway eventually led her to get together with some other women and form a mixed-race women's discussion group in 1993.

MICHELLE LA FLAMME

I have been involved in theatre for ten years and also managed to complete an M.A. in English. I am beginning to integrate all of my "identities" and express my passion and vision through performance, the written word and song. *Yo White Boy* is one of my pieces on a tape entitled *Void To Voice* — a compilation of dub poetry from artists of colour on the west coast, to be released in 1994. As mixed race people, we must claim our identities and challenge the singular definitions of self within the monotone world by extending boundaries of definitions. My mother is Metis and my father is Black and I claim their identities as well as my own uniqueness as a mixed race woman.

LEZLIE LEE KAM
A Callaloo-roti, Trini dyke, trying to survive this crazy world, always ready for a good lime and a cold beverage, but dreaming of being fed sweet, juicy mangos on a hot beach.

kim mosa mcneilly
She is currently taken with mastering the craft of weaving the multi-dimensional strands of her creative voice into a kaleidoscope of *soouull full* expression. She can be found beating the drum or dancing the beat — painting the dance or rhyming the *rainbow coloured harmonies* of her ancestral collage. Check her deft juggling skills as she keeps her eclectic ting flyin'!

LISA SUHAIR MAJAJ
She is writing a dissertation on Arab American literature. She lives in Massachusetts.

BARBARA MALANKA
She spent the first part of her childhood in New York City where she was born. Her mother is French Canadian catholic and her father was a Southern Black baptist. Currently, she lives with her partner in London, Ontario where she writes, paints and is trying to housebreak her two children and her Shih Tzu puppy.

KATHY ANN MARCH
Kathy Ann March was born in Kingston, Jamaica (Mona Heights), May 7th, 1962. She is currently working on a video production about issues concerning people of mixed race.

STEPHANIE MARTIN
Artist, born in Kingston, Jamaica. Lives in Toronto, Canada.

LORRAINE MENTION
Lorraine Mention is a 30 year-old Black woman child, daughter, sister, niece, granddaughter, cousin, friend, mother, lover, wife, student, warrior, spirit. She was the forth child that entered this world through the womb of her white mother which was the direct result of a union between her mother and her Black father. She was raised under the influence of her father's family from North Buxton, Ontario. Lorraine's mother's family immigrated from England some years ago.

MICHELE PAULSE
She currently lives in Toronto where she is employed with the provincial government, is studying toward her master's degree in Sociology at the University of Toronto, and is along with Rosamund, Tarik, and Aziza, constantly trying to figure out life. She is co-author of two children's books and has also published short stories.

NADRA QADEER
I am daughter of Mohammed and Susan, granddaughter of Reddy and Harry Silver and Magbool Begum and Shamas Din, great-granddaughter of Israel and Ester Silverman and Imam Din and Mehr'un Nisa. I was born in small-town Ontario and they never would have guessed it. I now live in Montreal. I study social work like my mother did and as her mother told her to. I am a Muslim, Pakistani, Jewish, American Canadian, and *I know who I am.*

YOLANDA RETTER
She is of Peruana/German heritage. She is a PhD student and transpersonal activist. She was born in Connecticut, grew up in El Salvador, spent 20 years in California and now lives in New Mexico.
Kukumo Rocks
African, Asian, Scots Performance Poet

STEFANIE SAMUELS
She is a Toronto born theatre artist and performer.

NONA SAUNDERS
I am a 43-year-old woman who has dealt with the quandary of 'where

do I belong' my whole life. My family roots are far-flung, from my father's Cree and French mother, to his Black father's ancestors as American slaves, to my mother's immigrant parents from Norway. I have published in *Fireweed* and the *Vancouver Sun*.

GITANJALI SAXENA
I am a videomaker and filmmaker currently living in Toronto.

SENI SENEVIRATNE
I am a writer and singer who has recently branched out into photography and I combine all three for performance. I was born in Yorkshire in 1951 to an English mother and Sri Lankan father. I now live in Sheffield with my teenage daughter. My work is published in various anthologies and on tape.

NGAHUIA TE AWEKOTUKU
Ngahuia Te Awekotuku was born and raised in the traditional Maori village of Ohinemutu, on the shores of Lake Rotorua in the North Island of New Zealand. Her tribes include the Te Arawa, Waikato and the Tuhoe peoples. Her maternal grandfather was of French background. Commited to indigenous rights, she remains active in the lesbian/gay and women's movements in Aotearoa. She has published two books, *Tahuri*, short stories and *Mana Wahine Maori - Selected Writings in Maori Women's Art, Culture and Politics*. Her work also appears in a number of periodicals and anthologies. She teaches Art History at the University of Auckland.

SHANTI THAKUR
She is an independent filmmaker who concentrates on social issues in general and intercultural issues in particular. She was producer/director of the documentary *Crossing Borders*. Her documentary *Domino* is a National Film Board of Canada production in association with her company, Lucida Films Inc. *Domino* will be distributed and available through the National Film Board.

S.R.W.
She is of British and West Indian ancestry. She was born in western Canada. She thanks Terrence Anthony, Nicole Jensen and Bradon Jones, her mixed race friends who have supported and encouraged her.

LISA VALENCIA-SVENSSON
I am a half-breed Filipina-Canadian dyke.

ANNE VESPRY
She is a Toronto dyke, fat-activist, and desk-top publisher.

NAOMI ZACK
She received her Ph.D in Philosophy from Columbia University in 1970 and left academia for twenty years. Since her return she has published the first philosophical critique of American categories of black and white race, *Race and Mixed Race* (Temple University Press, 1993). She is assistant professor of Philosophy at the State University of New York, at Albany.

SISTER VISION
Black Women and Women of Colour Press

was founded by Women of Colour in 1985. Sister Visions mandate and priority is publishing books by Black women, First Nations women, Asian women and women of mixed racial heritage.

The vision of Sister Vision Press came out of a need for autonomy, a need to determine the context and style of the work, words and images that are produced about us.

Our list features ground-breaking and provocative fiction, poetry, anthologies, oral history, theoretical writing and books for young adults and children.

A free catalogue of our books is available from Sister Vision Press, P.O. box 217, Station E, Toronto, Ontario, Canada, M6H 4E2, Phone (416) 533-2184